The Feminization of Development Processes in Africa

The Feminization of Development Processes —— in Africa ——

Current and Future Perspectives

Edited by
Valentine Udoh James
and James S. Etim

Westport, Connecticut
London

Library of Congress Cataloging-in-Publication Data

The feminization of development processes in Africa : current and
   future perspectives / edited by Valentine Udoh James and James S.
   Etim.
         p.   cm.
      Includes bibliographical references and index.
      ISBN 0-275-95946-5 (alk. paper)
         1. Women in development—Africa.   2. Women in public life—Africa.
      3. Feminism—Africa.   I. James, Valentine Udoh, 1952–   .
      II. Etim, James.
      HQ1240.5.A35F45   1999
      305.42′096—dc21   98–19300

British Library Cataloguing in Publication Data is available.

Library of Congress Catalog Card Number: 98–19300
ISBN: 0-275-95946-5

First published in 1999

Praeger Publishers, 88 Post Road West, Westport, CT 06881
An imprint of Greenwood Publishing Group, Inc.

Printed in the United States of America

The paper used in this book complies with the
Permanent Paper Standard issued by the National
Information Standards Organization (Z39.48–1984).

10 9 8 7 6 5 4 3 2 1

To the people of Ikot-Ekpene, Nigeria

Contents

Illustrations

Preface

A great deal of effort is being made in the developing countries to maximize the contribution of women in the development processes. In some countries most of the energy is spent at the menial and laborious bottom level of institutions, while in others serious institutional changes are being put in place.

Although the title of this volume might indicate that the work is about the feminization of development processes in developing countries as a whole, it should be emphasized that the chapters in this volume emphasize the African situation. There are occasions when broad generalizations are made about the developing countries, but the main thrust of this work is on Africa.

The history of development in Africa can be divided into three main categories—the precolonial era, the colonial era, and the postcolonial era. Many development experts and historians argue that the division of labor in the precolonial era in most African societies gave women the power and a voice that put them on an equal footing with men. This does not mean that there were not societies in Africa where women were treated on an unequal basis with the men.

The colonial era, it is argued, exacerbated the subordinate role of women. Colonial rulers established employment centers that led to men's leaving their rural farming jobs for the work in the towns established by foreign rulers. Men also left for plantations and mining jobs. The contacts made between foreign colonial rulers and African men led to the long-term working relationships and institutional establishment that excluded women.

This volume begins with an introductory chapter by one of the editors, Valentine Udoh James. James examines the "Trends and Conundrums in the Feminization of Development Processes in Africa." The chapter basically examines the theoretical foundation of development and the modification needed in applying development theory to embrace women's contributions in all levels of society.

Part II, Sociopolitical Development Processes, includes seven chapters. The situation of Nigerian women is discussed in Chapter 2 by Kofi Johnson and R. Babatunde Oyinade. This is an appraisal of the degree of women's participation in the political system in Nigeria. Johnson and Oyinade focus upon the struggles of two prominent Nigerian women: Oluwole (1905-1957) and Ransome-Kuti (1900-1978). Their roles in championing democratic reforms are discussed. Gender issues, the authors argue, have changed as women become more empowered. There are differences in the political involvement of women in the different eras of precolonial, colonial, and postcolonial times. The impediments that women confront should be removed in order for the country to benefit from their talents. Discrimination against women is still very rampant, and, as such, women do not feature in equitable numbers in government midmanagement and upper-management jobs.

Chapter 3, "Women's Empowerment and the Anthropology of Participatory Development" by Ester Igandu Njiro, discusses steps involved in empowering women so that they can be involved in significant roles in their societies. Njiro uses case studies in Kenya to explain the process and significance of empowerment of communities so that they can fend for themselves. The importance of building community capacities is very vivid in this chapter. The strength of Njiro's argument becomes clear as one examines issues of food security, workload for women, division of labor by gender and age, and women's groups. The implication of the anthropology of women's participation is central in this chapter.

In Chapter 4, Amy Beer and Christine List examine how the media discuss and portray feminism, issues of human rights, and the general idea of the role of African women in development. By looking at the works of some writers and some films, the authors attempt to indicate a trend and perspective that the public is given about African women. The general image of African women is a poor one. The authors call the reader's attention to what needs to be done in giving the improving efforts to include women in the key positions in development efforts. This recommendation with regard to the role of international community, especially the Western feminist, is one that should be taken seriously among academics and those in policy making in both African and foreign circles.

Ifeyinwa E. Umerah-Udezulu in Chapter 5 draws the reader's attention to the West African condition of development processes. The state plays an important role in setting the agenda for development, and in many cases the priorities of women do not rank very high in the African government's agendas. Umerah-Udezulu offers a different viewpoint on developmental processes. She gives a resounding analysis of the current feminist schools of thought and provides a unique analysis of the impact of patriarchy on development in West Africa.

In Chapter 6, Felix K. Ekechi offers the reader a discussion of the importance of women's efforts in the struggle for liberation. This is essentially a historical perspective that has contemporary significance. Ekechi claims that in precolonial African societies, women had a great deal of power and influence. He gives the reader ample examples to substantiate his argument.

In Chapter 7, Ambe J. Njoh explains the seriousness of gender-based discrimination, with specific emphasis on housing and development policies that impact urbanization and transformation of Cameroon societies. Discriminatory policies and practices against women have long-term sociological and economic ramifications, and Cameroon provides a classic example. Njoh makes a compelling argument for why discriminatory practices and policies should be abandoned.

In Chapter 8, Umerah-Udezulu strengthens the argument that was made by Njoh in Chapter 7. She provides a case study of the Ibo women in eastern Nigeria. Although the work reported in this chapter is based on the author's personal observations, the analysis and synthesis presented in this chapter are quite accurate in terms of what other researchers have observed. Umerah-Udezulu argues that the Ibo society values males, and so the ideas and perspectives of males predominate in key decision issues.

Part III contains chapters that devote their themes to educational, economic, and institutional development matters. Chapter 9 focuses attention on the education of women in Nigeria. James S. Etim argues that tremendous strides have been made in different levels of education in Nigeria. The author uses statistical data to show the improving trends.

In Chapter 10, Alice Etim provides one dimension of the development process where a great deal of attention must be paid in order to globalize women's entrepreneurship and make their businesses more successful. She makes the argument for the incorporation of computer technology in the development process for women.

In Chapter 11, Noble J. Nweze discusses, through a Nigerian case study, how to "mobilize and allocate household savings." He sees a great deal of advantage in promoting linkages between women's indigenous savings groups and community banks in Nigeria. Although many community banks have failed in Nigeria, the author thinks that the linkages could create a "win-win" or "symbiotic" situation.

In Chapter 12, Anthonia C. Kalu, provides an argument for why the role of individuals and therefore community-based efforts must be integral parts of political and economic development in Africa. The author explores the traditional views in contemporary literature, especially those of African women writers in making her recommendation for the direction of development in Africa.

Chapter 13 by Victoria Carchidi wrestles with the subject of development and women's writings as expressed by writers from Northern and Southern Africa. This chapter explains and discusses what the expectations, attitudes, and perceptions of women are with regard to development.

It is our hope that this volume will set the stage for many more interdisciplinary book projects on the feminization of development processes in Africa. Our effort to bring scholars of diverse disciplines together to speak to the issues concerning women's contributions to Africa's development is basically an effort to continue a dialogue that is gaining rapid attention globally. We hope we have added to the debate.

Acknowledgments

The inspiration for a book project such as this comes from many sources—the observations of what is going on in many developing countries with regard to women's roles in different spheres of life, discussions with colleagues in American universities and colleges and residents in developing countries, and dialogues in conferences, seminars, and classrooms. In organizing the *Feminization of Development Processes*, the editors realized that the most effective way to accomplish the task of covering the very diverse aspects of development processes that involve women is through a multidisciplinary collaborative effort.

Fieldwork in many parts of Africa exposes us to the conditions and plight of women in both rural and urban places. Among these women are our mothers, grandmothers, sisters, aunts, and distant relatives who spent some time in forming our thinking on the subject of development and implications for women. Some women in many parts of the developing world have succeeded in what they do, but others have not; this book attempts to explain the strategies for improving the condition of women and thus maximize their potential to contribute to the growth and development of their respective countries. Hence, our sincere gratitude must, first and foremost, be to the women who have formed our understanding of development dynamics (both in print and in face-to-face discussions), and our female undergraduate and graduate students for their unique perspectives in class discussion, and, of course, great credit must go to those women who work from international organizations (private voluntary organizations and nongovernmental organizations) who endeavor to ensure that development processes are sensitive to women's issues in the developing world.

I would like to express a most sincere appreciation to the chapter contributors of this volume for their quick and professional response to the many queries and for returning their manuscripts in a timely fashion for publication. I put many under a great deal of pressure, but having this book published makes it worthwhile. Finally, I would like to thank Melanie Marshall James for her continuing role as project coordinator.

I

Introduction

Trends and Conundrums in the Feminization of Development Processes in Africa

Valentine Udoh James

The introduction of gender issues into the discussion of development in the emerging nations of the world is a highly contested issue but needs consideration if the developing world is to maximize the amount of talents and knowledge necessary to combat poverty and to play an important role in global affairs.

Gender consideration is paramount in the discussion of development because it is necessary to understand the opportunities that are available to developing countries when women's roles are fully incorporated into the development processes of these countries.

The introduction of gender considerations into development planning in developing countries requires careful examination of the institutional arrangements: government policies, educational systems, cultural and religious norms, and the economic, political, social, and judicial systems. These variables play key roles in the development processes of developing countries.

It is common knowledge that patriarchal societies in the developing countries have had their development pace determined by men. The economic fate of these societies has remained largely in the hands of a few powerful elite (men).

DEVELOPMENT THEORY

Development theory is based on Western interpretations of the transformation of infrastructural, institutional, economic, and political variables in order to achieve standards of macroeconomic levels. The transformations are ongoing phenomena that are brought about through public and private efforts by assembling necessary resources in order to acquire the capacity to make the development changes. For most developing countries the transformations have been predicated upon Western ideas of how development should proceed and what the development should be based upon. For example, in many developing countries, the development of natural resources (renewable or exhaustible) has been seen as development. Natural resource exploitation has historically spurred development in emerging nations of the world.

Social sciences have provided the fundamental basis for development theory because they have pointed out the necessity for a contextual consideration of development processes to recognize the differences in societies: the cultural, historical, economic, and environmental differences that exist in societies. These differences, social scientists maintain, make it paramount to examine the uniqueness of societies.

Economic transformation of developing countries requires the operationalization of Western economic paradigms so as to link developing economies with the world markets. Goods and services in developing countries must be marketed in the global marketplace where free market enterprise system dominates, and the policies of Western industrialized countries predominate. Agendas for structural adjustment and other economic strategies are sometimes dictated by foreign banks and other international development agencies with their conditionalities for securing assistance. The democratization process and social and institutional reforms in developing countries are being influenced by Western ideas.

The development theory debate has revolved around two ideas: (1) basic needs and (2) comprehensive development. Women are very active and play significant roles in meeting the basic needs of their communities in developing countries. This is exemplified in their role in the agricultural sector and in keeping their families intact. In the comprehensive development of many developing nations where established institutions play important roles in employment and general resource allocation, women have been confronted by major traditional, cultural, and discriminatory barriers.

DEVELOPMENT SCENARIOS

The level of development in an emerging nation of the world can be examined in light of the degree of financial and technical support available from three sources: international community, national governments, and local administrations. The institutional structures left by the colonial rulers in most of these countries are proof of the link to Western philosophy of development.

Precolonial development witnessed little transformation in the developing countries. Changes were occurring at a very slow pace in communities across the developing world. Commerce was driven by local trade in local food produce and merchandise, and autonomy rules and norms were adhered to in the empires, emirates, towns, and villages. In Africa trade by barter and some aspects of profit-motivated economy existed during the precolonial era, in which customary or traditional norms governed the ethics or code of trade.

The colonial era truly monetized the economic systems in the developing world. The mode of exchange became money. One must realize that in the precolonial era, women played important and significant roles in the market scene. The colonial era emphasized male predominance in colonial government jobs. Men left the rural scene for cash-paying urban jobs or plantation jobs. It stands to reason that the international patriarchal concept of work was exacerbated in the developing countries during the colonial era. Thus, the legacy of the colonial administration is that men hold powerful positions in the development process and in institutions of government at national and local levels.

In contemporary Africa, Central America, and Southeast Asia, development is influenced by aid agencies such as the U.S. Agency for International Development (USAID), foreign governments, nongovernmental organizations (NGOs), and multinationals. The postcolonial era is one where development is governed by bilateral, multilateral agreements, loans, and technical assistance.

The questions that this chapter attempts to address are, What is the role of women, and what institutional problems exist that hinder full participation of women in the development processes? There is no doubt that, in many developing countries, culturally biased, pro-male based policies existed during the precolonial era and that the colonial era reinforced the distortions that existed in the economies of these countries. In all the eras of development, one thing is clear: there has always been a general low economic and social status of women.

However, it should be clarified that in some societies, women fared well. For example, the informal market sectors in many African countries have disproportionately large numbers of women, and women are known to be at the center of food production, processing, and distribution on the continent. But it should be made clear that modern technology for the development processes is controlled by men. Hence, macroeconomic inequality exists among men and women in the developing world. Lele (1991) makes this point vividly clear when she argues that the most pressing problems women farmers in the developing countries face include technology and institutional constraints, technical and financial support, and subsidy.

THE RELEVANCE OF FEMINIST DEBATE TO DEVELOPMENT PROCESSES

It was stated in an earlier section of this chapter that Western thought has guided the colonial and postcolonial eras of development in emerging nations of the world. Philomena Okeke (1996: 223) offers a cogent and compelling discussion of the implication of post-modern feminism on the study of African women. She argues that disparate interpretations and common themes can be found on the subject and suggests that "post-modern feminism has also waded into the arena of development theory and practices. Recent debates in the field have centered around the prospects for a dialogue that places the Women in

Development (WID) framework at the center, not merely to be informed by but also to inform the larger body of feminist scholarship. The flow of development expertise, critics argue, has tended to ignore (at enormous costs) the indigenous female knowledge bases" (225).

In generating knowledge about African women, indigenous perspectives are very limited, and, as such, the plethora of literature on African women is largely produced by Western women. The colonial legacy of Africa bears some of the blame for this phenomenon. Okeke (1996: 227) makes this point when she notes: "The colonial advantage has long been justified by white women's dominant presence in the study of African women." Much internationally funded collaborative research on the study of African women does not have indigenous African women scholars as the primary investigators.

International development agencies are influencing development in developing countries at a very rapid pace. In these international agencies indigenous women's perspectives are very much needed. Existing arrangements for research on African women's progress and the institutions in foreign and domestic countries need to be reexamined for "recalibration" so as to make the institutions more inclusive of African women's perspectives.

SPECIFICS OF NEEDED CHANGES IN DEVELOPMENT PROCESSES

The development process ideally involves four stages: planning and design, construction, implementation, and operation. In all phases of development gender should be an integral part of evaluation of how inclusive the system of development is.

Linking and De-linking in Development

Planners must be concerned about gendered impact of economic developments. As has been established in previous sections, men traditionally have been in control of the development processes (decision making) in the developing countries. In recent times (in the last decade) women have begun to make some inroads into the decision-making sectors of development processes in developing countries. The processes of development must be made to respond to pertinent issues of equity and efficiency.

A number of African women scholars, regardless of their disciplines, have wondered about the role of African thought and experience in the development of the continent. This question transcends one discipline. Kalu (1996: 272) ponders this issue when she notes: "To what extent is the African reality relevant to development for Africans on the continent and in the Diaspora? Can we develop without realizing, reconstructing, and validating our common heritage and essential connections and possibly, our origins?" Africans and African governments have continued to use development ideas emanating from Western developed countries, and both men and women of African descent have consistently questioned the appropriateness of such development ideas. Kalu (1996: 275) makes this point:

Our continued insistence on defining ourselves in Western feudal and capitalist terms maintains the pitfalls of Africa's underdevelopment. This viewpoint will continue to result in the implementation of development projects mandated by knowledge that alienates Africans from Africa's problems. The exploration of Africa's heritage and future development must be based on a well organized and systematic research program for understanding precolonial African societies.

Some scholars such as Kalu (1996) argue that precolonial African societies were structured in such a way that roles were well defined for both men and women, and the development that was emerging in African societies was in concert with the natural rhythm of events, and, as such, haphazard development was not present. Colonial and postcolonial eras in Africa brought in development that depended essentially on technical experts from developed countries or trained in developed countries. These individuals had/have access to the necessary technical expertise to perform development based on theories developed in Western institutions. This creates a relationship of superordination and subordination (Preston 1985).

Colonial and postcolonial development in the developing countries as envisaged by experts from the developed countries had to be modeled after (1) an ideology of authoritative intervention (growth theory), and (2) an ideology of elaborate intervention (this one could be argued to be an American style). This is the *modernization theory*.

African governments and others in the emerging nations of the world embraced the so-called ordered reconstruction and development of the growth theory. It should be pointed out that, although the early development fervor was spurred on by the defense of Western capitalist ideas in the face of the global depression and the cold war, contemporary development based on growth theory emphasizes structural adjustment, trade liberalization, devaluation, privatization, and market reforms. Within the growth theory emerges explanatory theory that appears to legitimate industrialization, urbanization, commercialization, and, generally, "construction." It should be recognized that the notions of planning that involves the initiation of activities related to the extraction, transformation, distribution, and allocation of resources fall in the domain of development assistance or aid. During the colonial era and still in the postcolonial era, the mode of engagement in developing countries was and continues to be the application of authoritative prescriptions for development, and Western ideas of development are central in the growth and development of emerging nations. Take, for instance, the creation of new towns (capital cities) in developing countries. The construction of a new federal capital territory (Abuja) in Nigeria could be examined as the application of modernization theory in a developing country. This capital city appears to be out of touch with some local realities in Nigeria. If one agrees with the argument made earlier that gender is a valid dimension along which to examine equity and efficiency of the development theories (impacts) on Africa, then the creation of new urban centers in Africa neglects the role of women.

Several studies indicate that growth and modernization in many developing countries have done little to improve the condition of women (Tinker and Bramson 1976; Kelly and Elliot 1982; Boulding 1976). Seabrook (1993: 163) makes a convincing argument about the plight of women and children as a result of development that does not look out for their interests:

It is a paradox that part of the "externalizing" of economic and social costs of development has been through forms of "internalizing" them: that is to say, individuals, especially women, have absorbed, secretly, privately, unspeakable burdens of social shame, disgrace and sorrow. These, too, need to be counted, before we can make any realistic assessment of profit and loss, advantage and penalty, gain and impoverishment, in our lives.

As was mentioned earlier, colonialism brought tremendous changes in women's position in African societies. It separated women from working side by side with men because it established jobs that took the men away from their families. The cash crop/plantation farms, civil service jobs, and the mines all took the men away from their villages, and it should be stressed that colonial administrators reinforced male biases. Women had few responsibilities in the governments. These, certainly, were significant setbacks (Snyder and Tadesse 1995).

Colonialism created state structures that hindered women's progress, and some traditional customs made it difficult for women to be completely equal with men. For instance, in many parts of Africa, women do not have complete land-use rights; inheritance of property goes only to male children, and women's share of capital resources is limited (Pankhurst 1992). There is no doubt that progress must be made by women so as to eliminate their alienation from the state governing body. Women's weak social, political, and economic positions lead to them being the least-skilled and least-educated majority with the worst-paid jobs.

Hence, efforts must be made to improve women's contribution in the following development processes: politics, institution building, infrastructure construction, education, agriculture, economy, information, and technology. Patriarchal cultures of the developing world have helped in exacerbating women's poor conditions in the developing countries, and, as such, grassroots empowerment and mobilization of women in urban and rural communities are necessary for the gradual improvement of women's conditions.

In dealing with the issue of feminization of development processes, one needs to address the subject of "gender concept." In defining gender, Ostergaard (1992: 6) contends:

Gender refers to the qualitative and independent character of women's and men's position in society. Gender relations of power and dominance structure the life chances of women and men. Thus, labor divisions are not fixed biology, but constitute an aspect of the wider social division of labor and this, in turn, is rooted in the conditions of production and reproduction and reinforced by cultural, religious, and ideological systems prevailing in a society.

It appears that the past and, in most cases, the present-day development processes subordinate women's efforts. Gender planning must be incorporated into the feminization of development processes. Moser (1993: 87) argues that gender planning in development process should include political and technical matter. It should assume conflict in the planning process that enhances transformation through rational debate. But one should understand that the concept of women in development may exacerbate the marginalization of the group because it connotes treating women as a special group. Ostergaard (1992: 7) suggests that the concept of gender in development is a more appropriate approach to envisage inclusion of women in the development process because of the abstractness of the concept and its openness for the realization of women's productive potential in development.

Experience in many parts of the developing world indicates that when women are involved in wage labor economy, they encounter tremendous discrimination and lower wage rates. Elias (1989) contends that areas of concern for integrating women's issues into development planning and management are

1. Women's participation in development through women's economic projects.
2. Women's involvement in management and decision making at all levels of governmental and nongovernmental organization.
3. The role and function of national mechanisms for women.
4. The role of training.

One way of addressing these concerns is by integrating these issues into the administration of projects and by having gender-aware development planning. Roy et al. (1996) contend that such integration is necessary because current development projects in Africa seem to marginalize women. For instance, large-scale agriculture absorbs land and economic resources, and, as such, women's subsistence agriculture suffers. Industrialized agricultural systems do not favor women. As a result of the marginalization of women due to past planning methods, contemporary administrations in many developing countries are attempting to put in place policies and programs that are designed to target women's interests. Moser (1993: 145) makes a significant contribution in the process of operationalizing procedures for implementing projects that would make possible efforts to achieve the objectives of improving women's contribution in development. Table 1.1 shows a detailed plan.

CONCLUSION

The beginning of feminization of the development process in the developing countries is to understand women's roles in these countries and to identify, early in development processes, what the hindrances to women's progress are in the specific societies. Influencing the power structure is paramount to the ability to change the impediments that make it impossible to elevate the status of women in developing countries. There are many success stories of how well women are doing in the economic development of these countries, but the majority of these success stories happen to be in the informal sectors of the economy. As Adepoju and Oppong (1994) observe in their study of gender, work, and population, African women play significant roles in the production and reproductive spheres in the developing world. The hindrances that women face compact their lifetime experiences into a short lifespan, and, as such, these countries cannot reap the complete benefits of women's contribution to these societies. The erosion of confidence brought about as a result of the hindrances must be stopped and reversed by instituting private and public ventures to assist women's aspirations. The challenges are internal in developing countries and external with regard to development assistance from industrialized nations. On the domestic front, the governments of developing nations must work to remove handicaps that stem from cultural biases that deprive full participation based on female gender. Certainly, religious and traditional beliefs seem to disregard the tremendous talents of women.

On the international scene, agencies (Non-governmental Organizations and Private Voluntary Organizations) must do more to educate and inform the general public in the developing world about the problems posed by gender biases. But caution must be exercised to understand the cultural context of developing countries' population. There is no doubt that there is development crisis in the developing countries, and part of the crisis is the plight of women in the development processes.

The Special Initiative on Africa that was unveiled on March 15, 1997, by former secretary-general of the United Nations Boutro Boutros-Ghali with assistance from the World Bank should enable development in Africa to be more comprehensive and inclusive ("Continental Developments" 1996). This $25 billion, ten-year program will address education and health care problems and promote sustainable development issues such as governance, peace promotion, and the improvement of water and food security. These issues are central to the feminization of development processes, and, if carefully and properly planned, designed, constructed, and implemented with gender concept in mind, women will begin to benefit from their hard work and contributions, but, more importantly, the societies as a whole will stand to gain in the short and long runs. Taking gender issues into account is bound to reflect a more equitable number of women in the governmental decision-making workplace as well as in industry, as can be seen in some developed nations of the world. This argument is supported by Jenson et al. (1988) work on *Feminization of the Labor Force.*

Table 1.1
Planning Procedures to Operationalize Women in Development (WID)

General procedures	Purpose	Type of country-specific procedure
WID mandate or policy	to define and legitimate WID policy	• parliament legislation • ministerial directive • internal guidelines • operational objectives
Plan of action	to provide WID operational strategies and procedures	• detailed plan of action • general action programs • WID strategy paper
WID specific sector guidelines	to provide sector-specific WID guidelines	• sector-level WID checklists • WID sector papers • WID manuals
Integrated WID criteria in sector guidelines	to integrate WID criteria into general sector guidelines	• sector guidelines • WID in office procedure
Country-level WID guidelines	to integrate WID concerns into country-level operations	• country-specific WID plans • country plan of action • country development strategy statement • country program / reports • country assessment WID papers
WID project guidelines	to integrate WID into the project cycle	• WID project cycle manual • WID project checklist • project identification document • project paper • checklist for participation of WID projects
Monitoring procedures	to monitor implementation of WID plan of action	• progress reports • built-in monitoring procedures • reporting to Congress

Source: Adapted from Moser 1993: 145.

Computer graphics: Melanie Marshall James.

There is, indeed, a need to redefine the workforce in many developing areas of the world so as to maximize human potential.

REFERENCES

Adepoju, Aderanti, and Christine Oppong (eds.). 1994. *Gender, Work and Population in Sub-Saharan Africa*. London and Portsmouth, NH: James Currey and Heinemann.

Arat, Yesim. 1989. *The Patriarchal Paradox: Women Politicians in Turkey*. Cranbury, NJ: Associated University Presses.

Boulding, E. 1976. *The Underside of History*. Boulder, CO: Westview Press.

"Continental Developments: United Nations Special Initiative on Africa." 1996. *African Research Bulletin* 33 (2) (April 10): 12477-78.

Ekechi, K. Felix. 1996. "Perceiving Women as Catalysts." *Africa Today* 43 (3): 235-50.

El-Bakri, Zeinab, and Ruth M. Besha (eds.). 1989. "Women and Development in Eastern Africa: An Agenda for Research." *Proceedings for the Workshop on Women and Development in Eastern Africa: An Agenda for Research*, held in Nazareth, Ethiopia. Addis Ababa, Ethiopia: Organization for Social Science Research in Eastern Africa.

Elias, Misrak. 1989. "Research Priorities on Women, Planning, and Management in Eastern Africa." In Zeinab El-Bakri and Ruth M. Besha (eds.), *Proceedings for the Workshop on Women and Development in Eastern Africa: An Agenda for Research*, held in Nazareth, Ethiopia. Addis Ababa, Ethiopia: Organization for Social Science Research in Eastern Africa.

Gower, Rebecca, Steven Salm, and Toyin Falola. 1996. "Swahili Women since the Nineteenth Century: Theoretical and Empirical Considerations on Gender and Identity Construction." *Africa Today* 43 (3): 251-68.

House-Midamba, Bessie. 1996. "Gender, Democratization, and Associated Life in Kenya." *Africa Today* 43 (3): 289-306.

Jenson, Jane, Elizabeth Hagen, and Ceallaigh Reddy (eds.). 1998. *Feminization of the Labor Force: Paradoxes and Promises*. New York: Oxford University Press.

Kalu, C. Anthonia. 1996. "Women and the Social Construction of Gender in African Development." *Africa Today* 43 (3): 269-88.

Kelly, Gail P., and Carolyn Elliot (eds.). 1982. *Women's Education in the Third World: Comparative Perspectives*. Albany, NY: SUNY Press.

Lele, Uma. 1991. "The Gendered Impacts of Structural Adjustment Programs in Africa: Discussion." *American Journal of Agricultural Economics* (December): 1452-55.

Moser, O. N. Caroline. 1993. *Gender Planning and Development: Theory, Practice and Training*. NY: Routledge.

Okeke, E. Philomena. 1996. "Postmodern Feminism and Knowledge Production: The African Context." *Africa Today* 43 (3): 223-34.

Ostergaard, Lise (ed.). 1992. *Gender and Development: A Practical Guide*. London: Routledge.

Pankhurst, Helen. 1992. *Gender, Development and Identity: An Ethiopian Study*. London: Zed Books.

Parpart, L. Jane (ed.). 1989. *Women and Development in Africa: Comparative Perspectives*. Lanham, MD: University Press of America.

Preston, W. P. 1985. *New Trends in Development Theory: Essays in Development and Social Theory*. London: Routledge and Kegan Paul.

Roy, C. Kartik, Clement A. Tisdell, and Hans C. Blomqvist (eds.). 1996. *Economic Development and Women in the World Community*. Westport, CT: Praeger.

Sahn, E. David, and Lawrence Haddad. 1991. "The Gendered Impacts of Structural Adjustment Programs in Africa: Discussion." *American Journal of Agricultural Economics* (December): 1448-51.

Seabrook, Jeremy. 1993. *Victims of Development: Resistance and Alternatives*. London: Verso.

Snyder, C. Margaret, and Mary Tadesse. 1995. *African Women and Development: A History*. London: Zed Books.

Tinker, Irene, and M. B. Bramson. 1976. *Women and Development*. Washington, DC: Overseas Development Council.

Wakoko, Florence, and Linda Labao. 1996. "Reconceptualizing Gender and Reconstructing Social Life: Ugandan Women and the Path to National Development." *Africa Today* 43 (3): 307-22.

II

Sociopolitical
Development
Processes

2

Women and Politics in Nigeria: An Appraisal

Kofi Johnson and R. Babatunde Oyinade

INTRODUCTION

This chapter focuses on women and their political participation and political development activities in Nigeria. It explores the role of women in the Nigerian political process, including their interest, participation, and representation in the political system. To do this, we examine the pathway of women in the political development process in Nigeria. The chapter examines the achievements and accomplishments of women and how far they have come to be part of a sometimes unpredictable political process. Finally, the chapter takes a look at the struggle of women and how they have suffered by the lack of representation and integration into the mainstream of the political process. This struggle is also induced by the lack of finances and family restrictions, which further hamper their involvement in the political process.

Nigeria is the largest and the most populous country on the African continent. It lies on the coast of West Africa. Nigeria came into being in 1914, having been amalgamated by the British colonizers. Colonial rule in Nigeria was a devastating period that completely diminished the influence of women in the country's political process. Their presence went unrecognized by the British colonizers by simply turning deaf ears to women's issues and writing them off as the British were establishing governmental and other political apparatuses. So, women suffered a great deal of indignation in spite of their enormous contribution to labor and the general economy of Nigeria. Compounding this neglect was the fact that the British colonists refused to acknowledge the importance of women in the national development and, as such, did little to enhance their education. This denial of educational opportunities would lead to women's not being part of government policy-making groups.

The politics of inclusion of women in government, to some extent, is an intricate part of modernization and development. Regardless of the type of inclusion, the idea of being part of the political process tends to conjure a sense of belonging in and to that political process, and, as such, a commitment is given to the process. Potholm (1970) wrote that one of the most important ingredients in developing policy is institutionalized flexibility, which he contends is the ability of the political system to deal with change, to meet new situations, to formulate new goals, and to process new demand and support.

WOMEN'S POLITICAL PARTICIPATION

Nina Mba (1982) defined politics as the resources and values that are allocated within a social unit for the purpose of meeting the needs and desires of its members. It is customary for countries to set up their political apparatus in a way that will tend to dictate the political process of the respective countries. Thus, within each political apparatus are political frameworks that fit into the system espoused by the country's leaders. While some countries practice the politics of integration and inclusion whereby all segments of the society are represented, others practice the politics of exclusion, whereby men dominate national politics. As a result, there is a considerable lack of participation by women. Women's participation in Nigeria's politics continues to be hindered by the traditional setup of loyalty to their men and the incomplete metamorphosis from old culture to modernity. Every region in Nigeria has stories of brave women who contributed to their respective communities. Such women were great because of their contributions to their people, trade, wars, and politics. Only a few of these women were able to accomplish greatness outside their men's command. Some of these women achieved much after the death of their husbands, and others went into oblivion.

Among the women of precolonial days who left an unforgettable legacy was Moremi of Ile-Ife, considered one of the greatest women of her time. She proved her worth by allowing herself to be captured by the masqueraders who constantly made life difficult for the people of Ile-Ife. Legend has it that, while in captivity, she learned the secrets of her captors, escaped, and revealed the techniques of the invaders to her people and organized them to fight and defeat them. In remembrance of her contribution, the people of Ile-Ife continue to celebrate the Egungun (an annual parade of masqueraders) festival to this day.

In the precolonial days, Nigeria had prominent women who helped to shape history. An example of such was Queen Amina of Zaria, who was the first woman to become the Sarauniya (queen) in a male-dominated society (Abubakr 1992). Queen Amina was said to have engaged in countless wars, reaching the northern banks of Kano and Sokoto and erecting walls as she pushed farther in an attempt to acquire territory after territory. Her reign brought prominence to the Hausaland. In recognition of her contributions, she was appointed Magajiya (one of the highest honors given to prominent women in Hausaland) (Abubakr 1992).

Another woman worth mentioning was Madam Tinubu, a business apprentice to her mother at an early age who became the most prominent nineteenth-century businesswoman. She became so influential that she succeeded in helping to restore Oba Akintoye to his throne in 1851. She once organized a campaign against wealthy immigrants that backfired. She was subsequently expelled from Lagos and moved to Abeokuta, where she became more prosperous and grew more powerful, contributing to the peace and prosperity of Abeokuta. For her many contributions, the chieftaincy title of "Iyalode of Abeokuta" was conferred upon her by the Alake of Abeokuta. Also, a Tinubu square in Lagos was named in her honor for the many contributions to development in Lagos. Other women trailblazers were Nana Asma'u Iyalode Efunsetan Aniwura, Charlotte Olajumoke Obasa, and Lady Olayinka Abayomi, who were activists for the women's cause during their respective times.

Deborah Pellow (1977) wrote that a woman's perception of social reality and her place in that reality—roles, aspirations, satisfactions—are governed, in part, by the sector of the society to which she belongs. The importance, role, and contribution of women to political participation in Nigeria went unrecognized for a long period of time. This is due to the fact that the politics of Nigeria had been dominated by men before and after independence. In a world where women outnumber men by a two-to-one margin, one would expect women to participate actively in the political structure of the country. Appropriately so, it is accurate to say that women participated silently in the political process of Nigeria for a long time through involvement in one way or the other. Male domination of the political scene led to the fact that women had minimal representation in both the federal and regional civil services. Thus, in 1954, as Mba noted, "there were only twenty three women in the civil service" (1989: 79).

Nigeria exemplifies the harsh reality of authoritarianism and lack of accountability. The urgent need for the country to begin the process of political democratization is increasingly being felt. The certainty of winners taking office and losers waiting for the next time around has long eluded most African countries, especially Nigeria. It is therefore ironic that since Nigeria attained independence in 1960, it has not sought constitutional transition from one government to the other. Instead, one military strongman has come after the other. Representation and participation, according to Joseph, Taylor, and Agbaje (1996), are two vital components in modern democracies. According to them, Nigeria is not a democracy. This is evident in the interim national government put together by the Abacha administration. Of the ninety-one-member Senate, there is no female, and of the 593 representatives, there are only two females, again a reflection of the limited formal political roles for women in Nigeria (cited in Joseph, Kesselman, and Krieger 1996).

In contemporary Nigeria, women continue to follow their husbands and are unable to stand on their own political beliefs. Men still dominate the political scene in Nigeria, and those women who have dared to participate have been overshadowed by men. Some women made their political moves behind their husbands' popularity, while others spoke only when their husbands were in danger. Examples are Chief (Mrs.) H.I.D. Awolowo, who was very effective while her husband was in jail for treason. Once her husband was released from prison, her political activities were surrendered to him. The same was true for Chief (Mrs.) Faderera Akintola, the wife of the slain former premier of the old Western Region of Nigeria. She was politically active for a short period after the death of her husband because to pursue her political aspirations without the support of her man would pose a direct challenge to the men in politics. Wives of other great Nigerian politicians were less active in the politics of Nigeria. This does not mean that they did not support their husbands while in power. Examples abound in the country: the late Mrs. Flora Azikiwe, the wife of the first civilian president of Nigeria, the wives of the Northern Region leaders (the late Alhaji Tafawa Balewa, the first prime Minister), the late Sardauna of Sokoto, Chief J. S. Tarka, and the late Alhaji Aminu Kano, to mention a few. None of the wives of these politicians actively participated in politics.

Under military rule, wives of military leaders, with the exception of Mariam Babangida (who was controversial), never participated in politics; once their husbands were eliminated or deposed, they disappeared from the political limelight. The educated women who were appointed to political positions got caught up in the political malaise, and their efforts to protect the good names of their respective families forced them to participate ineffectively in politics. Their accomplishments in politics are yet to be documented. Overall, preindependence politics and postindependence politics in Nigeria have given little or no room for Nigerian women to excel in their pursuit of political interests. For example, the wives of civilian politicians who were detained by the military were not given the chance to actively partake in the political process because their activities were considered threats to the ruling military rulers. Hence, those women who were active politically were silenced. Some even paid a greater price of death by assassination. An example is the assassination of the wife of Abiola under the Abacha's regime.

The contemporary political patterns in Nigeria still make women's participation a difficult saga. Many prominent researchers have focused on postindependence Nigeria, and their observations have been harsh and disturbing. Many of these researchers see corruption, repression, political decay, and violence as the predominant features of the new political landscape. Only a few women are brave enough to withstand the waves of the political storm. The frequent pronouncements by the army encouraging women to participate in the political affairs of the nation have not given enough assurances to respectable Nigerian women to partake, because of societal beliefs as to what a woman's role should be. Despite all the pre- and postindependence political upheavals, few women stand out in the political scene of Nigeria.

ANALYSIS OF TWO MODERN WOMEN

In a book titled *Nigerian Women in Historical Perspectives*, Bolanle Awe pointed out that the past two decades have witnessed all over the world a new interest in the role of women in society. Many women have contributed to their societies in different ways, some through trade, like Madam Tinubu, some in their professional way, such as Mrs. Kofoworola Pratt, who was dubbed "African Florence Nightingale" (Ogunsanya 1992), or some like "Madam Yoko: Ruler of the Kpa Mende confederacy" and Omu Okwei of Osomari. All of them contributed one way or the other to their societies.

This section focuses on the political contributions of two women who stood out and made significant and lasting impact in the political scene of Nigeria: Olaniwun Adunni Oluwole and Olufunmilayo Ransome-Kuti. They became legends, having set the groundwork for other women to follow.

Olaniwun Adunni Oluwole (1905-1957)

Ogunsanya described Adunni Oluwole as "not only as a female leader of great stature, but as one of the most colorful and dynamic political leaders of modern Nigeria" (1992: 126). She was born into the family of a famous warrior—Jalaruru of Eleta-Ibadan—in 1905 and was said to have inherited the fearlessness that distinguished her public career. Adunni spent her early years with the late Bishop Howells, the vicar of St. John's church Aroloya, Lagos. Adunni's political life started during the general strike of 1945 in Nigeria. As a religious person with a keen sense of social justice, she believed that "human endeavors should be governed by fair play" (126).

The strike of 1945 was triggered by inflation and economic hardship brought about by the aftermath of the Second World War. Adunni Oluwole was sympathetic to the cause of the strikers. She attended their meetings and encouraged them to uphold their principles until success would be theirs. She provided the strikers with financial and moral support, and the striking workers appreciated her generous support such that at her death in 1957 the two rival trade unions in Nigeria were united for the first time in appreciation for her services.

After 1945, Adunni Oluwole emerged as a champion of the worker's interest. She became a public figure not only in Lagos but throughout Nigeria. The strike convinced her that the only way for workers and other Nigerians to achieve better living conditions was to send the colonial exploiters away from Nigeria. After the strike she turned her attention fully to politics and became distinguished as a leader. She was always present at campaign meetings and lectures. In early 1954, Adunni Oluwole was one of the first women in Nigeria to form a political party (Ogunsanya 1992). The party became known as the Nigerian Commoners' Liberal Party. This became a confirmation of her interest in the welfare of ordinary folk. Her aims in founding the party were basically twofold: first, to oppose independence in 1956 in a motion proposed in 1953 by

Anthony Enahoro (a member of the Action Group) and second, to oppose the abuse of power by men who dominated the political scene.

Her opposition to Nigeria's independence in 1956 puzzled a number of Nigerians. However, Adunni Oluwole's rationale was influenced by her overriding interest for Nigerian unity and her belief that Nigeria could not achieve independence as a united country in 1956, because the northern politicians were not prepared for independence as one Nigeria (see Coleman 1958).

In spite of her opposition to independence in 1956, Adunni Oluwole's political goal was to achieve emancipation of Nigeria from the British and to uplift the sufferings of the ordinary person. Her party was well organized but lacked financial support. As a result, she was handicapped in realizing her objectives. To make matters worse, the newness of the party made it unattractive to the masses, and the fact that it was led by a woman made it unattractive. Adunni Oluwole was not elected to any political office, but her party scored a political victory when its candidate D.L.G. Olateju was elected from Ikirun in the former Western Region.

Oluwole's political career was short. It lasted only three years, but she left her imprint on Nigeria's political scene. She combined motherhood and public life. Adunni Oluwole was the torchbearer of emancipation of women in Nigeria. She was a trailblazer as an organizer and a forerunner of a political party run by a woman. Her career was cut short by death. On November 13, 1957, on her campaign trip to Ijebu-Ode, she suddenly fell sick and died at the age of fifty-two. She was mourned by her followers, particularly, the Nigerian workers. Adunni Oluwole's political career and struggles demonstrated the problems that Nigeria women face in a male-dominated political system.

Olufunmilayo Ransome-Kuti (1900-1978)

Funmilayo Ransome-Kuti was nicknamed the "Lioness of Lisabi Land" (Mba 1982). She attended Abeokuta Grammar School, graduated and became a teacher there, and later went to England to study music, education, and domestic science.

Funmilayo's political career began when she formed the Abeokuta Ladies Club in 1944, made up of Christian, educated women teachers and traders. The club would later take interest in issues of concern to illiterate market women. Having been informed about issues confronting market women by a friend, Funmilayo became interested in the market women's plight and began to work closely with them to achieve a common goal. The club would change its name to the Abeokuta Women's Union in 1946, and Mrs. Ransome-Kuti was named its president. This was the beginning of her political life.

The Abeokuta Women's Union's goals and objectives were to see to the social welfare of women across Abeokuta. Their aims were to work for the rights of women that were threatened by the Sole Native Authority, made up of men.

The authority was headed by the Alake of Abeokuta, Oba Ademola II, who, under indirect rule system, was a tool of oppression by the colonial oppressors. The women documented in great detail all the alleged abuses committed under the Alake (Mba 1982). These abuses included price controls, interference in trade, monopoly, exploitation, and a host of other human injustices. The Alake was forced to abdicate the throne to appease the people of Abeokuta. Mrs. Kuti continued to fight against unnecessary taxation of market women. She organized a well-orchestrated mass demonstration that was disciplined, and orderly with solidarity and described by Mba as very impressive.

Mrs. Ransome-Kuti was an eloquent and compelling speaker whose expressive, idiomatic language was superb, sharp, and brilliant. She used her brilliance to further her cause. Her prominence brought her in alliance with the National Council of Nigeria and the Cameroon (NCNC) but she decided to support the women's cause. All these accolades and prominence brought Ransome-Kuti to political limelight in Abeokuta, where she was nominated to represent Abeokuta province at a provincial conference for a constitutional proposal. In 1951, Mrs. Ransome-Kuti was defeated in her bid for the House of Representatives. She became the leader of the Abeokuta branch of the NCNC opposition party in the council. By 1949, her Women's Union metamorphosed into a National Women's Organization. She toured the country to plead her case before women in other parts of the country. She joined forces with the already established women's organizations in places like Enugu and Aba to form the Federation of Nigerian Women Societies. The organization agitated for the colonial administration to nominate women into local governments, to extend educational opportunities to women, and to improve the social status of women. Funmilayo was credited with founding the Federation of Nigerian Women, an International Women's Democratic Federation. She became the vice president in 1953. Mrs. Kuti was given international recognition and was invited to speak at the International Women's Organization (I.W.O.) conference in the United States but was denied entry visa, having been labeled a communist. She was not a communist, but when the question was asked of her, she replied that her father was a member of the African Farmers commune, and she said, if that made her a communist, then she is one (Mba 1982).

Mrs. Ransome-Kuti committed her life to democratic reforms. She once contested a seat to the House of Representatives on the NCNC platform but was scorned by men who believed that women had no place in politics: hence, they refused to support her candidacy. She broke away from the NCNC and formed her own political party, the Commoners' People's Party. As a result, she was expelled from the NCNC. Her party lasted a little over a year, but the imprint she left became a legacy for others to follow. Her bravery and courage were phenomenal. She was the first Nigerian politician to build bridges between the East and the West. She died in 1978, having laid the groundwork for a younger generation of women to follow. Throughout her life, she demonstrated love, and compassion and was a dedicated mother. Mrs. Ransome-Kuti was a great organizer and skilled politician. She committed her life to the emancipation of women even in an era of male domination.

GENDER ISSUES IN NIGERIA

Political participation in developed countries is a general phenomenon characterizing a truly democratic society. The right to vote and partake in political process constitutes luxury and the freedom long sought by so many people around the world. This participative process, in turn, permeates the smooth, effective, and efficient running of the government institutions that breeds accountability. In Nigeria, the reverse is the case.

The question now is, Why is it that the momentum of the precolonial days died with the passage of time? Among the many factors that seem to contribute to these deficiencies are tradition, the stereotyped role associated with being a woman, the lack of education, discrimination, and the role assigned to women. Women are said to be onlookers, the ideology was that a woman's place is in the home, and working outside the home became an abomination. Consequently, Nigerians developed their political system to conform with the political philosophies in existence. Hence, societal interactions are geared toward men only. Furthermore, women are expected to give birth to children, raise them, and ensure the continuation of the family. Nigerian women believe that politics is dirty. Based on this, they depended on men to do the actual mobilization of other women, which did little to enhance their political participation. Compounding this lack of political participation is the fact that a good number of people resides in the rural areas where there are no good roads, electricity, and means of communication, and hence they are cut off from the mainstream. Nigerian women are belittled in political matters. Their opinions are profoundly ridiculed as women's gossip. Their contributions are not taken seriously. In spite of their role in nurturing and maintaining life, Nigerian women's interests and opinions are considered secondary and are politically suppressed by their male counterparts.

Equally degrading was that the colonial rulers were primarily interested in formal education of men and not of women. The approach was to keep women as good housewives and competent mothers as opposed to being trained for careers outside the home. Discrimination against girls could be said to have begun at birth. The disadvantages of being a female are obvious within the society prior to the modern era. Lower life expectancy, minimum education, poorly paid jobs, lower status expectation, and very few rewards compared to men are common characteristics of circumstances that women confront. Thus, sex-roles differentiation and traditional ideological assumptions about women's place are linked to the unequal distribution of resources, rewards, rights, and authority between men and women, which, in turn, influence patterns of family and work life. This historic imbalance of power between the sexes has become a major obstacle in the pursuit of equality.

The political participation of women in Nigeria prior to and after independence varied significantly through time. In the northern part of the country, for example, women's participation is said to be nonexistent, whereas in the southern part of the country the same cannot be said of their accomplishments. Women fared better in the south than their northern counterparts. In the south, both the Yoruba and the Ibo traditions allowed women to play different roles and contributed enormously to the economic development of the southern part of the country. These women of the south were traders with significant roles in the marketplaces. They dominated every sphere of influence in the marketplace, becoming marketing trailblazers as they acquired economic importance, using their economic power to protest unfavorable political decisions and sometimes influence politics.

Feminist activities continued to be a hot agenda in Nigeria. The struggle for equality by women can be traced back to the infamous Aba protest of 1929, born out of women resentment of oppression. Although it was said to have been a misunderstanding of information concerning taxing market women, the idea of taxation angered the hardworking market women whose husbands were taxpayers. They eventually decided against any form of taxation that would tend to put an additional burden on them. Hence, a protest was launched in Aba and Owerri. The flame of the protest spread like an echo in the wilderness through some eastern provinces, including Calabar and Opobo. The event was considered "a knee slapper" to the colonial masters, who consequently ordered the protest to be stopped at all cost. Aba women defied the colonial order. At the end, more than fifty-three women were gunned down in Calabar province. Although the women failed in their attempt to overcome the oppressors, their actions went down in the annals of the history of Nigeria for challenging the colonial government.

In Nigeria politics has been dubbed a man's profession for as long as one can remember, and men continue to hold onto power by all means necessary. This philosophical ideology comes under the premise that women are much less inclined to partake in politics, hence are not featured in the so-called powerful political positions let alone contests for public offices. Whether or not this is a legitimate argument lies in the political imbalance and political disparities between men and women in Nigeria. Women continue to be relegated to a second-class citizen role when it comes to politics, as they have been considered unlikely to become actively involved in the politics of Nigeria. They continue to make up a share of disproportionately small share of voters. This is due, in part, to the fact that there were only three major elections in Nigeria since independence. They also disrupt the effective flow of government by suspending the legally constructed constitution and substituting decrees. Furthermore, the percentage of women who are active in public office remains relatively low in comparison to their male counterparts. Another problem is that Nigerians believe that by participating in politics, they have found a pot of gold, and the means to line their pockets with government funds. Politics has been dominated for a long time by men; therefore, women who go into politics face insurmountable obstacles of coping with the challenges and the day-to-day mudslinging that political dealings entail. It is also believed that political kingmakers tend not to look in the direction of women when considering those who will lead respective parties to victory; hence, they rarely select women candidates to chair party caucuses. Women outnumber men by more than two to one, yet they are seldom utilized to fill important political posts. Rather, some are used as campaign helpers, whose duties are to distribute leaflets and other campaign memorabilia.

Gender plays a significant role in Nigerian societies. Sexual discrimination in Nigeria occurs at an alarming rate, and this has led to male domination. Consequently, women are not offered key government positions. Considering the efficiency of women and their managerial roles at homes, one can say that they are more efficient than men. It is also appropriate to note that the job of childbearing and child raising is the most tedious and most demanding profession second to none and one in which no man can boast of any comparison. This prompted Margaret Mead as (cited in Elechi 1982) to point out that technology and new sources of power freed men, not women. She went on to say, "Equal education, political suffrage, freedom of occupation, the right to ownership of property, freedom to live an independent life, however necessary, are not satisfactory solutions to the problem of how women are to make contributions as individual human beings as well as in their roles as wives, and mothers and maintainers of the minutiae of individual lives" (1982: 76). In every society, socialization forms an integral part that helps to defuse the disparities between men and women on many fronts of political activities and attitudes.

Among the factors considered in bringing about a change in the structure of a society are education, occupation, and income. Education is and will continue to be in the forefront of any political awareness that will contribute to women's participation and involvement in the state and national politics. By Nigerian tradition too many women continue to remain housewives. The number of women in this group increases by the day due to lack of awareness and political participation. Thus, those who actively take part in the political process and other public affairs are not as many when the entire number of women in the country is taken into consideration. Furthermore, those who actively pursue careers outside the home have more to do on their return to their respective homes. Therefore, these women find comfort at home rather than being involved with the tedious tasks of politics.

WOMEN IN POSTINDEPENDENCE NIGERIA

During the 1960s, more Nigerian women than in the past were educated. As a result a few women were given political appointments. Notwithstanding; the limited resources for planning for national education Nigeria began to value education as a means of attaining higher standard of living. In spite of these gains, in the 1960s Nigerian women were not appointed to high-profile governmental positions. The military governments in the 1960s and the 1970s did not make concerted efforts to offer to draft more women into the political arena. Things began to change in the late 1970s because more women became assertive and educated, and, more importantly, they began to take a more active role in politics. This resulted in the election of Franka Efegbua to the Senate, followed by the appointment of Flora Nwapa, the noted novelist, as commissioner by the civilian administrator of the East Central State, D. Miller in the North Eastern State, and two in Oyo State, Folake Solanke and Ronke Doherty, along with Kofoworola Pratt in Lagos State, Mrs. Ebun Oyabola as the minister of national planning, Mrs. Elizabeth Irase, minister of state education, and Mrs. Janet Akinrinmade, minister of state internal affairs, and Mrs. H. A. Balogun was appointed the first female attorney general for Lagos State, an unprecedented scaling of hurdles for women. This is a very encouraging development in the history of the development of women in enhancing their status (Mba, cited in Pratt and Staudt 1989).

In the 1980s the military administration of Buhari issued directives to appoint women to government but failed to carry them out. But at the state level there was improvement. It can be argued that under the Babangida regime, women became involved, and Babangida seemed to have implemented the Buhari directives (Mba, cited in Pratt and Staudt 1989). The administration also set up a political bureau to continue to work and bring more and more women into the political mainstream. This was evident in the appointment of Professor Grace Alele as the first women vice chancellor of the University of Benin. In celebration of this august occasion, Babangida was quoted as saying, "Let there be known that here in Benin I believe we have started what appears to be a silent revolution to bring women directly into the mainstream of the government and administration of higher learning" (Adinuba 1990: 84).

SUMMARY AND CONCLUSION

As we approach a new millennium, there is an urgent need for change not only in the status quo but also in the attitude and political disparities born out of male chauvinism. The bone of contention in Nigeria has been the inability to overcome the problem of gender and the many divisions it has created. The need to begin to practice the politics of integration and inclusion as opposed to exclusion is now more evident than ever. Nigeria is a vast country whose human and other resources continue to be eroded by the hour due to the politics of exclusion. Women can no longer be excluded from the politics of Nigeria if Nigeria is to take its place as a leader in the African continent in the twenty-first century.

The politics of self-actualization should be a thing of the past, and the politics of inclusion for a united Nigeria should be operative across the board. Political disparities have created enormous problems in the past, and their continuing presence in both state and national politics poses grave danger for the future. Attempts should be made at all levels to bring about change in the political behaviors of all Nigerians. Women should no longer be left out of the political scene; they should be made to become flag bearers and should be heavily recruited by all political parties. For one thing, it is time to allow women to run for higher political offices and move within the hierarchy of leadership. After all, women have succeeded in bringing about political, social, educational, and economic gains in countries such as Israel, where the late Golda Meir ruled and effectively led her country to prominence. Consider also Eva Peron in Argentina and Margaret Thatcher in Britain, who actively oversaw the revival of the British economy as it progressed through the cold war era and was the first woman prime minister in Western Europe. Corazon Aquino brought credibility to the government of the Philippines after the Marcos era. She ruled the tiny archipelago island and saved it from anarchy and chaos. Chamorro of Nicaragua won a heavily contested election from the ruling Sandinistas and brought stability to the Central American republic; Indira Gandhi ruled India, the world's most populous democracy, for more than a decade with immeasurable success, and Beneazir Bhutto of Pakistan was elected to the post of prime minister on more than one occasion. Now in the United States for the first time in history, a woman has been appointed to the post of secretary of state.

Change is as inevitable as the coming of the seasons. It cannot be avoided, and, sad as it may seem, it is inescapable. According to Kegley and Wittkopf (1995), inevitably, the transformation of world politics now taking place will confront nation-states and other world political actors with new issues that cry out for novel means of addressing them. The winds of change sweeping through the world ought to serve as a serious lesson to Nigeria. Women's empowerment should be initiated and become attractive enough to alter the balance of power throughout the federation. Sustainable political development that will now put women at the forefront of the national agenda should be emphasized. Thus, a modernizing society like Nigeria needs to take part in the international division of labor, so that exogamous politicization roles may form the support of the society's modernization roles. Because modernization is said to be a special kind of hope, it has embodied within it previous revolutions of history and human desires. It thus became epic in scale and moral significance, even though its consequences might be frightening. Therefore, whatever direction it takes, the struggle to modernize is what has given meaning to this generation. It tests the cherished institutions and beliefs of the society. It puts society in the marketplace, and Nigeria is no exception. This struggle to modernize and to practice the politics of inclusion that takes into account the effects and roles of women in national government should be the cornerstone of every political debate and change. The divisions created in the country by the colonial master, Great Britain, and still allowed to remain are the real culprit that must be tried and put away forever. The time is now to put an end to the shameful political practices in Nigeria. The politics of exclusion has no place in modern society. Everyone in Nigeria, men and women alike, is part and parcel of the government. Therefore, to think that a part is better than the whole is not proper. It is as dangerous as ever for a given government not to give its population a voice in governing. It is even more dangerous to keep a population mute, ignoring their input and making only cosmetic changes. Nigeria should not let tradition supplant modernization.

Finally, we are in a new era of equality of gender, as the world continues to witness the era of space satellites, and technological advancement. It is easy to see that human beings generally are living in a rapidly changing society. Today, it is a common phenomenon that the survival of a society depends on its ability to educate its people irrespective of gender. It is believed that the goal of every political endeavor is to democratize its system to encompass everyone within the system. Therefore, politics of inclusion should be made to meet economic needs and cultural aspirations of the people. The system must educate the rural and urban dwellers, including the illiterate and the poor. After all, nations seeking political growth must never waver from allowing everyone to blossom. No nation can develop by neglecting its human resources. Women are Nigeria's greatest asset. They must be made to partake in local state and national politics. In the words of C. Don Adinuba (1990), "There is nothing in its character which fundamentally makes it impossible for Nigeria to become a stable democratic nation, rather than just a stable state. Few countries the world over are blessed with abundance of material and human resources as Nigeria." He went on to say that the country cannot afford to be a clay-footed giant. No nation is as much a beacon of hope to Africa and the Black world as Nigeria. For stability, economic prosperity, and development and for the interest of unity, let the politics of inclusion be the mission and goal, let the hardworking women of our great nation become the torchbearers.

Nigerian women must come to recognize that politics determines the allocation of all resources in society and that their alienation from politics means that their special interest will continue to be neglected. If Nigerian women are to achieve emancipation and equality, it is imperative for women in Nigeria to organize mass associations to assure effective political strategy. In addition, women's political activism should be geared toward putting pressure on the government to achieve a new Nigerian society that will be gender-blind.

REFERENCES

Abubakr, Saiad. 1992. "Queen Amina." In Bolanle Awe, *Nigerian Women in Historical Perspectives*. Ibadan, Nigeria: Sankore/Bookcraft.
Adinuba, C. Don. 1990. "Nigeria: The Making of a Nation." *West Africa* (Dec./Jan.).
Amadi, Elechi. 1982. *Ethics in Nigerian Culture*. Ibadan, Nigeria: Heinemann Educational Books.
Awe, Bolanle. 1992. *Nigerian Women in Historical Perspectives*. Ibadan, Nigeria: Sankore/Bookcraft.
Coleman, J. S. 1958. *Nigeria: Background to Nationalism*. Berkeley, CA: University of California Press.

Joseph, A., M. Kesselman, and J. Krieger. 1996. *Third World Politics at the Crossroads*. Lexington, MA: D. C. Heath.

Kegley, Charles W., Jr. and Eugene R. Wittkopf. 1995. *The Global Agenda: Issues and Perspectives*. 4th ed. New York: McGraw-Hill Publishers.

Mba, Nina E. 1982. *Nigerian Women Mobilized: Women's Political Activity in Southern Nigeria 1900-1955*. Berkeley, CA: Institute of International Studies, University of California.

Ogunsanya, G. O. 1992. "Adunni Oluwole." In Bolanle Awe, *Nigerian Women in Historical Perspectives*. Ibadan, Nigeria: Sankore/Bookcraft.

Pellow, Deborah. 1977. *Women in Accra: Options for Autonomy*. Algonac, MI: Reference Publications.

Potholm, P. Christian. 1970. *Four African Political Systems*. Englewood Cliffs, NJ: Prentice-Hall.

Pratt, Jane L., and Kathleen A. Staudt. 1989. *Women and the State in Africa*. Boulder, CO, and London: Lynne Riener.

3

Women's Empowerment and the Anthropology of Participatory Development

Ester Igandu Njiro

INTRODUCTION

The empowerment, autonomy, and improvement of women's political, economic social, and health status were one of the important issues discussed in a conference at Beijing. The purpose of this chapter is to highlight the current status of women's empowerment in the context of participatory development in post-Beijing Africa. Although the issues are broad and vary from community to community in each of the African countries, there are common factors that can be discussed broadly as applicable to the whole region of Africa. Lack of enjoyment by women vis-a-vis men of equal access to political influence, economic power, and social status is a characteristic feature of women in all the African countries.

Women all over Africa are facing threats to their lives, health, and well-being as a result of being overburdened with work. This is despite the international, regional, and individual efforts. Only modest progress has been achieved, and critical gaps continue to exist in several areas.

Anthropological analysis reveals several underlying factors that impede women's progress and perpetuate gender inequality. Poverty is the overriding cause for the continued power relations that impede women's empowerment at all levels of society in many of the African countries. Women's lack of income excludes them from the market, political, and social decision-making forums. Their inability to meet the most basic needs keeps them susceptible to exploitation by those with power for policy and development.

The chapter recommends changes that are specifically directed to policy and program action geared to improve women's access to secure economic resources and alleviation of workloads. This will entail full participation of both women and men if sustainable development is to be achieved.

Anthropology of people's participation in development is a complex concept that defies any simple definition. Participation is primarily concerned with broad commitment to redress the imbalances of development activities and to provide conditions under which people can take an active role in the development process. Development is a vast topic which deals with the dynamic processes of improving human life through systematic changes geared at betterment of human life. Human development entails a multidimensional process involving individuals and societies at both national and international levels. Individual development entails increased skills, capacity, freedom, creativity, self-discipline, and material well-being. Societal and national development entails a capacity to regulate internal and external relationships as well as a capacity to determine a nation's future destiny. As a holistic process, it involves changes in societal structures, attitudes, and cultural institutions, acceleration of economic growth, and eradication of inequality, poverty, and cultural values that discourage the betterment of human life. In practice, participation is conceived in two main ways: first, as development programs in which people's participation is often passive and consultative and second, where people are active in all aspects of social-economic development. Development at international levels entails a genuine concern for the welfare of the less fortunate people that goes beyond handing out leftovers.

In Africa, human development is hindered by a narrow range of choices manifested by several factors. Cultural institutions in many African countries have a rigid stratification enforced by traditional beliefs which minimize individual and societal initiatives and thus discourage human development. Factionalism, ethnic, racial and religious distinctions are emphasized bringing about kinship loyalties, regional identification and cultural conflicts. Other indices of lack of human development are ignorance in economic issues, low labor efficiency immobility and limited specialization in occupation and trade.

Disempowerment of women is another major impediment to development in many of the African countries. The way gender issues were introduced in Kenya and perhaps in most of Africa seemed to threaten the patriarchal status and left a trail of hostility that made the concept of women's empowerment offensive to every male who heard it. The concept originated in developed countries and was launched aggressively in Kenya and most of Africa by feminist trainers with the good intentions of uplifting the status of their sisters in the south (Munyakho 1995; Njiro 1995).

This chapter highlights some observations on the way women's disempowerment continues to be a hindrance to development in Africa, Kenya in particular. The problem is in the way concepts of women's empowerment were introduced. Concepts such as women in development (WID), women and development (WAD), and gender and development (GAD), which originated from developed countries, were launched very vigorously in developing countries by aggressive feminists whose intentions were to uplift the lot of women all over the world. Not much thought was put into the cultural orientation, and this may have brought about the misunderstanding and lack of implementation of women's empowerment programs. To date, a trail of hostility characterizes whatever efforts are made toward women's empowerment in Kenya and other parts of Africa. Patriarchy is greatly offended by any effort that can effectively change the situation, as was observed among communities around Mount Kenya, as shown in the following three study sites.

RESEARCH SITES FOR CASE STUDIES

The research that informs this chapter was carried out in Laikipia, Embu, and Tharaka-Nithi, the three districts surrounding Mount Kenya (see Figure 3.1).

Laikipia

Laikipia lies to the northwestern foot-zones (bottom area) of Mount Kenya. It is to the eastern side of the Rift Valley with an area of about 9,723 kilometers and is divided into five divisions of Central, Lamuria, Mukogondo, Ngarua, and Ruinuruti. The district is a level plateau bounded by the edge of the Rift Valley to the west and Mount Kenya massifs to the south (Njiro 1995). The altitude is, on the average, very high, with the north 180 meters and the south 2,100 meters above sea level. The drainage to the district is through Ewaso Nyiro River and its tributaries. These rivers have their sources in Mount Kenya and flow from south to north in the district.

This study was carried out in West Laikipia, which is 4,612 square kilometers in size and accounts for 47 percent of the whole district. The specific research sites were Ngarua and Rumuruti divisions, with a dry and cold climate. Rainfall is unimodal, and often there are no rains from August to March. Erratic rain amounts to about 600 millimeters per year. This climate affects the land use patterns, and the general impression is that of subsistence and poverty for a good number of farming households that were studied.

Embu

Embu is a district in the eastern province that lies to the southeastern foothills of Mount Kenya and has an area of 2,714 square kilometers. Up until February 1996, after the creation of Mbcere district, Embu district was divided into four division: Runyenjes, Manyatta, Gachoka, and Siakago. The altitude rises from 515 meters at river Tana in the East to over 4,570 meters on top of Mount Kenya. The drainage is provided by six major rivers and their tributaries: Rupingazi, Ena, Kavingazi, Thuci, Thiba, and Nyaniindi, whose sources are located in Mount Kenya. They flow from the north to the south of the district.

The research site was around the tea-coffee-dairy agroeconomic zone, which is found adjacent to the rain forest. The area has cool temperatures, about 12°C during the months of June, July, and August. The hottest months are December, January, and February, with temperatures ranging between 20.4°C and

Figure 3.1
Research Sites around Mount Kenya

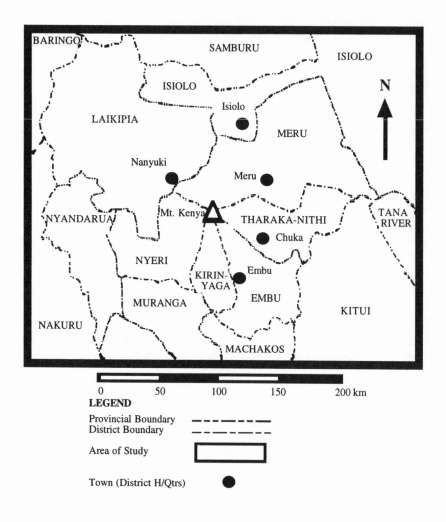

Source: Extracted and modified from the *District Development Plan*, 1994/1996.
Map drawn by: J. Kirema.
Computer graphics: Melanie Marshall James.

27.1°C. Rainfall is bimodal, with an average annual amount of 2,000 millimeters.

Tharaka-Nithi

Tharaka-Nithi is a relatively new district carved out of Meru on March 2, 1992, located to the east of Mount Kenya's peaks of Nyamene ranges. The district has an area of 2,136 square kilometers forming 21.53 percent of the original Meru district. It has five divisions: Mwimbi, Chuka, Tharaka North, Tharaka Central, and Tharaka South. The district is fairly flat with deep valleys along the following rivers: Thuci, Ruguti, Thanatu Ura, Mutonga, Nithi, and Tungu, all of which flow into the Tana. Most of these rivers have their catchment in Mount Kenya. Temperatures in the high altitude areas range between 17.0°C and 14.0°C, while the lowlands are hot and dry, rising to 37.5°C in the hottest month.

The research sites were Chiakariga Marimanti and Gatue in the lowlands of Tharaka South, central and north divisions. Rainfall has a bimodal pattern, with the rains falling in the months of March to May and October to December.

CASE STUDIES

Laikipia: Marginalization of Women in Household Food Security

In Ngarua and Rumuruti divisions, where this study was conducted, the people are small-scale farmers, squatters, and the landless. A focus on the relationship between marginality and household food security confirms the argument that, although marginalization and food shortage ideally affect members of the household, intrahousehold food distribution renders women and children more vulnerable. Malnutrition was confirmed in about 66 percent of the households as being a major problem. The consumption of food in these households lacked the required calories, proteins, and vitamins essential for the tasks that people engage in. The statistics for the children's nutrition revealed that only about 10 percent of those below six years were near the normal status of nutrition. Malnutrition is an indicator of poverty brought about by the constraints of low incomes. The situation for the women and children is aggravated by cultural beliefs and practices that relate to people's diets (Manguyu 1993).

Cultural factors play a significant role in conditioning the persistence of food habits and preferences (Guru 1980). Analysis of intrahousehold food distribution reveals a situation of contradictions where the women who are involved in all processes of food production, processing, and cooking are malnourished (Jellife 1962). Household food is unequally distributed. In the scarce-resource families of Laikipia, food is distributed according to concepts that proportionately favor men over women, adults over children, and boys over girls (see also Rothschild 1988). The notable discrepancy is where women are experts at production but have no power over distribution or even control over the benefits of the sold food resources. A situation where it is the prerogative of the men to distribute directly or to determine the pattern of distribution which invariably is in the interest of men against women and children, has been observed in many parts of Kenya (Rothschild 1988).

The cultural explanation for this imbalance is that a man, as the breadwinner for the family, should be served the largest and best portion of food at any given time. This is because the well-being of the household depends chiefly on the work and labor of the men. Such cultural norms have not taken note of the economic and social changes that have reduced the physical work of men. Nevertheless, social status and food habits are linked in such a way that distinctions based on class hierarchy make a difference. Desired foods are consumed by the privileged individuals who are accorded higher status (Caliendo 1979). Age and gender are other factors that determine food consumption in the sampled households. Children and the old people do not eat *Githeri,* a mixture of maize and beans, for it is difficult for them to chew and digest it. Pregnant women do not consume beer or other alcoholic drinks, for they could lead to miscarriages. Pregnant women also limit their intake of foods high in calories and proteins such as eggs, in order to prevent difficult deliveries due to cephalopelvic disproportion. These restrictions are, however, very loose and generalized and may not be zealously adhered to. When asked to identify foods beneficial for lactating and pregnant mothers, the same women listed milk, eggs, beans, and potatoes. The prohibitions are, however, maintained in subtle ways through a distribution system that allows only men to eat the best of what is available.

Foods of animal origin such as, meat, milk, and eggs are accorded higher status in the traditional food continuum (Swantz 1984). Thus, it was found that women are systematically deprived nutritionally by a cultural symbolism that gives men better nutrition regardless of the food situation of the community.

Table 3.1 shows the intrahousehold food distribution and the order in which food is served and eaten by respondents of the study sample. Table 3.2 shows the responses when respondents were further asked to rationalize the order of eating that they had given.

From Table 3.2, it is clear that as many as 92.4 percent of the respondents alluded to either traditions or respect as basic determinants of the women-biased eating order. The preferential social hierarchy that gives men top priority is reflective of the patriarchal cultural structure of the respondents. This bias is enshrined in the minds of the people such that women found it difficult to respond to questions that were tantamount to challenging patriarchal values that are supportive of male superiority and expectation for preferential treatment. In real terms the preferences are a relic of the past, as it can be argued beyond any reasonable doubt that women are the ones involved in breadwinner economic

Table 3.1
Eating Order by Households

	Frequencies	Percent
No Order	32	21.1
Father, Children, Mother	64	58.1
Mother, Children, Father	1	1.0
Children, Father, Mother	13	11.8
Total	110	100.0

Source: Adapted from Olenja (1990: 12).
Computer graphics: Melanie Marshall James.

Table 3.2
Reasons for Eating Order

	Frequencies	Percent
Tradition	47	42.7
Respect	54	49.7
Children Need More	7	6.4
Other Reasons	2	1.8
Total	110	100.0

Source: Adapted from Olenja (1990: 12-13).
Computer graphics: Melanie Marshall James.

activities, particularly in the resource-poor West Laikipia. Cultural values have not yet caught up with the realities of the situation.

Embu: Increased Workloads for Women in Tea-Producing Households

Tea production is a very labor-intensive agricultural undertaking. To be allowed to grow tea, one must own a piece of land on which to grow as well as have a reliable family labor. A survey carried out in the area of this study revealed that 55 percent of the sampled tea growers relied on family labor, and only about 10 percent were able to have hired labor. Family labor comprises a man, his wife or wives, and children. In many of the studied households men were found to be away in search of off-farm wage employment, while children were in school, and the only available family labor was the women. Even in households where men had not left, they preferred working on coffee, where the work is not as intensive as on the tea farms. Since in almost all the farms land is owned by men, they were the ones with the power to command the labor of women.

Tea plucking requires rising very early in the morning so as to cover a large area of plantation by one o'clock in the afternoon, when it is compulsory to deliver tea leaves to the buying centers. The chill of the morning dew leaves the pluckers wet up to the neck. The conditions of working on a tea farm are long hours of carrying a heavy basket while standing throughout the plucking period without breaks. The combination of long hours, poor conditions, and poor nutrition causes poor health and a state of continuous fatigue for those interviewed during this study (Olenja 1990). By the time they leave the buying centers, it is late in the evening, and yet they have to ensure that their families are fed for supper. This is the time men call *Marugia aka,* a derogatory term that mocks the way women literally run up and down the house and compound to fulfill their domestic duties.

There is no doubt that tea production has intensified the workload for women, especially because they have to combine the labor-intensive activities with those of catering for their households. Increased labor burdens for women are the result of entering into the commodity production at a subordinate position where property ownership, rather than labor inputs, is what counts. Their low economic status in the farming undertakings is the result of being viewed as belonging to the traditional subsistence economy while the men are in the modern sector. Consequently, they are regarded as unemployed laborers bound to accept whatever terms the employer (the men owners of the farms) offer (see also Fruzzetti 1985).

The situation on these tea farms is not all bleak, because in 78 percent of the households women have devised ways of bargaining for better terms. Despite their dominant position, men are careful not to annoy the women. One of the reasons for this is that women are the custodians of the symbolic values associated with the prestige and high status of their husbands. The prevailing relationships are those of mild conflicts that allow room for negotiations and venting frustrations by both women and men.

THARAKA: GENDER PERSPECTIVES FOR COPING WITH SCARCE FOOD RESOURCES

Division of Labor by Gender and Age

This study found an asymmetrical division of labor in Tharaka. In almost all crop cultivation activities, men are nearly always armchair managers, while women do the actual duties of food production, which include land clearing, planting, weeding, and protecting. All harvesting activities, including processing for storage, are the responsibility of the women. Men become active participants only when the harvest is abundant, and there are possibilities of selling the surplus amounts for cash. Then they provide transport and are very enthusiastic about the farm produce. Their keenness starts early when they build platforms to facilitate the complete drying out of grains and legumes on the farms.

Threshing and winnowing are almost always exclusively the work of women. Women and girls are also responsible for the processing, preservation, and storage of the grains. In addition, they are the ones who perform the food preparation, which includes fetching water and firewood, cooking, serving and washing of the dishes (Njiro 1995). Data from the field did not make it clear whether the Tharaka men know how to prepare the meals or just did not want to bother to learn.

Children often help their parents in agricultural, animal husbandry, and domestic activities. Boys do most of the herding, while girls do most of the domestic chores. Domestic duties are mainly tasks that deal with food production and provision of a clean and safe environment. Food shortages make women and girls seek ways to cope with the shortages. Alternative sources of food include gathering crops that grow in the wild. Even when there is flour to provide the main meals, women have to search for vegetables, legumes, and roots to be used as sauces and condiments. Women know where rare species of what makes up the relishes can be obtained. The author traveled to far-off areas where women got leaves from a variety of wild plants useful for relishes. Fruits and stems were also collected to be sold in the market. Many of the plants from which the leaves were obtained are drought-resistant and are used during periods of food scarcity.

Modern division of labor by gender and the migrations of some members of the household have intensified the Tharaka women's workload. This is because tasks of cultivation and animal husbandry that were performed by men are added to the women's arduous tasks of fetching water, gathering fuel, and looking for edible wild vegetables to eat. Child care, which involves feeding, cleaning, and training the children, is another task exclusively for the women. Health care for the family, which involves traveling long distances in search of health centers, and washing clothes by hand as well as cleaning the house and utensils, is also their duty. These activities are often viewed as noneconomic, for they are not income-generating and generally have no pecuniary remuneration (Mbilinyi 1990; Fruzzetti 1985). Guyer (1985) was right when she observed that procurement of diet is greatly feminized, and, in general, women cannot count on regular support from men. Table 3.3 depicts what this author observed in cultivation activities performed by females and males in Tunyai.

Table 3.3 also demonstrates that men's interest in farmwork is mainly for crops that have greater value in the market than for subsistence. They also tend to put their labor on those activities that have relatively fewer labor requirements. Table 3.3 also confirms that women spend much of their energy on subsistence crops that require protection. Women lose crops such as millet to the problems brought on by drought. Women's crops such as millet were labor-intensive. Even though maize does not require constant protection against birds, it is inadequate for food supply because it requires more rainfall than millet. So, by opting to plant maize in order to ease their labor requirements, men often end up losing the crop, which puts them under problems of food shortage.

During this study as many as 50 percent of the respondents, both husbands and wives, stated that they owned separate gardens. This was said to be one of the ways of coping with food shortages. Men, however, have the advantage of mobilizing the labor of their wives to work in their gardens, while women

Table 3.3
Division of Labor in Tunyai

	Males				Females			
	Pl	Wd	Ht	Mkt	Pl	Wd	Ht	Mkt
Maize	44	28	54	56	77	67	65	60
Millet & Sorghum	3	3	2	11	53	68	69	87
Green grain	15	18	20	24	13	13	16	16
Sunflower	5	5	5	4	5	6	6	6
Castor	5	5	5	4	7	7	6	5
Cotton	6	6	6	5	3	4	3	5

N = 30 males and 30 females (percentage of those above 15 years of age who work regularly on task).

Pl = Planting; Wd = weeding; Ht = Harvesting; Mkt = Market.

Computer graphics: Melanie Marshall James.

depend on their children, friends, and/or relatives for assistance. Women can obtain rights of cultivation from their natal homes. What is harvested from these separate gardens is available for the needs of all household members.

Thus, the conceptualization of a household as a place where resources are pooled and the benefits shared may not be a common feature in all the households. Consumption, it was noted, is not on an equal basis. For example, even though women in Tharaka control incomes accrued from their activities, they are responsible for very many household requirements. These include purchasing food, buying children's clothes, schoolbooks, uniforms, schoolfees, and transport, and paying market tolls. On the other hand, husbands use their incomes on what they consider productive investment (e.g., buying land, radios, and bicycles). The most visible expenditure of a number of men's income, however, is entertainment (i.e., buying beer and consumer goods and entertaining friends). In some few cases the needs of their households are considered only if there is money left for expendable purposes. However, these findings cannot be generalized for all the men because as many as 70 percent of those interviewed were very considerate in ensuring that their households are well supplied with basic needs.

One cannot, therefore, agree wholly with the views expressed by studies that stressed that a mother's income, rather than the overall household income, forms the significant factor in the status of child nutrition (ILO 1986). Thus, if men's incomes increase from agricultural production or other ways, the additional income may be used for the needs of their families.

These findings are a contribution to the Marxist-feminist scholarship that suggests ways in which patriarchal control within the family or kin group is linked to the division of labor by gender. As men become more involved in production for exchange, rather than for immediate consumption, the work of women is increasingly restricted to the domestic sphere. Similar views were earlier propounded by Hartmann when she wrote:

Dependence is a psychological and political economic relationship male control of women's labor power is the lever that allows men to benefit from women's provision of personal and household services including relief from child-rearing and many unpleasant tasks both within and beyond households. Patriarchy's material base is men's control of women's labor both in the household and in the labor market; the division of labor by gender tends to benefit men. (Hartmann 1981: 37)

Female Organization/Women's Groups

Written information describes the social structure of the Atharaka from a male point of view, and it was difficult to obtain information on women's participation and involvement in decision making. However, as seen in the preceding information, patriarchy dominates the Atharaka political and socioeconomic system. Males have a higher status than the females in most of the public decision making places. Lack of information concerning the role of women in politics and decision making has, in another context, been explained as due to the fact that most of those interviewed by ethnologists in Tharaka were men, and they may have been ignorant of the functions of women or afraid to disclose their secrets for fear of incurring the wrath of women councils (Hanger and Moris 1973).

This study established that there were women councils known as *kiama gia kagita.* These councils had the role of disciplining those who disobeyed or violated traditional law. Women also had important roles in religious ceremonies. In times of problems such as prolonged food shortages due to drought, the councils for women and for men met to make joint resolutions. This information is an indicator that traditional gender segregation was not necessarily oppressive to women. Current political situations of centralized political systems have eroded women's work, views, and position (Chalton 1984; Hartmann 1981), even though they have brought more women to the public.

The findings are opposed to the view that "the greater the involvement of women in nondomestic work the greater their status in their culture" (Chalton 1984: 25). Information collected during this study highlighted the high status of the role of women's groups in Tharaka traditionally.

In the past, women's groups catered to the personal, social, recreational, and ritual needs of individual women. Nowadays, women's groups in Tharaka, as in other parts of Kenya, go through four broad phases that overlap and often coexist within given groups. These are welfare, fund-raising, investment, and reorganization. In articulating these phases, women's groups are often equivalent to unions of the poorest of the poor (Holding 1942).

Two views were constantly expressed concerning the social functions of women's groups during this study. The first is that women manage to break out of male-dominated institutions that protect and oppress them (see also Nyaga-Mwanlki 1986 about women's groups in Mbeere). The second view places women's groups more explicitly within the existing relations of production. Women's groups are seen as the means of coping with the scarcity of resources in the context of changing socioeconomic situations. Such a view was important to this study, for women's groups are the local institutions that strive to cope with scarcity of food and other environmental resources in Tharaka.

Women had mixed views concerning their groups. Some preferred to work alone as individuals, and they engaged in making baskets and ropes and in other crafts. They are also extensively engaged in both formal and barter trade. Profits from their exchange activities as groups are so meager that many women expressed their dislike of the groups, while others had dropped out completely. As Sprig (1992: 346) propounded: "Some of the income-generation activities are really income preservation activities valued (really overvalued) because the family does not have to buy what the woman can make."

Other household dynamics noted during this study have to do with power relations between household members. As already pointed out, there is a situation of power inversion whereby children are, in some cases, the suppliers of the needed food in the households as well as the ones who pay fees and provide other requirements of their younger siblings.

Power restructuring is also becoming an important dynamic between husbands and their wives. Educated women with high-status jobs have changed attitudes toward what were accepted as gender-based roles, and they act in a manner that challenges the traditional roles that have held them in inferior positions compared to those of men (Sprig 1992). In Tharaka, as in other Kenyan societies, women are expected to be submissive to men. Nowadays, women who are relatively educated and have jobs are capable of buying their own lands, to which they have unlimited access and control. They also have the confidence and competence to nullify the habits of dependence that are the cornerstone of the Atharakas' patriarchal society. The market economy is thus raising women's marital powers, for many can now opt out of the subordinate roles and be independent. Nonetheless, discrimination against women still remains a common feature in Tharaka.

THREATS TO THE WELFARE OF WOMEN IN AFRICA

Beijing's platform of action singled out some of the causes for women's subordination. These include globalization of the economy, lack of contribution to the political power sharing, and health and reproduction rights. Women's low status is also traced to the lack of formal education and the fact that they are caught up in a vicious circle of poverty, pregnancy, disease, and premature death, particularly at childbirth.

This chapter focuses on the challenges that face those African countries that are keen on empowering women effectively for development. Empirical evidence from the case studies demonstrates the problem of women's empowerment.

Current status of African women is the result of their cumulated experience over the years. Figure 3.2 explains the interrelated factors that affect African women's well-being. Broadly speaking, we can summarize these factors as cultural traditions, powerlessness, education, economy, health, and environment.

Cultural Traditions

Although most cultural traditions in Africa regard the birth of a child as a joyous occasion, preference for sons is evident in the customs of many communities of Africa. Ordinarily, such preferences seem insignificant, but a deeper analysis reveals that this is the start of discriminatory practices against women and that it continues throughout their lives. Among the cultural practices that are obviously discriminatory against women are nutritional taboos, child marriages, wife inheritance, and traditionally sanctioned violence against women.

Nutritional taboos vary according to different cultures among the communities of Africa. Generally, foods rich in vitamins and minerals are proscribed by cultural norms. The consequences of depriving women of

Figure 3.2
The Interrelated Factors Affecting Women's Well-Being

THE VICIOUS CYCLE OF WOMEN'S HEALTH PROBLEMS

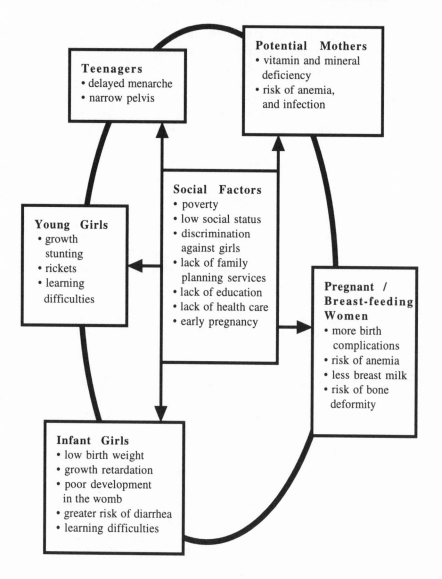

Computer graphics: Melanie Marshall James.

nutritious food are adverse effects on their health whereby many suffer toxemia and anemia, and many are vulnerable to infections due to low resistance to communicable diseases. Apart from the impact on the health of the mothers, malnutrition results in retardation or stillbirths.

In some African communities, female children are victims of early marriages whereby they are married off even before the first sign of puberty. Although these marriages are condoned by the communities, they are detrimental to the health of the young girl. Many of the child brides suffer from vesiovaginal and rectovaginal fistulae, kidney infection, and hypertension, among other ailments.

Widow inheritance is another punishment that women must endure. Despite the current medical reports that this practice facilitates the spread of sexually transmitted diseases, particularly the incurable HIV/AIDS, this practice is still allowed. No one should inherit the wife of any man suspected of having died from an unknown or incurable disease such as AIDS. Treatment should be sought for the wife or wives of such a person. Culture has a way of being blind to realities of contemporary societies in a place where many men are dying, leaving behind their wives. In some cases, makeshift cultural condemnation of the wives who are accused of being the murderers of their husbands is quickly bringing instant mob execution of the poor women. There must be an end to this practice.

Outdated cultural practices are detrimental to women, and the lack of legal recourse in some countries exacerbates the problem. Discriminatory practices have continued and are passed from generation to generation without rational evaluation of their negative impact on women. While we have lauded the need for maintaining valuable cultural practices to maintain the social and cultural identity of Africa, there is need to eliminate those that have outlived their usefulness. Continuous adherence to some of these serves to perpetuate male supremacy while suppressing the women. Obstructing one gender from a full and meaningful life is not conducive to human development. In this regard, violence against women must be discouraged.

Powerlessness

Power relations that discriminate against women in many African countries are not necessarily included in the law statutes of a country. There are, however, subtle omissions whose practical interpretation allows women's subordination. An example is the way constitutions of many African countries omit to include sex as a ground for discrimination and therefore punishable by law. Generally, the relationship between law and society in many African countries seems to give the state power to intervene on behalf of the offended family members only in issues brought to the public (Kabeberi-Macharia 1995). Family issues that are included within the law are registration of marriages, provision of social welfare, and whenever family matters are raised in courts. This legal system has the effect of adversely affecting women for many of the issues relating to their oppression, and their production and reproductive roles are not valued. The situation is worse with respect to violence and exploitation by the family members. In many cases women's oppression is traumatic to them, their children, and their families as a whole.

Education

Lack of formal education is a great disadvantage to girls and women. Illiteracy keeps women in subservient positions, as they lack what it takes to compete in the rapidly changing world. Although there has been a substantial increase in numbers of girls and women going to school, there are still few women engaged in professions that bestow recognition and influence (ECA 1989). Although there is widespread knowledge about the benefits of educating women, many African governments make no efforts to reinforce formal education for girls and women. In some places, the school curriculums are structured in such a way as to show that girls are not good students of science and technical subjects. This way, women are kept in their subservient roles, as they do not have what it takes to compete in the world.

Economics

The impact of changing from the traditional economies to Western free markets has resulted in extreme poverty in many African countries. Women are the poorest of the poor. Poverty at the national level is felt hardest at the household level. Poverty restricts people from making choices at various levels of life. Current structural adjustment programs' recommendation of severe cuts on the governments' spending on social services has an adverse effect on women whose position does not allow them sufficient flow of financial resources (Ouko, Riria 1993). Poverty is also brought about by illiteracy. Lack of knowledge and understanding of how economies work is found more with women than men. Lack of women role models in economics means lack of inspiration for younger women to pursue careers as economists.

Health

Poverty has serious adverse effects on women's health. Poor people have no means of obtaining adequate food, shelter, water, and sanitation. They cannot access appropriate and affordable health services, and they have poor understanding of health messages. Lack of health services leads to poor adjustments for survival and planning for the future. Poor people are not in a position to contribute to human development, as they are ever in ill heath. The health concerns of African countries include sexually transmitted diseases, cancers, difficult pregnancies, and disabilities. Women are facing these problems in ever-increasing numbers.

Although the health statistics have not been properly disaggregated in African countries, the World Health Organization estimates that of the 500,000 women who die from causes related to pregnancy and childbirth, 99 percent are from the developing countries, and about 50 percent of these are from Africa (Reid and Bailey 1995). In Africa about 80 percent of the births take place at home, where hygienic conditions are poor. Giving birth to many children is another problem that women in Africa suffer from.

WID, WAD, and GAD

Much of the current lack of women's empowerment in Africa and in Kenya may be traced to the way those in positions of power conceptualize equity between women and men. In my view the way these concepts were introduced is to blame. Without much cultural orientation, loaded key terms such as women in development (WID), women and development (WAD), and gender and development (GAD), among a host of others that challenged the supremacy of men in the African countries, were introduced. This could probably explain why many male-dominated African governments and NGOs have been reluctant to implement programs for women, even when these are essential for development. African women's empowerment sruggles have brought negative repercussions in rural areas, where in some households men continue to forbid women from participating in the women's group activities. The contempt was caused by the abrupt and aggressive lobbying by the North American feminists at high international offices. In many cases African heads of governments (men) did not understand the theories and practices behind the terminologies and acronyms of women's empowerment. We shall examine WID, WAD, and GAD to demonstrate the confusion of the meanings and assumptions that have continued to exacerbate the plight of women.

WID was first used as part of a deliberate strategy to bring in new research evidence (generated first by Ester Boserup 1970 and others) for advocacy on women's human rights. The North American feminists lobbied for change in the legal and administrative structures to ensure that women would be better integrated into economic systems. Action programs aimed at minimizing women's disadvantages in the productive sector were recommended. WID approaches were adopted by the international agencies.

The are, however, several shortcomings with this approach:

1. WID focused on the notion of development as a process of slow, but steady, linear progress. The solutions adopted were in areas of technological transfer and modernization. Benefits of development were meant to trickle down to women as their countries became modern.
2. The WID approach did not question the existing structures so as to find out why women fared badly from development processes. It was a confrontational approach that never examined the nature and the sources of women's subordination and oppression. Women were viewed as separate units of analysis

who were homogeneous. The diversity of women by race, class, ethnicity, and culture was ignored.

3. The WID approach concentrated only on productive aspects of women's lives. Women were viewed as agents of development processes rather than active participants and beneficiaries. The economic empowerment advocated assumed that access to income by women would change the gender relations at all levels, leading to a situation where women became full economic partners with the men. Women's groups in parts of Africa have never gone beyond being welfare groups.

Disillusionment with WID led to launching of WAD. WAD offered a more critical view of women's position than WID, but it did not undertake a full-scale analysis of the relationship between patriarchy, different modes of production, and women's subordination and oppression. Like WID, however, WAD's perspective assumes that women's position will improve if and when international structures become more equitable. How these could change was not stipulated clearly.

The GAD approach emerged in the 1980s and focused attention on social relations of gender. It questions the validity of the ascription of roles to women and men. Why have women been systematically assigned inferior roles? The GAD approach starts from a holistic perspective. It is concerned with women and men per se and also with the social construction of gender, the assignment of roles, and the responsibilities of both women and men. In contrast to WID and WAD, GAD welcomes potential contributions (not just productive and reproductive) within the context of the households and the public. GAD also emphasizes the participation of the State in promoting women's emancipation. It claims that it is the state's duty to provide the social services that women require.

CONCLUSIONS AND RECOMMENDATIONS

From the preceding information it is clear that, despite the pivotal link between women's empowerment and holistic and sustainable development, there is little progress toward achieving this goal in Kenya and some other countries of Africa. In many African countries, the current power relations impede women's attainment of empowerment. The challenge therefore is how women are to break the poverty trap that is the root to their lack of power. If the momentum gathered in Beijing is to be maintained, strategies to remove the obstacles in the way of women's progress must be devised. The following are the recommendations:

1. Women in Africa must remember the words of Nyerere which stressed that history shows that the oppressed can get allies from the dominant groups as they wage their own struggle for equality, human dignity, and progress. No one and no group can be liberated by others. The struggle for women's development must

be conducted by women not in opposition to men but as part of the social development for all the people.

2. Currently, African countries wishing to empower women must strike a balance between the demands of implementing structural adjustment programs (SAPs) and improving women's political and socioeconomic status. This is a major task, as SAPs entail measures that are detrimental to women's advancement.

3. In a situation of dwindling resources, it is going to require courageous men to integrate a gender perspective in the budgetary decisions on policies and programs to ensure equal participation and control by women and men in all the vital sectors of development.

REFERENCES

Boserup, Ester. 1970. *Women's Role in Economic Development.* New York: St. Martin's Press.

Caliendo, M. A. 1979. *Situational Analysis of Children and Women in Kenya.* Nairobi: United Nations International Children's Emergency Fund (UNICEF).

Chalton, S.E.M. 1984. *Women in the Third World Development.* Boulder, CO: Westview Press.

Economic Commission for Africa (ECA). 1989. "The Abuja Declaration on Participatory Development: The Role of Women in the 1990s." *The Outcome of the Fourth Regional Conference in the Integration of Women in Development.* Abuja, Nigeria: ECA.

Fruzzetti, I. 1985. "Farm and Health; Rural Women in a Farming Community." In H. A. Afsher (ed.), *Women: Work and Ideology in the Third World.* London: Tavistock.

Government of Kenya. 1994/1996. *District Development Plan.* Nairobi, Kenya. Government Press.

———. 1992. *Children and Women in Kenya: A Situational Analysis.* Nairobi: UNICEF.

Guru, G. 1980. "Pilot Scheme on Nutrition Education at Primary Stage in India." In H. M. Sinclair and G. R. Howart (eds.), *World Nutrition Education.* Oxford: Oxford University Press.

Guyer, J. F. 1985. "The Role of Women in African Economic Development." A background paper for *Development Anthropology.* Cambridge: Harvard University.

Hanger, J., and J. Moris. 1973. "Women and Household Economy." In R. Chambers and J. Moris (eds.), *Mwea: An Irrigated Rice Settlement in Kenya.* Munich: Wetforum Verlag, 209-44.

Hartmann, H. I. 1981. "The Family as the Locus of Gender, Class and Political Struggle: An Example of Housework." *Signs* 6: 372-75.

Holding, E. M. 1942. "Some Preliminary Notes on Meru Age-Grades." *Man* 42 (29-49): 58-65.

International Labor Organization (ILO). 1986. *After the Famine: Towards an Approach.* Geneva: United Nations Organization (UNO).

Jellife, D. B. 1962. "Culture Social Change and Infant Feeding Trends in Tropical Regions." *American Journal of Chemical Nutrition* 10: 19-45.

Kabeberi, Macharia. 1995. "Inequality: A Legal Analysis." *Gender Review* 2 (4): 23-24.

Manguyu, F. 1993. "Women, Health and Development." In *Empowering Kenyan Women*. Nairobi, Kenya: National Committee on the Status of Women (NCSW).

Mbilinyi, M. 1990. "Plight of Women Plantation Workers." In L. Sheikh-Hashin (ed.), *Tanzania Women Magazine*. Dar es Salaam: Tanzania Printing Press.

Munyakho, D. (ed.). 1995. *Gender Review*. Nairobi: IRIS.

Mwanlki, Nyaga. 1986. "Against Many Odds: The Dilemma of Self-Help Groups." *Africa* 56 (2): 211-57.

Mwenesi, H., and E. I. Njiro. 1995. *Towards a Healthy Women's Counselling Guide*. Geneva: World Health Organization.

Njiro, E. I. 1995. "Food. Culture and Environment: The Case of the Atharaka of Eastern Kenya." Ph.D. thesis, University of Nairobi, Institute of African Studies.

Olenja, J. 1990. "Marginalization and Household Food Security; Evidence from Laikipia District." Paper presented at a National Seminar on Women in Development at Pan Africa Hotel, Nairobi, Kenya.

Ouko, Riria. 1993. "Women and the Economy: Credit Issues." In *Empowering Kenyan Women*. Nairobi, Kenya: National Committee on the Status of Women (NCSW).

Petros-Barvazian. 1990. "Women's Health: A Global Challenge." In F. Staugard (ed.), *The Role of Women in Health Development*. Gotab, Stockholm, Nordic School of Health: World Health Organization.

Rathgaber, E. 1992. "WID, WAD GAD: Trends in Research and Practice." A paper presented at Gender Institute, Dakar, Senegal.

Reid, E., and M. Bailey. 1995. *Young Women: Silence, Susceptibility and HIV Epidemic*. New York: United Nations Development Programme (UNDP).

Republic of Kenya. 1993. *Laikipia District Development Plan*. Nairobi, Kenya: Government Printers.

Rosaldo, M. Z., and L. Lamphere (eds.). 1974. *Women, Culture and Societies*. Stanford, CA: Stanford University Press.

Rothschild, Safilios. 1988. "The Impact of Agrarian Reform on Men's and Women's Incomes." In D. Dweyer and J. Brup (eds.), *A Home Divided: Women and Income*. Stanford, CA: Stanford University Press.

Sprig, A. 1992. "Women Farmers and Food in Africa: Some Considerations and Suggested Solutions." In A. Hansen and D. E. McMillan (eds.), *Food in Sub-Saharan Africa*. Boulder, CO: Lynne Rienner, 332-48.

Staudt, K. 1997. "Agricultural Productivity Gaps: A Case Study of Male Preference in Government Policy Implementation." *Development and Change* 9 (3): 437-39.

———. 1987. "Un-captured and Unmotivated? Women and the Food Crisis in Africa." *Rural Sociology* 52 (1): 37-55.

Swantz, D. 1984. *Women in Development: A Creative Role Denied*. Uppsala: Scandinavian Institute for African Studies.

4

Looking at African Women: Media Representations of Feminism, Human Rights, and Development

Amy Beer and Christine List

INTRODUCTION

In the last several years, African and non-African feminists have engaged in a process of rethinking the role of international human rights and of international development policies in feminist struggles around the world. Informed, in part, by the discourse of Western academic feminism, the goal of this rethinking is to reduce poverty and stop the decline in material conditions for most of the world's women. Although much of the work is at the level of international organizations, there is an increasing trend toward grassroots organizing and international solidarity. Feminist activist media have become a popular method of depicting issues important to African women and of organizing international support for change of oppressive conditions and detrimental policies.

The authors of this chapter use four films on women's issues in Africa as entry points for an exploration of differing perspectives on gender, culture, human rights, and development in media representations of African women. *Warrior Marks* (Parmar 1993) is a documentary made to serve as an educational and organizing tool for the international movement to end female genital mutilation (FGM).[1] Our analysis concentrates on the film's position as a representation by Western feminists of FGM, an issue that the film describes as a violation of international human rights. *Finzan* (1989), directed by Malian Cheick Oumar Sissoko, explores the problems of marriage rights and FGM in Mali, revealing the contradictions created when a feminist African discourse is couched within a highly charged emotional framework. *Hidden Faces: A Look at the Lives of Egyptian Women* (Hunt and Kim Longinotto 1990), created for British television, is primarily an ethnographic documentary, and discussion centers on the film's questioning of the meaning of "women's issues" and "empowerment" in the discourse of feminism and development. Finally, *Women with Open Eyes,* directed by Togolese filmmaker Anne-Laure Folly (1994), is a video documentary that showcases numerous activist women's groups in West Africa. Our investigation of *Women with Open Eyes* looks at the positive strategies of self-representation deployed by the documentary's African director.

Until very recently, *Warrior Marks,* a collaboration between the director and the novelist Alice Walker, has been shown exclusively in the West, but the filmmakers have begun to show it in Africa as well.[2] By its internal discourse and its primary distribution in the West, the film situates itself as part of an international effort to mobilize women outside Africa. As such, it falls within an established tradition of solidarity work to promote the observance of human rights throughout the world. This analysis focuses on three strategies used by the filmmakers to legitimate participation of the film in these efforts. They are the equation of Walker's situation to that of women in Africa; the film's privileging of the expertise of an educated elite; and the invocation of international human rights as a solution to the problem of FGM.

According to Parmar, "*Warrior Marks* refers to the patriarchal wounds which women carry with them. As Alice says in the film, it is possible to use these wounds as a guide and an act of resistance" (Parmar 1993: 12). *Warrior Marks* is structured around Walker's statement of emotional connection to the issue of abolishing FGM. In one of the first scenes, speaking directly to the camera, Walker tells the story of her "visual mutilation" as a young child when her brother accidentally shot her in the eye with a pellet gun. After the incident, her brother was not punished, and Walker felt that her parents blamed Walker herself for the social and medical problems she suffered. Like women who undergo FGM, Walker asserts, she is the victim of patriarchy: "What I had," she says, "I realized only as a consciously feminist adult, was a patriarchal wound." As Walker interviews women who are active in the movement to abolish FGM, women who have undergone FGM, and women who perform the operations (known as "birthing assistants," as they often serve that role as well), Walker is audibly and frequently visibly present. The film also includes two interviews with Walker herself as the subject.

By designating herself as a spokesperson for African women on the issue of FGM, Walker drew criticism from human rights activists and film critics. After the U.S. release of *Warrior Marks,* Cylena Simonds reviewed the film for *Afterimage,* remarking:

The [film] raises old conflicts between Western and non-Western feminists. The continued condescension towards non-Western women, as well as less opportunities for them to express their views, impede the possibility of unity between Western and non-Western feminists. Unfortunately the tendency of Western scholars to see themselves as the champion of the "third world" is pervasive. Imperialist ideology is so indoctrinated into Western scholarship that well-intentioned feminists cannot understand why their intervention, which they see as clearly for the good of all concerned, is met with hostility, resentment, and lack of appreciation. As *Warrior*

Marks demonstrates, African-American and other women of color are not necessarily excluded from this legacy of self-righteousness. (Simonds 1994: 3)

Simonds bases her objections to the film on Walker's validation of her empathy and involvement in the issue through her "visual mutilation." Simonds also dislikes Walker's "subjective" treatment of the African women's rights advocates interviewed in the film. Finally, Simonds criticizes the film for implying that Western feminists "have won the war against sexist and genderist behaviors at home and must now move to liberate other women around the world" (Simonds 1994).

The issues raised by Simonds' critique of *Warrior Marks* parallel a more general debate on the interactions of Western feminism and African women. Chandra Mohanty reproaches Western feminist discourse for its tendency to construct "women" as a homogeneous group. Instead of researching "the material and ideological specificities that constitute a particular group of women as 'powerless' in a particular context," Mohanty writes, "the focus of Western work too often becomes a search for a variety of cases of 'powerless' groups of women to prove the general point that women as a group are powerless" (Mohanty 1991: 57). Mohanty asserts that Western feminist discourse constructs Third World women as implicit *victims* of a generalized male violence. Instead of theorizing and interpreting male violence within specific socioeconomic formations, Western feminism positions women as frozen into powerless (female) and powerful (male) groups of people, and constructions of "women of Africa" tend to be characterized by "common dependencies or powerlessness (or even strengths)" (Mohanty 1991: 59). This strategy assumes that women are always already constituted as sexual-political subjects prior to their entry into social relations, thus eliding the fact that women, as well as being implicated in forming these relations, are also produced through these relations. For Mohanty,

What is problematical about this kind of use of "women" as a group, as a stable category of analysis, is that it assumes an ahistorical, universal unity between women based on a generalized notion of their subordination. Instead of analytically *demonstrating* the production of women as socioeconomic political groups within particular local contexts, this analytical move limits the definition of the female subject to gender identity, completely bypassing social class and ethnic identities. (Mohanty 1991: 64)

The discourse of *Warrior Marks* exemplifies the practices that Mohanty criticizes. Walker conflates the patriarchy at the hands of which she suffered with the "patriarchy" that she names as responsible for the practice of FGM. At several points in the film, she either states, or concurs with an interviewee who states, that the practice stems out of men's need to control women. She overlooks the possibility of women's agency and ignores the notion that the roles of men and women could be socially constructed in different ways in different societies. For example, when one interviewee points out that FGM is not solely a practice performed by women on women, Walker dismisses the remark, insisting that it is something that men force women to do."It's like everything else to do with children," she states, "men don't want to do it—they don't want to brush their hair, they don't dress them, they don't feed them, they don't cook for them."

The documentary treats all women who are subject to the practice of FGM as similarly situated—there is no effort to distinguish any characteristics of class, culture, or ethnicity, leaving the viewer with the impression that the practice of FGM is universal in a homogeneous "Africa." This leads the film to lay the "blame" for FGM on a universal patriarchy, of which women who perform the operations and women who subject their children to the practice are the tools and the dupes. In one scene, Walker confronts a birthing attendant who refuses to reveal the details of the operation because it is a secret, telling her: "We know that when women are circumcised, the clitoris is removed. This is not secret." In fact, since the woman will not tell her what she does, and since it is no secret that FGM encompasses a range of practices, Walker unwittingly reveals that she has an inaccurate understanding of what the woman does, but it is clear from her accusatory remarks and her lack of respect for the woman's cultural taboos that Walker sees the woman as an agent of patriarchy and not as an individual actor.

Walker's confrontation with the birthing assistant illustrates another problematic tendency of Western feminism, that of privileging "the epistemology of experts over that of the women themselves, by positing that [the] expert knows what's best for women, even if they don't know it themselves" (Apffel-Margolin and Simon 1994: 35). *Warrior Marks*, by constantly spotlighting Walker's presence as the interviewer, the ruminator, and the consoler, makes her out to be an expert who is also the facilitator of the international exposure of African horrors.[3] The film does interview several African feminists who have struggled tremendously and at great personal cost to educate women about FGM, but the film cannot let their comments stand for themselves; instead, they must be frequently validated by Walker's murmurs of agreement. The film also creates a hierarchy of authority in the voices it presents. Walker, as the ubiquitous presence, is in the first rank. In the second rank are the leaders of several African organizations who are identified by name and title, who speak in French or in English, and who, if they speak in French, are translated by means of subtitles. The next level down is the "ordinary" women, women who have undergone FGM or whose children have been circumcised, who are generally not identified by either name or nationality, and whose words are translated by a voice-over. The result is that the voices of "experts" are privileged by allowing the viewer to hear them unmediated. By refusing the "nonexperts" a voice, the film seems to be invalidating their experience.

The cultural shortsightedness of *Warrior Marks* leads us to a larger question that has been raised by non-Western feminists, namely, whether solidarity projects initiated by Western feminists are merely remnants of colonialism. For Mohanty, such solidarity reinforces Western cultural imperialism and maintains "a very specific power in defining, coding and maintaining existing first/third world connections" (Mohanty 1991: 73). Mridula Udayagiri, however, cautions against Mohanty's "postmodern" position, which renders political projects impractical by creating unbridgeable divides between women (Udayagiri 1995). "If there is no connectedness between the two realms, 'us' and 'other,'" Udayagiri asks, "then how is it possible to form strategic coalitions across class, race and national boundaries?" (Udayagiri 1995: 166).

In its effort at solidarity, *Warrior Marks* poses a universal oppression that can be partially remedied by international human rights. Walker heartily endorses the suggestion of Efna Dorkenou, a well-known Somali activist against FGM, that FGM should be prohibited by the United Nations (UN) Convention on Torture,[4] and she adopts the slogan, "Torture is not culture." On one level, this slogan, in its guise of protecting women against men, is another example of the film's inability to permit African women to think for themselves, as it rejects the possibility that the people whose culture it is could either consider it to be part of *their* culture or have valid reasons for maintaining the practice. At another level, it could be seen as an example of the tendency of Western feminism to use Western standards and goals of rationality and individualism to judge the history and cultures of non-Western societies, a tendency that frequently leads to proposals of prescriptive solutions according to a set of legal, political, and social benchmarks that are considered critical, by Western women, in achieving a balance of power between men and women (Ong 1994).

The feminist discourse of *Finzan* (1989) is also based closely on notions of human rights. *Finzan,* a feature-length narrative directed by Cheick Oumar Sissoko, opens with a shot of a mother goat nursing her young and then cuts to a title page that quotes the following statistics from a 1980 UN Conference on Women report: "A world profile on the condition of women reveals the striking effects of double oppression. Women are 50 percent of the world's population, do about two-thirds of its work, receive barely 10 percent of its income and own less than 1 percent of its property." The statistics introduced in this initial scene align the filmic text with the UN's official social text on women, offering an economic framework for the analysis of African patriarchy as well as connecting the condition of African women depicted in the film to a global feminist analogy. The UN data reinforce feminist discourse as it has been articulated in the West, thus creating a margin of intellectual comfort for viewers who are watching from a Westernized feminist perspective.

The story in *Finzan* develops around two central characters. Nanyuma, the main character, becomes a widow as the film opens. According to village tradition, her brother-in-law, Bala, has the duty to take care of Nanyuma, and he must make her his own wife. Nanyuma refuses to marry him because he is an arrogant fool, and, moreover, she is in love with another man in the village. When the village chief orders her to marry Bala, Nanyuma runs away to the city, where she discovers a parallel society also plagued by sexism. Eventually, she is captured, tied up, and sent back to the village. Although forced to marry Bala, she continues to stand her ground against him by refusing to consummate their relationship. In the end, Nanyuma leaves the village to make her own way in the world.

Nanyuma's story is developed so that the audience witnesses the dynamics between genders, as various men and women from the village negotiate with the chief on behalf of Nanyuma. When the chief refuses to allow Nanyuma out of her marriage to Bala, the village women make a pact to not have sex with the men until Nanyuma gets her way. At another point in the story, the chief is sent to jail by the central government of the nation for refusing to give an unfair percentage of the village wheat in payment for the national tax. The women band together with the men of the village and march in protest to the jail, forcing the release of the chief. In this way, Sissoko avoids the trap of an "us" versus "them" reification of African patriarchy and instead proposes process and partnership as an integral part of the struggle for gender equality.

The secondary plot involves the character of Fili, a well-educated young woman who questions the village tradition of FGM. Fili rejects the excision ritual on feminist grounds, explaining that the procedure is an affront to her sexuality. In addition, Fili comes from a family of women who suffer from severe hemorrhaging. Her father, who is living in another village, forbids the excision on the grounds that she could die if forced to undergo the surgery. The movie constructs a subtext of tension between Fili's Westernized notion of her right to control her own body and the attitudes of traditional women in the village, who ridicule Fili, labeling her as dirty and antisocial. In one of the final sequences of *Finzan*, Fili is captured by a group of women in the village and excised against her will, as her own neighbors drag her into a corner and hold her down. We then hear Fili's blood-curdling scream. The scene effectively denounces FGM and seems to be intended to rouse an audience to the point of outrage.

Sissoko's overt manipulation of the dramatic form as a cinematic weapon against FGM has been questioned by film scholar Nwachukwu Frank Ukadike, who characterizes Sissoko's approach to the issue of FGM in *Finzan* as myopic and overly Westernized (Ukadike 1994). Ukadike faults Sissoko for failing to explain FGM in a historical context of African cultural rituals and traditions, and he accuses Sissoko of slipping into the trap of the many Hollywood films that portray African rituals as exotic aberrations from Western norms and decontextualize rituals so that they become pure shock effect for the audience. Ukadike concludes that *Finzan* has been extremely popular in the West precisely because the film manages to dislocate FGM from an African cultural context (Ukadike 1994). Ukadike's point is well taken. Nevertheless, it should be mentioned that Sissoko's human rights argument against FGM is not quite as reductionist as Ukadike believes. For instance, the village women are not constituted as a single voice of tradition. One of the women, in fact, goes to the chief on behalf of Fili, saying that she has learned that excision can cause death and sterility. The woman asks the chief to reconsider the excision because of the health risks to Fili. Sissoko also constructs a scene between Fili and Nanyuma in which Nanyuma, the woman who has fought hard for her right to marry and thereby has won the empathy of the audience, rejects Fili's explanation of the clitoris as an organ of the body. Nanyuma says the clitoris is dirty, and she chooses to stand on the side of tradition on the FGM issue, until the moment that she learns that Fili may die if circumcised.

Like *Warrior Marks*, *Finzan* represents FGM as a violation of human rights. Scholarly and popular criticism of the films exemplifies the contestation over international human rights standards between liberal Western feminists and advocates of a more informed and constructive engagement with "other" feminisms. Objectors to the use of an international, universal standard point out that human rights are derived from Western legal constructs of individualism that may be inapplicable to non-Western cultures (Lionnet 1995). On the other hand, enforcement of international standards of human rights can be a potentially effective weapon in struggles to seek relief from patriarchal systems of gender, race, and class-based oppression (James 1994). It is beyond the scope of this chapter to review the extensive debates on human rights and cultural relativism.[5] Rather, the focus is on the proposal made by *Warrior Marks* and *Finzan* that international human rights are an effective solution to the oppressive practices of patriarchy.

A brief history of the evolution of human rights law is helpful in understanding why it is an ineffective and cumbersome means for changing traditional practices. Human rights law evolved as a response to state abuse of fundamental human rights during World War II. It is important to distinguish between international human rights *principles*, which are enunciated, for instance, in documents adopted by the United Nations General Assembly such as the Universal Declaration of Human Rights, and international human rights *covenants* or *treaties*, which are ratified by individual member states of the United Nations and which are designed to punish abusers of human rights. The genesis of human rights law in curbing abuses of state power means that most of the covenants or treaties do not provide any international enforcement mechanism for violations of human rights by private individuals (Human Rights Watch 1994). For example, a woman forced to undergo FGM as a child could not sue the birthing attendant who performed the surgery under human rights law. In response to this omission, the human rights movement is working to enlarge the scope of treaties to prohibit states from condoning practices by individuals that are contrary to principles of international human rights law.

The Universal Declaration of Human Rights, adopted by the UN General Assembly in 1948, affirms the equal rights of men and women and specifically states that the rights and freedoms set forth in the declaration are a matter of entitlement without respect to any distinction such as race, sex, or national origin.[6] Nevertheless, international human rights instruments written since the declaration of 1948 have elided issues of woman's rights, which can be explained, in part, by the genesis of many of these instruments in nationalist struggles against colonialism. As Rey Chow points out, the needs of "women" as a category are frequently sacrificed for the "greater cause of nationalism and patriotism" (Chow 1991: 88). Furthermore, in nationalist struggles, a dichotomy is frequently constructed within national culture between material and spiritual worlds. Inner, spiritual space becomes identified with the feminine, and the role of women is naturalized as the protection of the spiritual qualities of national culture, which are seen as existing in the domestic or private sphere (Chatterjee, quoted in James 1994). Stanlie James uses the examples of revolutions in Egypt and Zimbabwe to argue that the result of this dichotomy is that, in return for gaining certain rights in the public sphere, traditional gender hierarchies remain in place in the private sphere, including in family relations (James 1994). While women may have increased access to such public rights as education and political participation, traditional practices that affect family relations, such as FGM, tend not to be addressed either at the national or international level.

As a result, although the status of women is addressed in various human rights instruments[7] (consolidated into the 1979 Convention on the Elimination of All Forms of Discrimination Against Women [CEDAW], human rights are a particularly ineffective means of abolishing practices (traditional practices) such as FGM that are considered to exist in the private sphere of the family.[8] CEDAW itself has minimal provisions for enforcement, and there is no procedure for accepting complaints against individuals. "[I]nternational human rights standards require states not to enforce, or condone the enforcement of, reproductive and sexual norms through violent or sexually discriminatory means" (Human Rights Watch 1994), but in practice, the lack of an enforcement mechanism at an international level means that protection of many of the rights agreed to in CEDAW depends on the enactment of national legislation that then can be enforced only in local legal systems.

While several African governments have moved to protect woman's rights in the public sphere, the enactment of legislation and the implementation policies to protect rights in the private sphere have been slower (James 1994). Even if national legislation exists, however, as Florence Butegwa points out, national legal systems themselves are often a primary obstacle to the enforcement of recognized rights:

Members of the police force often refuse to accept and to record a complaint from a woman against her husband or member of her family. The police treat such complaints as a private family matter. Judicial officers, including judges, have yet to understand women's special concerns and fears. The technical nature of the entire court process—including the pleadings, court language, and the demeanor of the judge and counsel to the process of cross-examination—is a hindrance to the exercise of rights by women. (Butegwa 1993: 41)

Butegwa supports the enactment of legislation to outlaw traditional practices, pointing out that many "so-called customs" have been discarded, except those that "concern women and are meant to subordinate them" (Butegwa 1993: 40). However, the cost of exercising rights as an individual may be social ostracism, and, accordingly, the promotion of human rights must be a community project (Butegwa 1993). Sissoko illustrates this problem in *Finzan* by showing the futility of Fili's Westernized approach to asserting her human rights. As an individual agent within a community organized around a different set of standards, Fili's rationale that she alone should determine what happens to her body holds no legal or social credence. The standard maintained by the community of village women is enforced. Fili's statement only serves to fire up the indignation of the elders, who are suspicious of her precisely because she has been exposed to a different set of values when she left to study in the city.

The conflict between Fili and the women in the village can be transposed onto other debates on FGM. Lionnet, writing about the criminalization of FGM under French national law, characterizes the controversy as a polemic opposing "two apparently conflicting versions of human rights, one based on the Enlightenment notion of the sovereign individual subject, and the other on a notion of collective identity grounded in cultural solidarity" (Lionnet 1995: 155). As a possible solution to this problem, Lionnet suggests cooperating with African countries that are struggling to replace certain traditional cultural norms, rather than imposing a new norm from above (Lionnet 1995). Rhonda Howard, a professor of human rights law, also endorses this approach. While she condemns FGM, Howard refuses to categorically attribute the practice to "gross misogyny," and she notes that adult, educated women voluntarily undergo the surgery. Howard advocates an educational campaign about the health risks of the practice and national legislation guaranteeing a woman's right to refuse the custom. For Howard, change in the situation of women will result from three kinds of change: economic development, ensuring both that basic needs can be met and that women can have comparative "leisure" to devote to assuring other rights; the implementation of civil and political freedoms to assure women the possibility of organizing and to promote public debate; and legislation that protects the rights of women, as individuals, to opt out of customs and norms (Howard 1984).

This brief discussion illustrates that "human rights" may not be the most effective tool to eliminate traditional practices such as FGM. This is not to say, however, that concepts such as human rights, which may be formally expressed in international instruments in Western terms, do not have their counterparts in other cultures, or that Western women have no role to play in supporting the struggles of non-Western women. The examples of *Warrior Marks* and *Finzan* underscore problematic tendencies of a Westernized view of feminism and human rights, but the project of solidarity as a matter of political expediency should not be dismissed. In the next section of this chapter, our discussion of *Hidden Faces* and *Women with Open Eyes* suggests that there are techniques of filmic representation that are less troublesome but are effective in constructing international awareness of complex issues that affect the lives of African women.

Hidden Faces: A Look at the Lives of Egyptian Women (Claire Hunt and Kim Longinotto, 1990) is a documentary based on the return of Safaa Fathay, a woman who grew up in the southern part of Egypt, to her home country after ten years in Paris. Fathay's return was precipitated by an offer to work as an interviewer on a documentary film about Egyptian feminist Nawal El Saadawi.[9] Like *Warrior Marks,* this documentary is structured as a personal essay, beginning with Fathay's description of her identification with the writings of Saadawi, as a young woman, and ending with her disillusionment with Saadawi. "We had wanted to make a film which linked Saadawi's life with the kind of women in her stories," Fathay says at the end of the film, "but the issues had seemed so much more alive in my family than around Nawal."

The film opens as Fathay and the film crew travel to Kafr Tahla, Saadawi's home village, where Saadawi has called a meeting to discuss problems with a bee-keeping cooperative. As the filmmakers arrive, Saadawi is involved in an argument with her assistant, Aziza, whom Saadawi has just slapped, apparently for arriving late to a meeting. "I'm like a grandmother to you," Saadawi says, "If I slap you, you must accept it. If you don't I can't trust you. I gave you a sewing machine. I favored you most of all. And now you do this to me." This scene introduces the theme of class division that runs throughout the film, which becomes centered around the uneasy balance between Saadawi's empowerment and development efforts with the actual concerns of members of Fathay's family and their household and her friends from university.

By contrasting Saadawi's demeanor in the village, where her empowerment project is primarily economic, and in the city, where she focuses on women's sexual liberation, the viewer is introduced to the complexity of the concepts of "empowerment" and "development." This is also brought out by scenes at Fathay's family home, where her brother-in-law, Mustapha, epitomizes patriarchal authority, forcing his very young son, Wa'el, to eat and ordering his wife to put on her head scarf before she may eat the food she and her mother have prepared. An interview with the housemaid, a girl named Sayeda, shows that development is not simply a matter of improvement in economic status. Although Sayeda has improved her situation by coming to work for Fathay's family, Mustapha has forbidden her to learn to read and write. "What I would really like," she says, "is to be educated like Wa'el."

Through interviews with Fathay's friends from the university and female members of her family, Fathay also introduces a conflict between women's development and religious fundamentalism. One friend describes how, after her marriage, her husband continuously demanded that she increase the portion of her body that she veiled. On the eve of the wedding of another friend from the university, the friend explains her decision to begin wearing a veil after her marriage: her religion requires it, she says, and it is "more modest," "better protection." At the wedding, we see the men dancing exuberantly, while the women sit and watch. In the final scenes, Fathay discusses the issue of FGM with her mother, aunt, and cousins, all but one of whom have had genital surgery. The older women, except for Fathay's mother, describe it as an aesthetic choice; the cousins say that they realize now that it is not required by Muslim law but that, at the time, they thought it was necessary.

The style of *Hidden Faces* is very different from *Warrior Marks* and *Finzan*. Although Fathay's readings from the works of Saadawi and Fathay's remarks punctuate the scenes of the lives of Egyptian women, often ironically, the film takes a much less didactic tone by allowing events to unfold before the camera. For instance, when Fathay interviews the friend who is about to be married about her decision to wear the veil after her wedding, the interview takes place in the friend's bedroom, as she prepares for her wedding. Fathay's tone is one of curiosity, rather than harangue. The viewer is able to understand that Fathay's friend's decision to adopt a practice that reinforces traditional gender hierarchies is not made out of ignorance, and another interview with a friend who left her husband over the issue of veiling demonstrates that Egyptian women can and do resist oppressive practices.

The film leaves the viewer with an impression that, although there may be isolated empowerment efforts, religious fundamentalism means that private relations within the family continue to be dominated by patriarchal customs. With respect to the question of development policies, the film raises issues about the meaning of development and the failure of feminist efforts to create a global shift in development priorities throughout Africa. Historically, development policies have not recognized gender differentials, despite the fundamental economic importance of women's work and the disproportionate effect of poverty on women (Jahan 1994). Prior to the 1980s, most "development" projects initiated by international financial institutions such as the World Bank (WB) and the International Monetary Fund (IMF) were large-scale projects aimed at developing an industrial infrastructure. In the worldwide recession and debt crisis of the early 1980s, structural adjustment programs (SAPs) were introduced by the WB and IMF, ostensibly to reduce the debt burden of Third World borrowers. The net effect of SAPs, however, has been both to increase the debt of many countries and to decrease both economic opportunities and social services for men and women (Nzomo 1995; Michel 1995).

In response to the official lack of attention to the role of gender in development policies, in the last twenty years, proponents of "women in development" (WID) have managed to establish a place for gender in the policy and action programs of most international development agencies and in many countries, especially those dependent on foreign aid.[10] Initially, the WID approach, within the international agencies, focused on setting up women's policy offices in both the agencies and national governments to develop policies, and strategies and implement actions designed particularly for women. The result of these programs was to increase awareness and understanding of gender issues within these organizations and to increase women's participation in development concerns (Jahan 1994). However, numerous questions remained unaddressed, and material living conditions for most of the world's women decreased significantly over the decade of the 1980s and continue to decrease in the 1990s (Michel 1995; Jahan 1994).

In *Hidden Faces*, we see a multifaceted approach to development. On one hand, there are women's economic development initiatives, such as Saadawi's bee-keeping and goat-raising ventures. On the other, we see Saadawi attempting to raise women's awareness of gender inequality among the women in the village and in a therapy session and seminar in Cairo. Saadawi's efforts to expand the application of development initiatives beyond economic development are reflected in postmodernist critiques of the WID approach, which problematize its essentialization of the "poverty" of Third World women in Western terms:

In development rhetoric, poverty shares the status of the veil, *sati*, or genital mutilation in much of Western/ized feminist rhetoric; symbols of oppression, tradition and patriarchy, these are practices and forces to be eradicated. Once again, the equation of women with culture and with poverty, and poverty with economic backwardness, utilizes women's position in society to measure that society's progress, as an index of its civilization/ modernity. (Apffel-Margolin and Simon 1994: 33)

Recent alternative approaches to gender and development draw on the insights of both socialist feminism and postmodern feminism, but they also attempt to use the work of Third World women's feminist writings and grassroots feminist organizations to inform their work (Chowdry 1995). These approaches share a deep suspicion of existing "modernization" projects as protecting and expanding the interests of capitalism and the Western world, which are often interpreted as incompatible with the needs and goals of Third World women (Chowdry 1995). One such approach, known as the "empowerment" perspective, calls for a serious focus on indigenous grassroots movements (Chowdry 1995). Rather than seeing the interests of men and women as fundamentally opposed,

women and men are not necessarily poised antagonistically against each other, nor are all women joined by the invisible strands of sisterhood. Elements of class, ethnicity and race intersect with gender to form alliances between men and women. [The empowerment perspective calls] for the redistribution of power, both internationally and nationally, so that poor women can participate in controlling and influencing the directions in which development occurs. The adoption of empowerment strategies by grassroots organizations is a practical alternative to the top-down strategies adopted by WID. (Chowdry 1995: 38)

Women with Open Eyes, directed by Anne-Laure Folly, a Togolese filmmaker, is a video documentary that strongly advocates empowerment strategies pursued by African women in indigenous resistance movements. The documentary comprises seven different segments, dealing with an aspect of women's struggles in Burkina Faso, Mali, Senegal, and Benin: forced marriages, AIDS, FGM, social struggle, survival, the economy, and political life. The multiple-segment structure helps the video avoid essentializing, by showing each issue as only one of many concerns of the movement. For example, the section on the topic of FGM is brief but effective, containing primarily interviews with women who have formed their own organizations against FGM. These women are well-poised, effective public speakers whose voices give agency to the African continent. In stark contrast to *Warrior Marks*, African women in *Women with Open Eyes* speak for themselves. Unlike in *Warrior Marks*, in this documentary, the FGM practitioner, or excision woman, as Folly refers to her, is not depicted in a dichotomous or adversarial relationship to other African women, nor is she shown as a player in a binary opposition of tradition and progress. Rather, the cultural and historical context of the practice is discussed, and the belief systems underlying the ritual are addressed, so that the filmmaker does not demean or patronize any of the women shown in the tape. The relationship between the FGM practitioners and anti-FGM advocates is explained in terms of patriarchal structures that bind the FGM practitioner to her traditions, a different strategy from what Parmar and Sissoko take in their works.

One of the more empowering episodes in the documentary shows the participation of African women in the economic sector. This section gives examples of African women who dominate certain industries, including wholesale distribution of rice, wheat, sugar, and fabrics. Images of women who are not impoverished shatter the illusion of "women as victims" that Mohanty and others criticize. The video paints the women's movement in Africa as a large, progressive movement of women from a variety of social positions, and it refuses to single out FGM and poverty as the principal issues of importance to African women. *Women with Open Eyes* does, however, also address the issue of poverty. In the section on forced marriages, African women activists provide a cogent analysis of the political-economic foundations of the system, explaining how forced marriages maintain a patriarchal structure of inheritance in which women have no control over the wealth of their husbands and are therefore left in poverty if they divorce or are widowed, thus creating a class of "potentially poor" women.

Projects such as *Women with Open Eyes*, *Warrior Marks*, *Finzan,* and *Hidden Faces* illustrate the difficulties of balancing political pragmatism and ethical representation. Each of these films raises vital issues affecting women not only in Africa but in the so-called First World as well, as the distance between the two becomes ever closer and farther at the same time. As the contrast between the practices of the four productions shows, certain strategies of representation, while attempting to bridge the divide between Western and other feminisms, tend only to reinforce historical hierarchies. The task of the filmmaker, as well as the academic, is to negotiate this contested terrain, balancing the need for strategic political universalism with the use of techniques that allow women to represent themselves and to be represented in their differences. There is a place for solidarity, but that place seems to be increasingly designated as one of support, using the resources of the West to assist in publicizing and educating through the media and financially contributing to the struggles of women who are redefining issues of human rights and development, rather than persisting in the colonialist notion that Western feminism and its notions of human rights and development can or should represent a global standard.

NOTES

1. Practices of ritual surgery on female genitals range from a ritual nicking of the clitoris with a sharp instrument to removal of virtually all external genitalia. Although the term "female genital mutilation" is inherently value-laden, we use its abbreviation in this article as a convenient shorthand for a range of practices. FGM has been the subject of much recent discussion in the media, popular literature, and scholarly work. The enormity of the attention can be observed from the use of FGM as a primary example to illustrate issues analyzed in many of the works cited in this chapter. While this chapter frequently refers to FGM, the debate over FGM is not intended to be its focus.

2. One of the recent showings was at a "human rights awareness workshop" organized by Amnesty International in Bolgatanga, Ghana, for African men and women "dedicated to the abolition of female genital mutilation" (Walker 1997: 54).

3. Walker again positions herself as the agent of change in a recent piece for *Ms.*, where she writes: "Presenting my own suffering and psychic healing has been a powerful encouragement, I've found, to victims of mutilation who are ashamed or reluctant to speak of their struggle" (Walker 1997: 54).

4. FGM is obviously extremely painful, and numerous studies have shown that it may have long-term deleterious effects on women's health. Nevertheless, it is not torture, in the sense of this UN Convention, which defines torture as a state practice. The purpose of this remark is not to quibble with the film's use of the term "torture" but rather to note, as will be discussed further, that international human rights law was never intended to protect individuals from nonstate actors.

5. The notion of "universal human rights" is thoroughly discussed in Alison Renteln's *International Human Rights: Universalism versus Relativism*. Renteln, a professor of international law, proposes comparative, cross-cultural research of ethical principles to discover whether moral equivalents of the Western basis for human rights exist in other cultures. For example, her comparative study of the principle of retribution shows that the notion of retribution tied to proportionality is extremely widespread, if not universal (Renteln 1990: 88-137).

6. For a history of the development of the major human rights instruments, see Renteln (1990: 17-38).

7. These instruments include the 1952 Convention on the Political Rights of Women, the 1957 Convention on the Nationality of Married Women, and the 1962 Convention on Consent to Marriage.

8. The dichotomy between public and private rights can also be observed in the reservations (i.e., refusals to accept) to provisions of CEDAW that would affect woman's rights in the private sphere. For example, Egypt (one of the state drafters of CEDAW, which implies a certain commitment to improvement of the status of

women) lodged reservations to Article 16, which deals with the equality of men and women in all matters relating to marriage and family relations. In a more extreme example, Malawi expressed reservations to all provisions that would require immediate eradications of traditional customs and practices.

9. Saadawi has played many roles as the promoter of feminism in Egypt, as a doctor, as the author of numerous books, including *The Hidden Face of Eve*, which deals with the subject of FGM, and as the promoter of "self- help" projects for women financed by funds that Saadawi has raised outside Egypt.

10. A brief history of WID is contained in *The Elusive Agenda: Mainstreaming Women in Development* (Jahan 1994).

REFERENCES

Apffel-Margolin, Frèdèrique and Suzanne L. Simon. 1994. "Negotiating Positions in the Sustainable Development Debate: Situating the Feminist Perspective." In W. Harcourt, ed., *Feminist Perspectives on Sustainable Development*. London: Zed Books.

Butegwa, Florence. 1993. "The Challenge of Promoting Women's Rights in African Countries." In J. Kerr, ed., *Ours by Right*. London: Zed Books.

Chatterjee, Partha. 1990. "The Nationalist Resolution of the Woman Question." In K. Sangari and S. Vaid, eds., *Recasting Women: Essays in Indian Colonial History*. New Brunswick, NJ: Rutgers University Press.

Chow, Rey. 1991. "Violence in the Other Country: China as Crisis, Spectacle, and Woman." In C. Mohanty, A. Russo, and L. Torres, eds., *Third World Women and the Politics of Feminism*. Bloomington: Indiana University Press.

Chowdry, Geeta. 1995. "Engendering Development? Women in Development (WID) in International Development Regimes." In M. Marchand and J. L. Parpart, eds., *Feminism/Postmodernism/Development*. London: Routledge.

Folley, Ann-Laure, producer/director. 1994. *Women with Open Eyes*. California Newsreel.

Hosken, Fran. 1981. "Female Genital Mutilation and Human Rights." *Feminist Issues* 1 (3): 13-21.

Howard, Rhonda. 1984. "Women's Rights in English-Speaking Sub-Saharan Africa." In C. Welch, *Human Rights and Development in Africa*. Albany, NY: SUNY Press.

Human Rights Watch. 1994. *The Human Rights Watch Global Report on Women's Human Rights*. New York: Human Rights Watch.

Hunt, Claire and Kim Longinotto, producers. 1990. *Hidden Faces*. WMEN.

Jahan, Rounaq. 1994. *The Elusive Agenda: Mainstreaming Women in Development*. London: Zed Books.

James, Stanlie. 1994. "Challenging Partriarchal Privilege through the Development of International Human Rights." *Women's Studies International Forum* 16 (6): 563-78.

Lionnet, Françoise. 1995. *Postcolonial Representations: Women, Literature, Identity*. Ithaca, NY: Cornell University Press.

Michel, Andrée. 1995. "African Women, Development and the North-South Relationship." In M. Dalla Costa and G. F. Dellacosta, eds., *Paying the Price:*

Women and the Politics of International Economic Strategy. London: Zed Books.

Mohanty, Chandra. 1991. "Under Western Eyes: Feminist Scholarship and Colonial Discourses." In C. Mohanty, A. Russo, and L. Torres, eds., *Third World Women and the Politics of Feminism.* Bloomington: Indiana University Press.

Nzomo, Maria. 1995. "Women and Democratization Struggles in Africa: What Relevance to Post-Modernist Discourse?" In M. Marchand and J. L. Parpart, eds., *Feminism/Postmodernism/Development.* London: Routledge.

Ong, Aihwa. 1994. "Colonialism and Modernity: Feminist Re-presentations of Women in Non-Western Societies." In A. C. Herrmann and A. J. Stewart, eds., *Theorizing Feminism: Parallel Trends in the Humanities and the Social Sciences.* Boulder, CO: Westview Press.

Parmar, Pratibha. 1993. "Interview with Pratibha Parmar." *Black Film Review* 1 (3/4) (Autumn/Winter): 12-13.

Renteln, Alison. 1990. *International Human Rights: Universalism versus Relativism.* London: Sage.

Saadawi, Nawal. 1981. *The Hidden Face of Eve: Women in the Arab World.* London: Zed Press.

Simonds, Cylena. 1994. "Missing the Mark." *Afterimage* 2 (21) (March 1994): 3.

Sissoko, Cheick Oumar, director/producer. 1990. *Finzan: A Dance for the Heroes.* California Newsreel.

Udayagiri, Mridula. 1995. "Challenging Modernization: Gender and Development, Postmodern Feminism and Activism." In M. Marchand and J. L. Parpart, eds., *Feminism/Postmodernism/Development.* London: Routledge.

Ukadike, Nwachukwu Frank. 1994. *Black African Cinema.* Los Angeles: University of California Press.

Walker, Alice. 1997. "You Have All Seen." *Ms.* 7 (5) (March/April): 53-59.

Welch, Claude. 1995. *Protecting Human Rights in Africa: Roles and Strategies of Non-Governmental Organizations.* Philadelphia: University of Pennsylvania Press.

5

The State and Feminization of Developmental Processes in West Africa

Ifeyinwa E. Umerah-Udezulu

INTRODUCTION

This chapter to offers an alternative explanation to the dominant schools of thoughts on the developmental processes in Africa. It briefly analyzes and critiques the prevailing scholarly positions on developmental politics. Adopting a feminist standpoint on women and development, the discussion includes: a review of literature on women and development; time series analysis and an examination of machinery of dominance and the nature of developmental process in Africa; case studies of developmental process in West Africa and women's contribution from there; and finally, whether bringing women back into the developmental processes is a necessary alternative or an evil.

Several diplomatic historians and practitioners alike are exploring many options for attaining sustainable development in the developing countries. Three dominant scholarly positions emerged: the linear stages of development,[1] the modernity variant,[2] and the dependency and underdevelopment affiliates.[3] The linear framework underwrites a uniform approach to development, which Rostow and Organski substantially articulate; they delineate six stages of development: traditional societies, preconditions for takeoff, takeoff, drives toward maturity, age of mass consumption, and the search for quality.[4] The takeoff phase particularly relates to the developing states, because at that era, it holds promise of growth when they surmount the obstacles to development. Their argument assumes that growth is evolutionary and, furthermore, that the developmental trends exhibited by the West would simply be duplicated by Third World nations through the employment of technical know–how and investments from the West. The Third World countries, in this instance, African nations, would then abandon their orthodox and imputed approaches to development. They will embrace the procured archetype of advanced industrialized nations. As a result, these nations will then become developed like the Western industrialized nations.[5]

However, the modernity framework, whose major proponent was Samuel P. Huntington, attempts to sidetrack the shortcomings of the unilinear proponents. He recognizes that political transition serves as a direct outcome of socioeconomic conditions propounded by the unilinear model. He therefore concentrates on issues of order, stability, and harmony as analytical focal points of any developmental process. Huntington argues that stability is precursory to the expeditious function of social and pecuniary of modernization.[6] Yet, when he adds that technological advancements and, economic and political progress as part of the modernization process would, in the absence of an effective check-and-balance device, lead to political decay, Huntington seems to backslide from his main thrust. Such a mistake emanates from his placing strong emphasis on containing change, which is precursory to political and economic instability encountered by developing states. Therefore, he should not have argued for the establishment of a controlling mechanism by which they would monitor the distribution of information in the developing nations.[7] Even though Huntington makes a strong case about containing change, which seems autocratic, he nonetheless considers systemic equilibrium, rather than probable turbulent requisitions of a participation and mobilization nexus.

In a subsequent study, Huntington and Nelson analyzed five ideal blueprints of development: liberal, bourgeois, autocratic, technocratic, and populist models.[8] In each of these types, these scholars explain how the differing patterns of political participation impact on the levels of economic and social integration. For instance, the establishment of electoral and legislative institutions earmarks the bourgeois pattern of development to cater to the interest of the nascent middle class. High political participation characterizes the populist model. These five models of development were nonetheless ideal and cannot be actualized in the state system, especially African countries, when taking into account the social, economic, and political divergence of these states.

Other interesting analysis on modernization includes David Apter's illustration, patterned after the parameters of domination, namely, the "secular-libertarians" or pluralist systems and "sacred-collectivity" or mobilizing systems.[9] This analysis evaluates features of modernization intrinsic to the structural functional arrangement. For instance, the secular libertarian typified the contemporary U.S. system of arbitration and negotiation among competing interest groups. Distinct and dynamic leadership distinguishes the sacred-collective version depicted by the postcolonial nations, political indoctrination, and the establishment of mass party, as modeled by the subsequent governments: Egypt under Nasser, Ghana under Nkrumah, and China under Mao. However, Apter acknowledges limitation of the reconciliation system due to the discordant and highly sectionalized groups of the Third World nations, primarily African states. Nevertheless, he surmises that the reconciliation system will transcend the impediment to development and will result in "consummatory of values" geared toward elimination of oppression.

Apter's study is not without criticism. Pasquino argues that Apter's theory is too extensive and lacks operationalization.[10] Also, he faulted Apter's study for concentrating solely on the ability of the existing order rather than on its dictates and imprecisely formulated only three stages—traditional, transitional, and modern. Finally, African scholars have challenged the study for subscribing to the ideal types, which they have proven incorrect propositions.[11]

Furthermore, other scholars have challenged the unilinear and modernization methods on several fronts. First, by Portes argues that these theorists disregard the structural considerations involved in developmental process.[12] Second, they criticized these schools for overlooking the implications of economic development following the endorsement of the so-called modern values about the constraints of systemic atrophy of some Third World nations.[13] Finally and most important, these writers overlooked the impacts of development on gender integration.[14] The significance of this last point is elaborated throughout this chapter. The preceding critique on the unilinear and modernization theories involves their statements that development transpires as a unitary occurrence. Consequently, they did not take into consideration the structural forms between multifarious participants on the global arena.[15] Also, these writers overlook the significance of transcontinental advancements on pecuniary and ethnic arrangements intrinsic to the Third World states overall and, basically, to African economies.[16] Due to underdevelopment, the people of many Third World nations continue to be isolated from contemporary global establishments.[17] The major proponents of the underdevelopment theory argue that global capitalism functions to underdevelop the Third World nations.[18] They argue that Western capitalism failed to improve materially the lives of masses in most of Third World nations. With the deteriorating economic and political conditions in Africa, the United Nations Economic Commission for Africa (ECA) joins hands with others in articulating the demands for a new international economic order, to salvage these depressing conditions of African countries. Although the standpoint is valid, the theorists, like others mentioned earlier, fall short of addressing one crucial setback to development: the importance of gender to sustainable development.

These viewpoints essentially conclude that the position of women extemporaneously will be enhanced during economic advancement. Women are expected to obtain more passageways to economic assets and to profit from acceptance of contemporary values relating to the functions of women. On the contrary, some scholars argue that because patriarchal convictions have been buttressed instead of being denounced, women in the Third World have sacrificed their position as a direct result of development.[19]

Collectively, these conceptual frameworks have centered on androcentric economic and social establishments. The theoretical inadequacies in the two theories illustrate that gender is not perceived as central to developmental processes. One cannot successfully evaluate the process of development without taking into account most of the developing economies' population, which consists of women. According to research, women include 3 billion of the 5.5 billion people in the world system.[20] Women in African states constitute more than 50 percent of the population. Considering these numbers, the place of women in the patriarchal African state systems should be addressed. Women are central to social, economic, and political advancements of these nations.

The theories concerning women and development are traced back to the 1950s and 1960s. The development and feminist schools of thought are precursory to the theories on women and development. Six theories emerge from women and development standpoints: human resource development, welfare, antipoverty, empowerment, equity and human rights, and efficiency approaches. The human resources' standpoint maintains that sustainable development is not obtainable in the absence of women's integration into the state system.[21] This approach contradicts the argument that the gains from development filter down to women. Laying strong emphasis on nature's endowment of the high proportion of women as opposed to men in any given African country, these theorists argue that women must be educated, and have access to technology, income, and policy-making positions to effectively compete in the state arena.

The welfare alternative stems from the premise that women are subservient beneficiaries of the developmental process because of their biological typing as mothers and wives. As this assumption holds, population growth is usually the major analytical focal point. Hence, emphasis is placed on the relationship between maternal health care concerns, family size, and well-being. Consequently, they encourage the provision of health care resources in relation to maternal and child welfare. The dominant voice of this school is the United Nations Children's Fund (UNICEF), UN High Commission for Refugees (UNHCR), and United Nations Fund for Population Activities (UNFPA). The major setback of this theory is that it overlooks the essence of women's contribution to both public and domestic realms. Also, because of the employment of the concept of welfare, the theory may be subscribing to the state of dependency, rather than self-reliance.

The World Bank and the International Labor Organization (ILO) expound the antipoverty viewpoint to women and development. Women are the major focus, because of the hierarchical insertion of women in the state system. The World Bank earmarks women to achieve population control and to combat poverty. Consequently, it establishes small-scale, income-generating businesses. These kinds of projects, though minuscule, assist in giving some African women hope and support of achieving self-sustenance.

Another segment of the women and development perspectives, notably, women's empowerment, emerged in the mid-1980s. Its basic objective is the formation of the Development Alternatives with Women for a New Era (DAWN).[22] This school maintains that divergent backgrounds such as class, race, and history serve as the determinant factors in women's experiences. Because they perceive that all women are poor and oppressed, they underscore the importance of creating awareness of women's situation and mobilizing grassroots groups as a strategy to achieving empowerment. Women's empowerment and autonomy are obtainable when women achieve sustainable education and, have land and financial resources. This standpoint is essential for African women to emerge as major participants in the African state systems. It paves the way for African women's rights to be recognized.

The equity and human rights approach to women and development argues for the equality of women for actualizing women's integration in the state system. This school recognizes that the inequality between women and men is precursory to resolving the developmental problems facing Africa. It therefore places huge emphasis on obliterating some legal constraints against women's integration in the state system.[23] Achieving equality for all women is the main thrust of the UN Commission on the Status of Women (CSW), which established the Convention on the Elimination of Discrimination against Women (CEDAW). Their slogan that "women's rights are human rights" in the 1990s is adopted by the UN Commission on the Status of Women's Origins in the Commission on Human Rights. As the human rights issues in Africa are often orchestrated by African female lawyers, they bestow attention on reforming laws affecting land ownership, and inheritance, particularly in relation to women and children. African states would operate more efficiently when African women receive the due process of law. Even though hereditary laws vary among countries, those laws favor men in the majority of the patriarchal African state systems.

The efficiency method is geared toward development and places a strong emphasis on increasing productivity to bolster the high caliber of living.[24] It argues that women's participation in the developmental projects will accelerate growth, because women compose over half the labor force and contribute heavily to various economic affairs. As time progresses, this school shifted its focus in the 1970s and emphasized the impact of the market on development when the structural adjustment programs (SAPS) are initiated. This approach fails to take into consideration the impact of global political, economic, and technological determinants on the developing countries' capabilities to sustain themselves. Furthermore, its policy prescriptions, such as excessive reductions in government personnel and activities, dependence on the private sector for economic boom, and participation in the free markets of the world economy, are criticized. These cutbacks further led to economic deficits and massive unemployment, situations that adversely affected African women's social, economic, and political welfare.

Finally, the concept of gender flourishes in the 1980s and supersedes the terminology of women and development.[25] They evince gender as a social misrepresentation of identity. According to this standpoint, the anticipations and commitments of women and men in the state system are not always biologically given and therefore, are socially alterable. The gender construct is best suitable in addressing the impact of the patriarchal strongholds on the domestic and public spheres in Africa and applies very well to this discourse.

Many woman-centered scholars argue that women's interests are not articulated in the state system. They contend that sexism in the state system has created a kind of dualism where gender differentiation blinds the elites.[26] The African state system is divided into two pyramidal horizons, the private (domestic) and the public (civic). In the domestic arena, the male is the traditional head of the household, and the female bears and raises children. The civic frontier that the economic, social, and political institutions represent is capital-oriented and encourages individual competition at the expense of the less viable group. In this carefully structured domain, the male is the political and economic elite. This analysis is classified as the dialectic gender ordering, which is another terminology for capitalist patriarchy, a concept propounded by Zillah Eisenstein.[27] Her analysis though Eurocentric, is pertinent to the African situation because the African states are part of the global system. These states have, across time, been penetrated in various degrees by both indigenous and extrinsic capitals. Consequently, in the African state system, the public and private spheres are hierarchical, and both structure each other.

Based on the United Nations' analysis, women rarely account for 1 or 2 percent of senior management positions in the political and economic sectors of the world system. Furthermore, it states that it will take a century of rigorous effort and serious planning before women are fully integrated into the state system,[28] even if women, according to such UN reports, made up more than half the global population, stood for one-third of paid labor configurations, accumulated only one-tenth of worlds' income, and controlled less than 1 percent of the world's resources.

Men, on the other hand, dominate the workforce and the political arena. Men are better paid than women, and, as some women are unemployed, women are described as the army of reserved labor. No matter where women are employed, they are found in the lowest rank of the labor pool. In brief, the feminist theory of the African state system maintains that the state system is gendered. The female constitutes a separate class from the male. Generally, in the state system, the female has been the proletariat, and the male the elite.[29] For instance, in the private and the public spheres, the African males who have been the traditional head of household are also the secretary-general of the United Nations, chairperson of the Organization of Petroleum Exporting Countries (OPEC), Organization of African Unity (OAU), and the Economic Community of West African States (ECOWAS), and the president of any given African country. Therefore, in the hierarchical realms of the global, regional, and state political and economic systems, the African male dominates. The African woman, on the other hand, lacked access to this structured and yet differentiated economic and political arrangement.

Generally, in feminist thought, the concept of capitalist patriarchy is most frequently employed to denote a structure of masculine domination or a sexual system of power.[30] Though their conclusions may differ, there may be a consensus among feminist logicians that the contemporary state system, whether socialist or classist, is patriarchal.[31] For instance, Carole Pateman claimed that the notion of patriarchy unquestionably translated the intricacies of control and repression of women in the state system.[32] According to Eisenstein, patriarchy denoted a pattern of social interactions closely linked to hierarchical relations between men and women. Such interactions manifested in such a fashion that men benefit more than women in the system. Sandra Goldberg argues that capitalist patriarchy is universal if one extended the concept to embrace any system of organization—political, economic, industrial, financial, religious, or social—in which the formidable number of upper positions in the hierarchy is occupied by males.[33] Nancy Frazer contended that capitalist patriarchy depicted an elaborate structure controlled by the state in which the constituents act as affiliates positioned as economic and political proxies struggling against one another.[34] The consequence of such association is that one group came out dominating the other. The state in Africa promoted the procurement mechanisms in gender-distinctive modes. For instance, the African states authenticate the groundwork for groups to become accustomed to its governmental visions of acceptable gender exchange. African states' decision-making processes in relation to their political economy are gender-based. The outcome is that, with a few exceptions, men are the official breadwinners, and women are commissioned to work subserviently in the African economy and to invigorate male workforce productivity through home labor. The nature of work for the majority of African women includes food production, water fetching and gathering of firewood, and producing for home consumption, besides functioning as an army of reserve labor. In the political arena, African women are rarely visible. African men are the dominant actors presiding over the military or civilian types of governments.

PATRIARCHY, POLITICAL ACTORS, AND DEVELOPMENT IN AFRICA

According to Frazer, nation-states have the responsibility to represent the interest of the citizenry.[35] Nevertheless, the women and men as citizens of African states are not equally positioned. Women do not receive equal shares of the African states' political and economic resources. Rather, women have become passive laborers, docile and relegated to the bottom of the sphere, while men are active participants running the state system from the top down.[36] The number of women in decision-making positions such as heads of nations, senior members of government and parliament, corporate executives, and high-level officials in any given geographical area is an indication of a distorted, gender-based balance of power and influence. The dominant political actors in the United Nations and African states' domains are largely male.

African Women as Participants in the United Nations

The UN is a dominant international organization instrumental in articulating human rights, and it seems that this entity is supportive of women's integration into the state system. In fact, the charter of the United Nations, incorporated in San Francisco in June 1945, is the leading universal agreement to mention in precise details the equal rights of women and men: "the United Nations will place no restrictions on the eligibility of men and women to participate in any capacity and under conditions of equality in its principal and subsidiary organs." This allegiance is emphasized in an "open letter to women of the world," from men's representatives and counselors at the first General Assembly of the UN and was recited by Eleanor Roosevelt. "We hope that women's participation in the work of the UN may grow and increase insight and skills."[37] Yet the proportion of women participants as UN professional staff is very low. This pattern of minuscule participation is a replica of the vertical inclusion of women at the national level. In 1949, the ratio of women on the United Nations professional staff at all levels stood at 23.4 percent.[38] However, this number declined to 14.7 percent in 1975 and showed a significant increase within a year at 29.5.[39] The following represented the break down of the numbers of women on the professional staff: senior management, 2 percent; senior professional positions, 4.3; about 16.1 percent in the midlevel professional staff; and 30.3 in the junior professional level.[40]

Even if the rate of women's participation on the UN professional staff is higher than the rates of individual nation-states, the proportion is still low when considering the integrationist standpoint of the United Nations. In 1993, women constituted 29.5 percent of the UN professional staff, and only 12.6 percent of women were employed on the senior management positions. Only 16.2 percent of the senior professional level is presided over by women, and for the midlevel and junior professional positions, the numbers were 32.2 and 47.8 percent, respectively.[41]

In 1995, of the fifty-nine people serving as undersecretaries-general only four are women. These women made history when three of them were appointed by the former secretary-general, Boutros Boutros-Ghali. It is worth mentioning that only a fraction of women have worked for the specialized agencies. In 1975, for instance, the proportion of women assisting on the UN specialized agencies was 11 percent, compared to 15 percent in the Secretariat. The quantity has multiplied to 25 and 30 percent. Women's affiliation to the senior management of the UN programs and agencies in 1993 was much less than at other professional levels. In the majority of the cases, it was less than 10 percent. Women's representation was better in UNICEF at 17 percent, and only three of these institutions are administrated by women—United Nations Population Fund with 25 percent of women, the World Food Program with 25 percent, and United Nations Environment program, 20 percent. The top administrations in the UN Development Program and the Office of the United Nations High Commissioners for Refugees are approximately 12 percent women.[42]

From the inception of the UN about 36 peacekeeping operations have been initiated, and women's active presence is negligent. This palpable omission is even more pronounced in security-related operations. For instance, since 1988, the UN had engaged in twenty peacekeeping operations, and no woman had performed on the military peacekeeping staffs. From 1957 to 1979, 6,205 troops were supplied, and only five were women.[43] Between 1989 and 1992, the number of women involved in the UN security operations rose to 1 percent, and only 255 women assisted. In 1993, this figure grew to 2 percent. It is obvious that the degree of women's involvement in the UN security-related operations is determined by various countries' policies. While some nation-states blatantly restrict women's involvement in their military personnel, only a fraction approve their women serving in that capacity. Nonetheless, some women have assisted due to the enlargement of the United Nations civilian segment. For instance, between 1957 and 1991, the figures ranged from 5 percent to 23 percent. In 1993, women formed one-third of the international civilian staff. About 50 percent of the all-civilian peace and security mission in relation to the UN Observer-Mission to South Africa are women. Just as the hierarchical gender segregation of the labor force is a structural feature in the state system, such differentiation is a duplication in dominant international organizations, such as the UN. Women serving on the UN civilian staff are found at the lowest level of the strata. The UN had established one of the successful peacekeeping operations in Namibia. This effort was attributed to the method of staff selection, in which emphasis was placed on experience and regional balance. Because of this arrangement, 40 percent of those professional staffs were women. Also, women held three of the ten senior field positions. In the eighty-nine autonomous or specialized UN agencies, no woman has been commissioned as the chief administrator. Table 5.1 shows the number and percentage of West African women involved in the capacity of the UN professional staff.

The number of women from Niger Republic to serve the UN professional staff is only four, and this constitutes 50 percent of women from that nation serving the UN. In 1985, sixteen women representing Nigeria are grouped under this category, and they make up 6.3 percent of the UN personnel representing their country. For Liberia in 1984, only eight women functioned under this typing, and they formed only 37.5 of Liberians in that merit. In 1992, Benin had only six women, characterizing 16.7 percent of the total number of people to officiate in that degree. Burkina Faso in 1987 had only seven women on the UN professional staff and stood for 14.3 personnel of that nation's representatives on UN professional staff. Chad had only three women to serve, and the year is unknown. In 1994, Cameroon had fourteen women, and they profiled only 21.4 percent of those total representatives. Cote d'Ivoire had only twelve women, and they stood for only 16.7 percent of the country's staff to fare in that caliber. In 1983, Gabon had two women on their UN professional staff, constituting 14.3 percent of that nation's participants in that position. The number of women officiating on the UN professional staff from Senegal in 1988 numbered fifteen,

Table   5.1

West   African   Women   on   the   UN   Professional   Staff

Country	Number of Women	Percentage of Women	Year of Entry
Benin	6	16.7	1992
Burkina Faso	7	14.3	1987
Cameroon	14	21.4	1994
Chad	3	0.0	——
Cote d'Ivoire	12	16.7	——
Gabon	2	0.0	1983
Gambia	7	14.3	1993
Guinea	6	16.7	1982
Guinea Bissau	1	0.0	1985
Liberia	8	37.5	1984
Niger	4	50.0	——
Nigeria	16	6.3	1985
Senegal	15	33.3	1983
Sierra Leone	15	26.7	1988

Source: Adapted from United Nations Secretariat. 1994. "Composition of the Secretariat," Wistat (A/48/559); UN on the Convention for the Elimination of Discrimination against Women. 1994. "Report on the Committee on the Elimination of Discrimination against Women (Thirteenth session)." (A/49/3 8) unpublished.

Computer graphics: Melanie Marshall James.

and such data amounted to only 33.3 percent of Senegal's personnel. In 1988, Sierra Leone had fifteen women, and they embodied only 26.7 percent of their nation's representatives serving in that field. Finally, Guinea Bissau had only one woman in 1985 meeting that classification. These figures suggest that from 1982 to 1994, the number of African women participating on the UN professional staff varies across nations and times. These numbers depict the most salient truth that West African women remain significantly underrepresented in the most important international organization that is in the forefront in promoting woman's rights. African women are not equally positioned as men in the United Nations, and this incidence filters down to governments of African states.

African   Women's   Involvement   in   African   Politics

Table 5.2 displays the percentage of parliamentary seats allocated to West Africa in 1994. The pattern remains obvious: African women are not integrated

Table 5.2
Percent of Parliamentary Seats Occupied by Women, 1994

Country	Upper Chamber	Lower Chamber
Benin	—	6
Burkina Faso	—	6
Cameroon	—	12
Chad	—	16
Cote d'Ivoire	—	5
Equatorial Guinea	—	9
Gabon	—	6
Gambia	—	5.9
Ghana	—	8
Guinea	—	—
Guinea Bissau	—	—
Liberia	—	6
Niger	—	—
Nigeria	—	—
Senegal	—	12
Sierra Leone	—	—

Source: Adapted from The Statistical Division of the UN Secretariat. *Women's Indicators and Statistical Database*. # E.95.XVII.6.

Computer graphics: Melanie Marshall James.

into the upper chambers of their governments. In the lower chambers, the numbers range from none in countries such as Nigeria, Guinea, and Guinea Bissau, to six in Benin, Burkina Faso, and Liberia, to eight in Ghana, to nine in Equatorial Guinea, to twelve in Cameroon, and to sixteen in Chad. Although none of the West African nations have women in the upper chamber of their parliaments because of their variant regime types and the patriarchal nature of the existing governments, some countries have better representations than others. For instance, Cameroon had twelve, and Chad sixteen women. Even in the areas where women preside, the evidence suggests that women direct nonvital offices in comparison with their male counterparts. This data support our standpoint, which argues that women are not fully incorporated into the West African parliamentary governments. For African states to progress, they must establish balance among gender groups. That African women make policy contributions must become a reality.

From the era of independence to recent years, the majority of African countries have been governed by men. The only two exceptions were Burundi and Rwanda, where Sylvie Kinigi and Agate Uwilingiyimana fared in 1993 as the interim prime ministers of their respective countries. Accessible information justifies my claim of microscopic participation of women at the parliamentary level. According to the UN, the percentage of women in decision-making political positions in Northern Africa in 1994 was zero. For Sub-Saharan Africa, the figure was 4.4 percent.[44] In 1994, South Africa had twenty women in the lower chamber of parliament, and Seychelles had twenty-seven. For the upper chamber of the parliament, only Swaziland had up to twenty women, and other African nations had fewer than twenty women in both houses of the parliament in 1994. In fact, the average number of women in parliamentary assemblies for Sub-Saharan nations virtually remained stagnant between 1987 and 1994. The numbers were about 7.5 percent in 1987 and about 8.5 percent in 1994. For Northern African countries, the numbers rose from about 3.8 percent to around 4.5 percent.

Of all the governmental sectors examined, African women seemed to have made sizable progress in the legal spheres of their countries except the UN. None of the eighty-nine judges chosen to serve at the International Court of Justice since 1945 have been women. Nevertheless, the percentages of African women in law and justice, for Northern African countries were 16.7 and 6.9, respectively, for Sub-Saharan Africa. Women are gradually advancing in legal affairs. In 1991, Nigeria had fifty female judges serving as members of the International Association of Women Judges. The seemingly high presence of women judges in Nigeria, though an indication of progress, does not negate the marginality of women's interest in the Nigerian legal system. The Nigerian legal sphere establishes legal guidelines, commonly shared by either customary laws or laws enacted by political authorities who are largely males. The existence of multiple legal spheres due to diverse ethnic groups in Nigeria and other African nations impacts women's status. For instance, there are some variations by countries in courts' definitions of crucial areas of woman's rights, such as marriage, divorce, property ownership, and child custody. These issues determine African women's access to means of production: land labor, and capital, and all these, in turn, affect the values attached to kinship, women's access to education, and, eventually, the degree of women's involvement in politics. Some African governments are notorious in their lack of recognition of electoral laws and boundaries. The Nigerian case is particularly crucial, because men have usurped the military and civilian governments, and, in so doing, the vital contributions that might have been made by various women intellectuals as top-level politicians are forfeited.

The UN also reported 5.8 ratios for women in Northern African nations in the executive offices and 2.8 percent for women in Africa south of the Sahara.[45] Even when a few women occupy ministerial and senior-level positions, the nature of appointments is nonstrategic and did not contribute in advancing women's stake in the African state systems. The types of political appointments extended to women are ministers of women's affairs, cultural affairs, social development, education, and so on. For such offices, African women are found to have the most representation. For instance, except for Northern Africa, which has 1.6 percent of women in high-level social positions, the social ministries of other African states had 12.5 percent women.[46] Yet, African women's political participation after independence is minimal as opposed to the precolonial period.

Before the manifestation of colonial legacies, many African women have been major actors in the politics of their precolonial societies. Some women exercised great authority as political leaders, counselors, and spiritual heads. For example, the queen mother under the Asante empire shared power with a male counterpart, legislated in the court system, and rendered decisions in the absence of the chief.[47] According to Awe, the *iyalode* had administrative power over all Yoruba women and represented their interests in the king's legislature.[48] The prominent position of many African women changed following the onset of colonialism in Africa. During the colonial era, European powers introduced differing legal and cultural structures that incapacitated African women's historical cornerstones of power. Consequently, African women are transformed into political and economic proletarians. The transformation of African women became a permanent condition following the statehood of African nations, and this marginal status of Africa in government extends into the modern era. Table 5.3 explains the ratio of West African women in government ministries.

In 1987, the numbers of women at the ministerial and subministerial levels were low. For instance, in 1987, there were no women in the ministry in the Republic of Benin. Nonetheless, evidence in 1994 disclosed a significant improvement, bringing the number of such women representatives to 9.5 percent.

Information relating to Burkina Faso established that there were 11.5 and 13.2 percent of women representatives at the ministerial and subministerial levels, respectively, in 1987. However, in 1994, evidence revealed that the country had only twenty-seven women ministers, at a ratio of 7.4, and forty-three women in the subministry, at a ratio of 14.0.

In 1987, statistics on Cameroon reported women occupying ministerially and subministerial offices at the percentages of 6.5 and 21.4, respectively. There was a decrease in 1994 in the ratio, projecting women's presence at 2.9 percent in the ministry and 4.8, at the subministerial level.

Available data on Chad supported our premise, illustrating that women fill state positions in very insignificant numbers. For instance, in 1987, the country had only zero percent of women in the subministry and 4.2 percent in the ministry. In 1994, merely 5.0 percent of women served in the ministry, positioning twenty women in that capacity and only eight women officiated in the subministry bringing the quota to 0.0 seats.

Cote d'Ivoire registered 9.5 and 2.4 percent of women in the ministerial and subministerial bureaus, respectively, in 1987. However, in 1994 there were some improvements in the placement of twenty-six women controlling 7.7

Table 5.3
Percentage of West African Women in Decision-Making Positions in Government Ministries

Country	1987		Ministerial in 1994 Total % by Women		Submin in 1994 Total % of Seats	
	Min	Submin				
Benin	0.0	0.0	21	9.5	2	0.0
Burkina Faso	11.5	13.2	27	7.4	43	14.0
Cameroon	6.5	21.4	34	2.9	62	4.8
Chad	4.2	0.0	20	5.0	8	0.0
Cote d'Ivoire	9.5	2.4	26	7.7	21	0.0
Equatorial Guinea	0.0	33.3	25	4.0	10	0.0
Gabon	2.0	17.6	29	6.9	17	11.8
Gambia	5.9	7.1	16	0.0	42	7.1
Ghana	0.0	22.7	28	10.7	26	11.5
Guinea	0.0	0.0	22	9.1	53	7.5
Guinea-Bissau	4.5	0.0	24	4.2	21	19.0
Liberia	10.5	0.0	19	5.3	5	0.0
Niger	0.0	2.3	20	5.0	31	19.4
Nigeria	0.0	5.8	34	2.9	18	11.1
Senegal	12.0	——	29	6.9	7	0.0
Sierra Leone	0.0	5.0	22	0.0	85	2.4

Source: Adapted from UN. 1994. "Distribution of Seats between Men and Women in the 178 National Parliaments in 1994." #18.Add.2IRev. 1.

Notes: Min represents ministerial, and submin stands for subministerial appointments.

Computer graphics: Melanie Marshall James.

percent of the seats in the ministry and twenty-one women who presided in the subministry, representing 0.0 percent of the seats.

Equatorial Guinea had 0.0 and 33.3 percent of women in the ministry and subministry in 1987. Notwithstanding such a poor performance, in 1994, twenty-five women were nominated as ministers, retaining 4.0 percent of the seats, and ten women filled 0.0 percent seats in the subministry.

For Gabon in 1987, women made up only 2.0 and 17.6 percent of the number of representatives in the ministry and subministerial levels, respectively.

Such figures slightly improved in 1994, placing twenty-nine women in the ministry at the rate of 6.9 percent, while seventeen women fared at the subministerial level, making up only 11.8 percent of such seats.

In 1987, Gambian women engaged as presiding ministers and subministers overseeing 5.9 and 7.1 percent of the seats; and in 1994, sixteen women were selected as representatives of 0.0 percent of the seats, and forty-two women were nominated as subministers, symbolizing only 7.1 percent of the nominees.

For Ghana in 1987, the congruity of women as ministers and subministers stood at 0.0 and 22.7 percent, respectively. In 1994, twenty-eight women were selected as ministers, occupying 10.7 percent of the seats, while twenty-six women served as subministers, and the parity was 11.5.

The findings on the percentage of women employed as ministers and subministers by the Federal Republic of Guinea establish that women in that region represent only 0.0 percent for both offices; in 1994, however, twenty-two women fared as ministers at the ratio of 9.1 percent, and fifty-three women participated at the subministerial level, and they carried 7.5 percent of the seats.

The facts on women's representation at the ministerial and subministerial levels in Guinea Bissau held that in 1987, they succeeded at the ratio of 4.5 and 0.0 percent, respectively. Such figures increased to 4.2 percent for twenty-four women in the ministries and 19.0 percent for twenty-one women at the subministerial level in 1994.

For Liberia, in 1987, 10.5 and 0.0 percent of the seats were occupied by women at the ministerial and subministerial departments, respectively. In 1994, nineteen women served at the ministerial level, occupying 5.3 percent of the seats, and at the subministerial position, only five women were nominated, which indicated only 0.0 percent.

Data on the Niger Republic indicated that, in 1987, women represented 0.0 percent at the ministerial level and 2.3 at the subministerial tier. But in 1994, twenty women became ministers, controlling 5.0 percent of the electoral positions, and thirty-one women were chosen at the subministerial level and carried 19.4 percent of the seats. Data from Nigeria in 1987 suggested that women controlled only 0.0 and 5.8 percent of ministerial and subministerial, respectively, posts in 1987. Furthermore, in 1994, thirty-four women were selected as ministers, and these women formed only 2.9 percent of the nominees, and eighteen women officiated at the subministerial capacity, 11.1 percent of the total seats.

Women composed 12.0 percent of ministers in Senegal in 1987, and the number of women in the subministerial office was unknown. Later in 1994, twenty-nine women became ministers, and they occupied only 6.9 percent of the allocated seats; seven women fared at the subministerial rank, carrying a miserly 0.0 percent of the seats.

Finally, in 1987, the statistics in Table 5.3 revealed that Sierra Leone placed 0.0 and 5.0 percent of the seats occupied by women at the ministerial and subministerial ranks, respectively. In 1994, twenty-two women became ministers, controlling 0.0 percent of the seats, and the eighty-five women governing at the subministerial level filled only 2.4 percent of the slots.

These data support the research standpoint that women are not fairly represented in the various national and local governments in Africa. There is also a lack of uniformity on the levels and rates of representation, which vary by year and country, and type of regimes, that is, whether the state has a military or civilian type of government. It is noteworthy that a high population of women in a given African country and the levels of education do not guarantee that most of these African women participate as ministers or subministers. Men still dominate in the governing process in Africa. These factors support our claim that, because of the patriarchal nature of African countries, African women are still underrepresented at the ministerial and subministerial levels.

It is a known fact that African women are underrepresented in the African political arena. Some segments of African women participate in politics, as opposed to African men, who dominate the political arena. African women's invisibility is pronounced at all levels of government in various African countries in the postcolonial era. For example, the UN reported in 1986 that women occupied an average of 6 percent of all national legislature seats.[49] Only about 20 percent of African countries had women as cabinet officials. Except for Botswana, where a woman served as a foreign minister, the rest of the women officials presided over nonstrategic positions, such as ministers of community development, cultural affairs, nutrition, and social development. It is possible that women are better represented at the local level, but information is unavailable to justify this claim. Generally, African women have not fared as military officials because of the segregated nature of the postcolonial military regimes. Very few African women have made headway at the supranational level. For instance, in 1986, only forty-seven UN women's officials out of thousands of African men were participants, and only two of those were directors.[50]

Women's absence in national government may be due to several interrelated determinants. First, the formation of political class following independence had men at the forefront of the political realm, with people like Kwame Nkrumah, Nnamdi Azikiwe, Obafemi Awolowo, Julius Nyerere, Jomo Kenyatta, and Kenneth Kawunda bearing the political banners of their respective nations. The political class established then, though dynamic, with a high incidence of military interventions, was exclusively male. From the era of independence to the postmodern era, African women have not yet emerged from the "backyards of African political arenas," because they lack a political base.

Another logical inference relating to African women's political alienation is that politics is perceived by most Africans as a relatively male domain, an area in which women are disabled and uninvited. Prospective female political aspirants are often intimidated, and this discourages their activism. African women who aspire to become politicians are often called derogatory names and have no institutional backing. Even when a few succeed in becoming politically involved, they function in a male-dominated world and consequently adopt a masculine political stance. They collaborate with male party officials, accede to their platforms, and compete on those goals. These contradictory stances cause stumbling blocks to African women's formation of a viable political class.

Furthermore, most African women who are active in politics form a tiny minority, and these women are different from the rest of African women. They are more accomplished, and, consequently, their interests reflect their elite class affiliation, rather than their gender background. For example, in Uganda and Kenya, the dominant women's association actively lobbied for amendments in the divorce laws to favor their immediate class interest and not for Ugandan and Kenyan women overall. The National Council of Ghanian Women campaigned for the establishment of child care in the school system in the urban areas,[51] a standpoint that if approved, would cater only to the interest of wealthy women in the urban areas, neglecting the rural areas, where a vast majority of African women are located.

According to Staudt, some African elite women strongly influence constructing opinions that safeguard their upper-class status and discredit and subordinate women overall.[52] Geisler argues, for instance, that the state uses the elites among African women to foster its own interest.[53] The Zambia's UNIP Women's League Acts compels the elite members to abide by the Zambia ethical code. These women, in return, agreed to spearhead the state's crackdown of prostitutes, black market traders, and any Zambian woman's association involved in illegal activities.

The states' use of women as tactics to subject other women is not restricted to Ghana and Zambia. In Mali, the women's group the National Union of Malian Women (UNFM) is forbidden from enlisting in activities other than the ones approved by the state. Lastly, the women's auxiliaries in the Kenya's political party were forbidden from publicly campaigning on any political platforms. These examples illustrate the reasons for the minimal engagement of African women in politics. These are compounded by lack of access, exclusion, and neglect. The consequences of such actions are that African women do opt to prevaricate state authority and/or when they become active in the public sphere, they fail to promote women's agenda due to lack of awareness or because of pressure by the state.

Other factors relating to African women's absence from politics are based on the following concerns. Most African women realize that they are shunned, and harassed, and they feel defenseless. Another factor relates to systemic inadequacy. The educational systems are not directed to properly advance potential political leaders. Education provides a bridge to establishing political clout, largely because knowledge is precursory to political ascendance. Thus, policies put in place today will directly affect the eligibility of future generations of prospective African women politicians. Therefore, lack of strategic know-how in politics has forced African politicians to exclude women in the political arena.

African Women in the Economic Arena

Historical findings suggest that African women's collaboration in economic life is widespread all over the continent. In many parts of Africa, particularly during the precolonial era, the gender classification of labor designated cultivation to women. They also engaged in barter with their produce, while men were mostly involved in hunting. But there were instances where division of labor was not clearly defined along gender lines. For example, West African women work with their men. Nevertheless, women most of the time shoulder the obligation to grow cocoa in parts of Nigeria. Ethiopian women simultaneously gleaned and harvested as their men cultivated the fields.[54] Generally, African women farm on the communal property temporarily apportioned to them by their elders, mostly male kindred.

Apart from farming, African women were busy with other kinds of economic activities during the precolonial era. Some of them undertook commercial ventures with the European merchants and at the local level. For instance, the West African merchant-princesses were renowned for their vast wealth and overseas commercial dealings. Petty trading and agricultural activities were common occupation for African women.

Apparently, during the early periods, African women had an exalted status as opposed to their European counterparts. While there was a class distinction between African women and their men about status, there might be an equilibrium of power in relation to economic obligations. There were comparable gender-based establishments catering to the needs of these groups. In southwestern Nigeria, women's courts were commissioned to impose fines, and women served as market officials regulating prices and mediating between disputing parties. Among the Bemileke female farmers in Cameroon, was a specialized group responsible for representing the interests of the farmers. Men and women in the area collaborated in some capacities in overseeing the affairs of the state, and in some special circumstances some men and women concurrently wielded high power.

Paramount transformations became evident in the colonial era as the colonial masters ushered in a new economic system, such as cash cropping and subsequent technologies. They also negated African women's role in the societies and introduced their gendered depiction of women, the Victorian concept of womanhood. Such notions characterized women as only reproducers and restricted them to the domestic sphere. Men, on the other hand, are perceived as go-getters and therefore could freely undertake political and economic responsibilities. The types of obligations given to African men by the colonial officials immensely contributed in reversing the division of labor between women and men in Africa. Men had the advantages of being educated, and employed and had access to other state resources.

Men became less involved in the traditional farming processes as they migrated to towns, and worked on mines and plantations because of the shifting patterns of Africa's political economy due to the colonial presence. Men's absence created a vacuum that the African women had to fill. Not only did they farm, but they took care of domestic obligations such as raising the young, nursing the sick, and taking care of the elders.

African women suffered a major drawback with the introduction of land settlement and consolidation programs that recognized men as heads of households and accorded them title deeds, even as absentee landlords. Such standpoints contradicted the user-rights tradition that promoted woman's rights and involvement in farming the family land.[55] Following the establishment of the permits, women's entitlements to the land proceeds diminished, and womanhood and women's work in the precolonial periods were devalued.[56]

The consequence of such policies created a huge uproar among African women. Africa's women farmers and merchants carried out their dissension of colonial policies that deprived them of their rights to engage in, and benefit from, economic activities. The colonial authorities refused to concede to the women's appeal to preserve subsistence crops due to their resolve to uphold the market economy. For example, in the 1940s and 1950s, women in Cote d'Ivoire, Cameroon, Uganda, and Sierra Leone challenged the introduction of cash crops such as coffee, sisal, and tea. The opposition arose because the cultivation was restricted to arable land, and these women complained that the crop required extra attention besides daily heavy workloads. Kenyan women in 1902 stationed their opposition against unfair labor practices by the colonial administrators.[57] The "Women's War" was an antitax uprising by the Ibo women in eastern Nigeria, opposing the colonial powers.[58]

African women endured in their quest to engage in economic activities in spite of the obstacles posed by the colonial policies. For instance, in 1950, western Cameroonian women teamed up to develop corn mill societies and established cooperative stores, built storage units for their corn and worked together to promote their interests. As a result, the membership reached a peak of 18,000 women, having more than 200 branches.[59] According to Boserup, some African women employed other tactics, such as demanding wages for their labor or threatening to divorce their spouses due to economic hardship introduced by these changes.[60] Over time African women have formulated some pattern of unified movements to help bolster their fecundity to make up for the socioeconomic incongruities because of unfavorable colonial policy choices. These could be in the form of protest, or communal activities.

Notwithstanding highly orchestrated attempts, the colonial legacy with its market economy left a lasting imprint on the African family system and the subsequent division of labor emanating from such arrangement. Some women-centered scholars argued that the colonial periods earmarked the inception of Africa's degeneration in food production.[61] This interesting notion, besides population crisis in Africa, attracted the attention of the ECA in 1970s, and such intervention led to the initiation of rural development policies with a special emphasis on women's integration.

Table 5.4 indicates the percentage of West African women engaging in economic activities by professional groups. These groups are classified as professional technicians, administrative and managerial, clerical, retail, services, and agriculture. It is worth mentioning that affiliation with one of these occupations is not rigid. Usually, most West African women are involved in more than one form of economic activity. These involvements cut across the immediate occupational boundaries, extending into other areas. For example, a West African woman may be a farmer and a retailer, or she may be a clerk or a teacher and engage in agriculture and/or retail, and vice versa.

Table 5.5 details the 1990 percent distribution of West African women in the labor force. The categories are grouped under the following headings: employers' own act workers, unpaid family workers, and employees. Forty-seven percent of women in the Republic of Benin are classified as working under the Employer's Own Act Worker, 40 percent are grouped as unpaid workers, and 21 percent are described as employed.

Cameroon had one of the highest number of unpaid family workers, and 70 percent of its female workers are tabulated under this distinction, and only 10 percent are listed under the employment scheme. Chad had no record of its women's involvement in any of these typings. While Cote d'Ivoire had 17 percent of its women ranked under the Employer's Own Act worker, 62 percent of these women were recorded as unpaid family workers, and only 7 percent are clustered under the employment bracket. Equatorial Guinea had 74 percent of its women recorded as unpaid family workers, 17 percent are itemized as self-employed, and 11 percent as employed.

Table 5.6 depicts the percentage distribution of the labor force classified according to gender. Women, for instance, are more likely than men to engage in agricultural activities. Conversely, there are more men than women employed in industries, with the exception of Cape Verde, where slightly more women are featured than men. The figures on the service sector also showed a slight increase in favor of women for Ghana and Nigeria. The rest of the countries in the table employed more men than women in the services. Table 5.6 confirms our claim that more women work in the agricultural divisions than men, and more men are hired in the service-related arena and in industries. Even when more women than men are employed in a given area, these women are vertically integrated, whereas men are horizontally integrated in the public sphere. African nation-states need to reverse this arbitrary trend and include women as active participants in all sectors of the state system.

Bringing Women Back into the Developmental Process: A Necessary Alternative or an Evil?

The nature of the contemporary African state system is patriarchal, which has resulted in the hierarchical structure of the states' apparatus. The leading economic and political institutions are hierarchically structured and gendered.

Table 5.4
Indicators on West African Women's Economic Activity
Professional Groups, 1990

Country	1994 Women	1994 Men	% of Women	Profes-sional & Tech-nical	Admin. & Manage-ment	Cler-ical	Retail	Ser-vices	Agri-cultural
Benin	75	88	47	43	7	32	1,303	33	27
Burkina Faso	75	93	45	35	16	48	194	28	99
Cameroon	39	86	32	32	11	45	66	46	100
Cape Verde	33	90	32	94	30	114	234	134	66
Chad	22	59	21	—	—	—	—	—	—
Cote d'Ivoire	47	87	34	18	—	23	109	30	59
Equatorial	52	82	40	37	2	19	55	20	83
Guinea	—	—	—	—	—	—	—	—	—
Gabon	45	82	37	—	—	—	—	—	—
Gambia	56	91	39	36	17	38	40	68	118
Ghana	51	81	39	55	10	42	807	53	90
Guinea	55	89	38	—	—	—	—	—	—
Guinea Bissau	55	90	39	35	9	26	6	9	2
Liberia	35	87	29	33	12	44	116	15	100
Niger	78	93	47	—	—	—	—	—	—
Nigeria	45	87	35	35	6	23	177	13	36
Senegal	51	86	38	20	4	26	30	156	1
Sierra Leone	37	82	32	47	9	70	222	18	122

Source: Adapted from International Labor Office. *Current Estimate and Projections: Year Book of Labor Statistics*. Geneva, 1994.

Notes: Admn. stands for administrative.

Computer graphics: Melanie Marshall James.

This interchange, which is based on the instant gratification of one gender group, has resulted in one gender's manipulating and controlling the other. The consequence of the politics of gender has resulted in the leaving behind of a vital

Table 5.5
Percentage Distribution of West African Women in Labor Force, 1990

Country	Employer's Own Act Workers	Unpaid Family Workers	Employees
Benin	47	40	21
Burkina Faso	16	66	13
Cameroon	39	70	10
Cape Verde	46	54	32
Chad	—	—	—
Cote d'Ivoire	17	62	7
Equatorial Guinea	17	74	11
Gabon	—	—	—
Gambia	44	64	20
Ghana	56	63	24
Guinea	19	60	43
Guinea Bissau	1	4	10
Liberia	47	65	13
Niger	17	24	15
Nigeria	36	46	15
Senegal	—	—	—
Sierra Leone	24	74	20

Source: Adapted from Statistical Division of the UN Secretariat. *Women's Indicators and
   Statistical Database* E.95.XVII.6.
Computer graphics: Melanie Marshall James.

segment of Africa's human resources—women—and created a significant vacuum
in combination with other variables for the developmental process of African
states.

African women used to be horizontally integrated in the state system during
the precolonial era. Following the onset of colonial administration and after the
sovereignties of these countries, African women became disfranchised politically
and economically. In the resultant hierachial public and private domains, African

Table 5.6
Indicators on the Economy and Women's Work: Percentage
Distribution of Labor Force by Gender, 1994

Country	Agriculture		Industry		Services	
	Women	Men	Women	Men	Women	Men
Benin	64	54	4	12	31	34
Burkina Faso	85	85	4	6	11	9
Cameroon	64	51	4	16	32	33
Cape Verde	14	50	31	30	54	21
Chad	80	75	2	7	19	18
Cote d'Ivoire	62	50	8	13	30	38
Equatorial Guinea	82	38	3	22	15	39
Gabon	84	63	3	18	13	19
Gambia	91	74	3	12	6	14
Ghana	50	55	17	20	33	24
Guinea	84	70	6	14	9	16
Guinea Bissau	91	72	2	6	7	22
Liberia	82	65	2	13	16	22
Niger	92	84	0	4	8	12
Nigeria	67	64	7	16	26	20
Senegal	87	72	4	10	10	18
Sierra Leone	78	56	4	22	17	23

Source: Adapted from International Labor Office. *Current Estimate and Projections: Year Book of Labor Statistics*. Geneva, 1994.
Computer graphics: Melanie Marshall James.

women are far from becoming political, social, and economic elites due to unequal gender exchange of these processes.

To reverse the process, there is a great need to adopt a holistic approach wherein the goal of one cannot be actualized in the absence of the prosperity of the other. African nations need to draw the line between instant and delayed gratification. Instead of excluding women and thereby promptly indulging themselves from readily available positions at the national and local levels and consequently marginalizing women as actors, these states should become strategists in their planning. They should delay the immediate yield of being the paramount actors and include women as dominant actors in the state's arena. They should create a response to the other, perceiving the other as an end, not a means to an end. This preemptive strike of delayed gratification would, in the long run, benefit, rather than hurt, Africa. This type of design also encourages states to establish laws that would grant women both legal rights and access to the state systems. African states need and should change laws restricting women's leadership and involvement in state affairs and create more opportunities for women to excel in the economic, social, and political realms of the state. This increases sustainability of the family and public spheres, not from the perspective of patriarchy but from a standpoint of mutual support and respect. These changes would, in the long run, lead to increased marketability and conventionality of Africa's vital resources in the global arena. Africa will then reach the ethos of sustainable development when policymakers take political and economic inventory and take correct assessment by bringing women back into the developmental process. The implementation of the correct values will achieve the long-awaited sustainable development.

NOTES

1. Nisbet, R. A. 1969. *Social Change and History.* New York: Oxford University Press.
2. Huntington, S. P. 1965. "Political Development and Political Decay." *World Politics* 17 (April): 386-430. Huntington, S. P. 1968. *Political Order in Changing Societies.* New Haven, CT: Yale University Press.
3. Chodak, S. 1973. *Societal Development: Five Approaches with Conclusions from Comparative Analysis.* New York: Oxford University Press.
4. Rostow, W. W. 1960. *The Stages of Economic Growth: A Non-Communist Manifesto.* Cambridge: Cambridge University Press. Organski, A.F.K. 1965. *The Stages of Political Development.* New York: Alfred A. Knopf.
5. Portes, A. 1976. "On the Sociology of National Development: Theories and Issues." *American Journal of Sociology* 32: 55-85. Todaro, M. P. 1985. *Economic Development in the Third World.* New York: Longman.
6. Huntington, S. P. 1965.
7. Huntington, S. P. 1968.
8. Huntington, S. P., and Joan M. Nelson. 1976. *No Easy Choice: Political Participation in Developing Countries.* Cambridge: Harvard University Press.
9. Apter, D. 1965. *The Politics of Modernization.* Chicago: University of Chicago Press.
10. Pasquino, G. 1970. "The Politics of Modernization: An Appraisal of David Apter's Contributions." *Comparative Political Studies* 3 (October): 297-322.
11. Ibid. 314-18.
12. Papanek, H. 1978. "Comment on Gusfield's Review Essay on Becoming Modern." *American Journal of Sociology* 83: 157-71.
13. Portes, A. 1976.

14. Tinker, I., and M. Bramsen. 1976. "The Adverse Impact of Development on Women." In *Women and World Development,* ed. I. Tinker and M. B. Bramsen. Washington, DC: Oversea Development Council, 22-34.

15. Frank, A. 1966. "The Development of Underdevelopment." *Monthly Review* 18: 17-31.

16. Chase-Dunn, C. 1975. "Dependence, Development and Inequality." *American Sociological Review* 40: 720-38.

17. Rubinson, R. 1976. "The World-Economy and Distribution of Income." *American Sociological Review* 41: 638-59.

18. Baran, P. 1988. "On the Political Economy of Backwardness." In *The Political Economy of Development and Underdevelopment,* by Charles Wilber. New York: Random House. Frank, A. 1988. "The Development of Underdevelopment." In *The Political Economy of Development and Underdevelopment,* by Charles Wilber. New York: Random House.

19. Nash, J. 1983. "The Impact of the Changing International Division of Labor on Different Labor Force." In *Women, Men and the International Labor,* ed. J. Nash and M. Fernandez-Kelly. Albany: State University of New York Press, 3-38.

20. Jacobson, J. L. 1994. *Gender Bias: Roadblock to Sustainable Development.* Washington DC: Worldwatch Institute.

21. ECA. 1971. *Factor Affecting Education, Training and Work Opportunities for Girls and Women within the Context of Development.* Addis Ababa: Economic Commission on Africa.

22. Sen, G., and C. Grown, 1987. *Development, Crises and Alternative Visions.* New York: Monthly Review Press.

23. Robertson, C., and L. Berger. 1986. *Women and Class in Africa.* New York: Africana Publishing.

24. Boserup, E. 1970. *Woman's Role in Economic Development.* New York: St. Martin's Press.

25. Rathberger, E. 1991. *Operationalizing of Gender and Development.* Washington, DC: Association on Women and Development (AWID).

26. Delphy, C. 1984. *Closer to Home: A Materialist Analysis of Women's Oppression.* Amherst: University of Massachusetts Press. Eisenstein, Z. 1989. *Capitalist Patriarchy and the Case for Socialist Feminism and Political Theory.* Stanford, CA: University Press.

27. Eisenstein, Z. 1981. *The Radical Future Liberal Feminism.* New York: Longmans.

28. UN. 1995. *The World's Women 1995: Trends and Statistics.* New York: United Nations Publications.

29. Delphy. 1984; Eisenstein. 1989.

30. Rowbotham, Sheila. 1983. *Dreams and Dilemmas.* London: Virago Press, 208-9. Disch, Lisa. 1991. "Toward a Feminist Conception of Politics." *Political Science and Politics* 24: 501-4.

31. Kramarae, C., and P. Treichler. 1985. *A Feminist Dictionary.* Boston: Pandora Press, 323-24. Bledsoe, Timothy, and Mary Herring. 1990. "Victims of Circumstances: Women in Pursuit of Political Office." *American Political Science Review* 84: 213-23. Boserup. 1970.

32. Pateman, C. 1989. *The Disorder of Women: Democracy, Feminism, and Political Theory*. Stanford, CA: Stanford University Press. Simon, R. J., and J. M. Landis. 1989. "Women's Place and Men's Attitude about a Woman's Place and Role." *Public Opinion Quarterly* 53: 265-76.

33. Goldberg, S. 1979. *Male Dominance: The Inevitability of Patriarchy*. London: Abacus.

34. Frazer, N. 1989. *Unruly Practices: Power, Discourse, and Gender in Contemporary Social Theory*. Minneapolis, MN: University of Minnesota Press.

35. Frazer, N. 1986. "Women, Welfare and Politics of Need Interpretation." *Hypatia* 2: 85-120.

36. Umerah-Udezulu, I. 1997. "The State and Interplay of Gender and Class on the Emergence of Women as Political Leaders in the Developing Countries." In *Capacity Building in the Third World*, ed. Valentine James. Westport, CT: Greenwood Press.

37. Charter of the United Nations. 1946. Article 8 and Official Records of the First Session of the General Assembly, Plenary Meetings of the General Assembly, Verbatim Record, January 10-February 14: 403.

38. Data for 1949 are derived from the report of the secretary-general on the participation of women in the work of the UN (E/CN.6 1132).

39. UN. 1976. The Reports of the Consultative Committee on the Administrative Questions (CCQ-SEC-368 PER) February 12.

40. UN. 1994b. The Reports of the Consultative Committee on the Administrative Questions (ACC/1994/PER/R. 13).

41. Ibid.

42. UN. 1994a. Reports of the Consultative Committee on the Administrative Questions (CCQ-SEC-368 PER) and (ACC/1994/PEWR. 13).

43. UN. 1995. UN. Department of Peacekeeping Operations (DPKO): Peacekeeping activities, various years.

44 Division for the Advancement of the United Nations. 1994. *Worldwide Government Directory*. Washington, DC: Belmont.

45. Statistical Division of the United Nations Secretariat. 1994. *Women's Indicators and Statistics Database*, No.1 8/Add. 2/Rev. 1. Geneva.

46. United Nations. 1995.

47. Aidoo, A. A. 1981. "The Asante Queen Mother in Government and Politics in the Nineteenth Century." In *The Black Women Cross-Culturally*, ed. F. C. Steady. Cambridge, England: Cambridge University Press.

48. Awe, B. 1977. "The Iyalode in the Traditional Yoruba Political System." In *Sexual Stratification: A Cross-Cultural View*, ed. A. Schlegel. New York: St. Martin's Press.

49. Africa Rights Monitor. 1990. "A Woman's Right to Political Participation in Africa." *Africa Today* 27: 49-64.

50. Ibid.

51. Bessie, House-Midamba. 1990. "The United Nations Decade: Political Empowerment or Increased Marginilization?" *Africa Today* 37: 37-48.

52. Staudt, K. 1986. "Class Stratification and Its Implication for Women in Politics." In *Women and Class in Africa*, ed. I. Berger and C. Robertson. New York: Africana Publishing Company, 197-215.

53. Geisler, Gisela. 1987. "Sisters under the Skin: Women and the Women's League in Zambia." *Journal of Modern African Studies* 25: 43-66.

54. Pala-Okeyo, Achola. 1985. *Towards Strategies for Strengthening the Position of Women in Food Production: An Overview and Proposals on Africa.* Santo Domingo: INSTRAW.

55. Parpart, J., and K. Staudt. 1990. *Women and the State in Africa.* Boulder, CO: Lynne Riener.

56. Van Allen, J. 1972. "Sitting on a Man: Colonialism and the Lost Political Institutions of Igbo Women." *CJAS* 6 (2): 165-81.

57. Presley, C. A. "The Mau Mau Rebellion: Kikuyu Women and Social Change." *CJAS* 22: 485-510.

58. Van Allen. 1972.

59. Snyder, M. 1991. *Gender and Food Regime: Some Transnational and Human Issues.* Iowa City: University of Iowa Press.

60. Boserup. 1970.

61. Pala-Okeyo. 1985.

6

Historical Women in the Fight for Liberation

Felix K. Ekechi

INTRODUCTION

The subject of the "African woman" has received considerable scholarly attention since the 1960s, thanks in part to the feminist movement. Of the many areas of feminist scholarship, the issue of gender inequality in Africa, especially in politics, has been of particular concern. Hence, attention is often drawn to "the age-long prejudices" and traditional "constraints" that have seemingly prevented women from full participation in African political affairs. Thus, Dr. Nina Mba writes, "In Africa, a woman's status is enhanced by the number of children she has. This emphasis on childbearing is a considerable constraint on women's participation in politics because a political career requires spending a great deal of time in activity away from home."[1] Susan Onyeche, a Nigerian feminist lawyer, wrote in a similar vein in 1992. In a paper delivered at the International Federation of Women Lawyers (Imo State chapter), held at Owerri, Nigeria, she reminded her predominantly women audience of "the age long prejudices that have militated against [women's] realization of [their political] rights." She added that, "societal norms ... expect [women] to be seen and not heard." However, she strongly urged her women compatriots not to be held back by "social norms" but "to participate actively in politics and the governance of this nation."[2]

Let me emphasize that African women have traditionally wielded considerable influence and authority in society. In fact, they have played active roles in the political affairs of their societies, both in the precolonial and colonial times, and women today continue to make their voices heard.[3] Indeed, they are by no means shy in articulating their grievances, whether these are social, economic, or political in nature.[4] African male leaders seem to be listening, even though their actions may not often match their rhetoric. In any case, President Ibrahim Babangida of Nigeria in 1989 remarked, "There are compelling reasons why African women must be integrated in the development process. First is their numerical strength. They are industrious and enterprising.... They are good managers.... No national programmes will be meaningful and thorough if women are not fully involved."[5]

That women have been part and parcel of the African political landscape is not in question, for historians and anthropologists have amply documented this fact.[6] For purposes of clarity, it may be necessary to broaden the concept of "politics" to include women's resistance to colonial or postcolonial overrule. After all, as Professor Falola has correctly pointed out, "Resistance is politics." Indeed, "Conflict is an expression of politics; it is public, challenging, and result oriented."[7] For this reason, women's resistance movements, whether collective or individualized, are treated as political actions. Better still, as the title of this chapter indicates, such movements may be regarded as illustrations of the liberation struggle.

This chapter, therefore, focuses on two related issues: the role that African women have played in the struggle for liberation from European imperialism and women's struggles to free themselves from marginalization in modern African politics. Essentially, this study provides portraits of women whose names certainly appear in Africa's historical past but who have not received the special attention they deserve in the historical literature relating to liberation. We are thus concerned here with the activities of selected African women who, in one form or another, contributed to the liberation struggle.

Even a cursory examination of the African historical record reveals a host of names of women leaders or activists who have, in their different ways, fought for the liberation of their societies from European imperialism. Examples of such women nationalists abound, and they include historical figures like Empress Taytu of Ethiopia (treated in this chapter), Queen Nzinga of Angola,[8] Madam Tinubu, "the famous Egba [Yoruba] woman" of Nigeria,[9] and Nehanda of Zimbabwe (c.1863-1898),[10] to name but a select few. Others, as this study illuminates, confronted the colonial powers head on or sought to end the marginalization of women in society. Our approach here is comparative; hence, examples are drawn from Nigeria, Ethiopia, and Kenya.

The first set of Nigerian women activists discussed here may be viewed as the early champions of cultural nationalism, for they felt compelled to challenge European pretensions of cultural hegemony. Yet studies of African nationalism, or, perhaps more specifically the liberation struggle, tend to concentrate on the activities of men, while the roles played by women are, by and large, relegated to the background. This chapter seeks, therefore, to redress this imbalance or, as some would say, benign neglect.[11] But let us define what exactly is meant by the expression "struggle for liberation." In the existing literature on the liberation question, there is often the tendency to associate this expression with violence or armed resistance. This is clearly the case with reference to the nationalist movements in Algeria, Angola, Guinea-Bissau, Kenya, Mozambique, Namibia, South Africa, and Zimbabwe. The "colonial situation" in these states, of course, made armed resistance inevitable. In this study, however, especially in the first two Nigerian precolonial examples cited, the focus is not on armed resistance, even though violence did erupt in, say, the Nigerian Women's War of 1929 and the Kenyan women's protest movement of 1922. But violence was incidental to the expressions of political agitation directed at the British colonial administration. However, as discussed later, the Nigerian protest movements of the 1840s and 1860s were essentially peaceful protests organized by women in response to missionary iconoclasm.

The Christian missionaries who came to Africa in the nineteenth century arrived, of course, with preconceived notions of Africa. To them, African culture was "paganish" and African society, in general, uncivilized. Hence, they felt compelled to subvert the social and cultural order and to replace it with European ("Christian") civilization. This was then considered the missionaries' "civilizing" mission. Thus, as one critic put it,

The missionary ... made it his business to destroy, usually without inquiry, and failed to recognize that the structure he was destroying had not only sent its roots very deeply, but had also thrown out its tendrils widely, so that its destruction involved vital wounds in many aspects of economic and social life. In destroying the religion, or rather in destroying or undermining its rituals and beliefs, he was at the same time and unwittingly destroying all that gave coherence and meaning to the social fabric.[12]

NIGERIAN WOMEN AND THE POLITICS OF LIBERATION

Nigerian women, as discussed later, proved to be active defenders of traditional African religion as well as the customs and practices (Omenani/ Omenala) that gave "coherence and meaning to the social fabric." In this regard, women may be seen as the earliest cultural nationalists. As a matter of fact, the pioneer missionaries in Eastern Nigeria perceived women so. But, on the other hand, they naturally saw them as the chief enemies of the Christian movement.[13] Eastern Nigerian women's early encounter with the Christian missionaries began in the 1840s. To begin with, European missionary enterprise in the area, as is true of all of Africa, was unpopular. This was largely because missionary evangelization entailed the destruction or undermining of traditional religious beliefs and the introduction of a new vision (the missionaries') of society. In essence, acceptance of Christianity implied the adoption of new cultural values. But Nigerian women, acting as the defenders of tradition, or the "guardians of their communities' spiritual health," mounted a stiff opposition against missionary propaganda. Take, for example, the case of Calabar women, whose resistance movements are recounted in missionary writings. The pioneer Presbyterian missionaries established a mission in Calabar in 1846. Not only did the missionaries convert some of the local people to Christianity, but they fervently preached the abolition of time-honored African marriage institutions, such as polygamy (polygyny), and other societal customs and practices, such as the killing of twins. The missionaries' preaching against the latter landed the pioneer missionaries in trouble with the local women. Here was a classic case of the clash of values.

According to missionary accounts, Calabar women presented "the greatest opposition" to the missionaries' new vision of the social order, especially with reference to the twin question. This report by the pioneer Presbyterian missionary the Reverend H. M. Waddell provides us with some understanding of the early missionaries' encounter with Calabar women:

> At all the stations it was determined, if twins were born in the towns, to bring both mothers and children to the mission houses.... At Creek Town some of the principal men could be depended on to aid our design.... [But] To our surprise, the greatest opposition we met came from a quarter from whence it was least expected, the women themselves.... Preaching on Christ the Light of the World, I referred...particularly [to] infanticide as beyond most bad customs unnatural, above most crimes heinous and unaccountable.... But the elderly ladies of the town...murmured and contradicted us.... They repudiated the doctrine of twins as monstrous and abominable, and spat out in disgust at the mention of such a thing.[14]

Traditionally, twin births were abhorred, being viewed as abnormal. Hence, the babies were generally disposed of, and their mothers were, at times, banished. Thus, the women's "sharp" protest against the missionaries' proposals was consistent with the people's beliefs and worldview. Their action was evidently a rejection of missionaries' cultural imposition. In essence, whereas the women stood for the preservation of the existing social order, Rev. Waddell thought otherwise. "Their opposition ... presented a new illustration of our subject, evincing the darkness, depravity, and deadness of mind and heart, which prevailed where the light of Christ had never shone."[15]

That women wielded considerable moral authority in society is illustrated by the positive response from the traditional rulers. Requested to consider the missionaries' proposals, the king and his counselors sided with the women and thus affirmed the legitimacy of twin immolation. Not only did they explicitly warn that "the old customs of the country [must] not be changed," but they further cautioned that "any man keeping those women [with twins] and their children would be blown out of town."[16] In this case, Calabar women had clearly demonstrated their moral authority as the staunch defenders of their society's spiritual health. Yet, the victory was short-lived; for the custom of twin immolation ultimately ended with the advent of British colonial rule in 1900.

As in the Calabar case, missionary-induced changes aroused a new social consciousness about missionary work in Igboland. Alarmed at the rapid rate of culture change, as evidenced in the conversions to Christianity, the adoption of new cultural values, the ever-increasing decline of the influence of traditional religion, and the growing disrespect for authority, exemplified in the attitudes of the Christian zealots toward the elders, Igbo women embarked on what might be called a "purity campaign." Their declared objective was the restoration of the traditional social order, now being threatened by missionary activities. This campaign, which began in 1864, took various forms and involved women from several Igbo towns east and west of the Niger River. Reportedly inspired by the spirit-medium called Odesoruelu ("Restorer of Traditional Life"), the women traveled from town to town preaching the message of peace and cultural renewal. They pointed to the negative impacts of missionary work, as evidenced in the adoption of foreign lifestyles, the disrespectful behavior of Christian converts toward the ancestral religion, exemplified in the desecration of religious shrines, and so on. These women messengers of liberation also called attention to the disturbing decline of social and moral values. Also of concern was the spread of new diseases (such as smallpox and influenza), believed to have been brought by the missionaries. Finally, the women expressed grave concern over the sociopolitical divide that then bedeviled the society. In short, missionary evangelization not only was believed to have brought religious polarization but had also accentuated social and political conflicts. The women's central message was this: the Igbo people should return to their ancestral religion and strictly adhere to its precepts. Unless this was done, the women messengers of liberation warned, the society would witness untold disasters.[17]

Again, as in Calabar, Igbo women had projected themselves as the true "guardians of their communities' spiritual health."[18] Apparently influenced by the women's messages and warnings, the political leaders, as in Calabar, listened and thus enacted legislation prohibiting, among other things, conversions to Christianity and the adoption of foreign lifestyles, like the wearing of European clothes. To further dramatize the point, the elders ordered all schools and churches closed indefinitely.[19] Here again, women have played the role of catalysts. In any case, it might be said that the women's cultural protests anticipated those of Edward Blyden and Casely Hayford, the indefatigable defenders of African life and culture from European assaults.[20] By extension, the women's obviously antiforeign ideology may be seen as resonating in the African nationalist movements of the 1950s and 1960s. In that case, Nigerian women certainly "played important, even crucial, roles in the denouncement of nationalist politics."[21]

EMPRESS TAYTU AND THE ITALIANS

Empress Taytu was the wife of Emperor Menelik II (1844-1913) of Ethiopia. She was a beautiful and brave woman. The Italian ambassador in Ethiopia who encountered her during the Ethiopian-Italian conflict described her as, indeed, "very brave.... In sum, she is a great lady, who perhaps in another milieu would have been a Christiana of Sweden or a Catherine the Great of [Russia]."[22] However, Empress Taytu's patriotic zeal seemed to have more forcefully impressed the ambassador, for, in fact, he perceived the empress as Italy's greatest antagonist. Indeed, historical accounts present Empress Taytu as a remarkable woman who played a vital role in the preservation of Ethiopian independence and sovereignty. In the process, she certainly left an indelible mark on the history of Ethiopia.

Ethiopia was, of course, one of the African states that the Europeans sought to colonize during the scramble for Africa in the 1880s. But Italian imperialistic ambitions in Ethiopia were foiled as a result of Empress Taytu's moral and political influence on her husband, Emperor Menelik. This section, therefore, focuses on the role Empress Taytu played in the politics of European colonization of Africa. In summary, it is well to note that Italy, like the other European powers of the nineteenth century, sought to acquire colonies in Africa, notably Ethiopia. The basis of the Italian imperial ambition in Ethiopia was the treaty of "amity and commerce," otherwise known as the Treaty of Wichale, which Emperor Menelik signed with Italy on May 2, 1889. Interpretations of the treaty, however, particularly Article 17, varied. Whereas the Italians claimed that Ethiopia ceded part of its country to them, the Ethiopians argued that no such cession of territory was ever contemplated. Consequently, a serious diplomatic wrangling developed in 1891, when the Italians formally declared Ethiopia an Italian protectorate.[23] During this diplomatic conflict Empress Taytu emerged as perhaps the most uncompromising advocate of Ethiopian independence.

When, during the negotiations, it appeared that Emperor Menelik was about to make concessions to the Italians, the empress reportedly stood firm against any compromises with Italy. In her impassioned speech opposing Italian claims, she is said to have boldly reminded Menelik of the supreme sacrifice of his predecessor, Emperor Yohannes (d. 1889). Here is part of her entreaty with Emperor Menelik: "How is it that Emperor Yohannes never gave up a handful of our soil, fought the Italians and the Egyptians for it, even died for it, and you, with him as an example, want to sell your country! What will history say of you?"[24] In addition, the empress reportedly taunted and "raved at Menelik" and even described him as being "weak and stupid." Worse still, she exposed "her finest part towards [Emperor Menelik]," this being a symbolic African gesture of contempt.[25] If, therefore, Emperor Menelik seemed even remotely willing to accommodate the Italians, Empress Taytu's taunts certainly assured him that she was not on his side. As a matter of fact, Italian negotiators seemed convinced that the possibility of any compromise with Ethiopia had become impracticable. Hence, they placed the responsibility of "any rupture with Italy" on the shoulders of the empress.[26] Indeed, "this stubborn woman," as one Italian diplomat described the empress, had become a thorn in the flesh of the Italians. Not only did she put pressure on her husband not to make any concessions to Italy, but she insisted that no diplomatic courtesies should be accorded to the Italians in any diplomatic correspondence with them. More seriously, Empress Taytu strongly urged Menelik to unilaterally abrogate the hated Treaty of Wichale. When the Italian diplomat learned of this, he cautioned that annulment of the treaty might cause Italy to "lose its dignity." The empress retorted in kind: "We too must retain our dignity," adding, "you want other countries to see Ethiopia as your protégé, but that would never be."[27]

As the diplomatic negotiations degenerated into claims and counterclaims, Empress Taytu finally urged Menelik to call off all negotiations, annul the Treaty of Wichale, and brace for war with Italy. "I am a woman," she said, "and do not love war, but [rather] than accept this [treaty] I prefer war."[28] War with Italy thus seemed inevitable, given, as the Italian diplomat observed, that the empress had become the most "persistent advocate of force against Italy." Continued the diplomat, "Emperor Menelik would have [perhaps] come to some reasonable compromise" but for Empress Taytu's "stubbornness and intransigence."[29] He was probably right, for the emperor finally took a more decisive action toward the Italians. In annulling the Treaty of Wichale, the Emperor stated firmly, "[This] country is mine and no other nation can have it." The annulment ultimately led to the outbreak of the historic Ethiopian-Italian War of 1895-1896. Menelik, it seemed, entered the war with some trepidation. "Not only do I dread this war, but the thought of shedding Christian blood also saddens me."[30]

Of course, the Italians were humiliated at the Battle of Adowa in 1896, thanks, in part, to Empress Taytu, who proved to be the catalyst for decisive action. In the words of an Ethiopian scholar, "The victory [at Adowa] was a tremendous lift for the Ethiopians. Fear of the white man's invincibility was laid to rest."[31] In addition to its psychological impact, the victory also ensured Ethiopia's political independence. Henceforth, Ethiopia became the symbol of African resistance to European imperialism. Interestingly, "thousands of Ethiopian women," mobilized by Empress Taytu, fought bravely in the war. As a matter of fact, "The logistics of [the] military campaign were heavily dependent on the thousands of women who carried on their backs what could not be loaded on a mule," including dead and wounded soldiers.[32]

MADAM NWANYERUWA AND WOMEN'S MILITANCY

Let me now direct attention to another courageous African woman, Madam Nwanyeruwa Ojim of Nigeria. Madam Nwanyeruwa was a typical village woman, an illiterate. But she was a woman who, like Mrs. Rosa Parks of the United States,[33] refused to see the colonial government as "a leviathan to which one is forced to acquiesce."[34] For all intents and purposes, Madam Nwanyeruwa literally "rang the bell" that summoned the women of Eastern Nigeria together. Her stubborn resistance to perceived oppression sparked the Women's War of 1929.

The story of Madam Nwanyeruwa is intimately linked to the history of British colonialism in Nigeria. Thus, as the commission of inquiry report of the Women's War noted, Madam Nwanyeruwa "is and still remains a name to conjure with" in the history of female militancy in Nigeria.[35] We are faced here with two critical questions: first, what were the circumstances that brought this illiterate village woman into the political limelight? and second, what role did Nwanyeruwa play in the ensuing political drama? To begin with, it is important to note that the British imposition of direct taxation on Eastern Nigerians provoked the women's antitax rebellion, known popularly as the Women's War (Ogu ndom or Ogu Umunwanyi). Direct taxation was first introduced into Eastern Nigeria in 1928. By all accounts, it was an unpopular innovation. Hence, complaints about the tax and the tax census that preceded its collection were widespread. But despite serious "misgivings" about the tax, official reports indicate that its collection in that year went on remarkably well. In the words of the lieutenant governor, "The result [of the collection] far surpassed] my expectation."[36] However, attempts to compile the tax list for the 1929 tax year proved ominous.

As was the case in 1928, native court chiefs (known as warrant chiefs) were instructed to produce a list of taxable adult males. Accordingly, one Chief Okugo of Oloko, in the then Bende division, enlisted the assistance of a schoolteacher, Mark Emeruwa. In the process of the enumeration, conflict erupted. In brief, Mark Emeruwa had come to the residence of one Mr. Ojim, where he met one of his wives, Madam Nwanyeruwa Ojim, who was preparing palm oil. He thereupon began to ask her a number of questions. Mr. Emeruwa is said to have requested that Madam Nwanyeruwa count the number of people and livestock in her household. Considering this rather too intrusive, Madam Nwanyeruwa replied by asking Emeruwa whether, in fact, his mother had been counted. Details of what then transpired are obscure, but Madam Nwanyeruwa's protest reportedly led to an altercation between her and Emeruwa. At that point, it seemed, there occurred some pushing and shoving, resulting in Madam Nwanyeruwa's distress call to other women in the neighborhood. According to one historian, "Nwanyeruwa ran [out] to inform other women who were holding an already scheduled meeting" nearby. The women's response was dramatic. They "at once proceeded to 'sit on' Emeruwa and [Chief] Okugo and sent messages with palm leaves to neighboring villages, which in turn sent messages to other villages."[37] The women's revolt was now onstage.

But why did the women respond in the manner that they did? Well, the rumor was actually in the air that women were about to be taxed, just as the men were. The women thus considered the proposed tax as an added financial burden inasmuch as most of them actually paid their husbands' and/or sons' taxes. Besides, the decline in the prices of locally produced goods (especially palm oil and palm kernel) and the rise in the prices of imported products had already become sources of grievance and agitation. Thus, faced with the prospect of taxation, the women naturally raised an alarm. Not only did they question British colonial administration's right to impose taxes on the colonized, but the women invoked their "natural right" of exemption from taxation. "We women are like trees which bear fruit.... [Therefore] women who bear seeds should [not] be taxed." They added, "It is not fit for men to pay tax even."[38] If, as Professor Afigbo contends, the women had already "made up their minds to resist" the taxation,[39] then the Emeruwa-Nwanyeruwa imbroglio must have provided the pretext for the tax rebellion.

Whatever the case, what followed was, indeed, revolutionary. Women from almost every division in Eastern Nigeria rose up against the British colonial government and its agents. Significantly enough, these women acknowledged Madam Nwanyeruwa not only as their recognized leader but also as "the voice of all the women." Hence, the women of Oloko and others from elsewhere brought money contributions to Madam Nwanyeruwa, ostensibly to "thank her [for] preventing women [from] paying tax."[40] Unfortunately, the women's revolt was marked by violence, as women, outraged by the actions of the chiefs and the colonial administration, attacked the colonial chiefs. Most of the chiefs were actually beaten up, and their houses were demolished. Also, their caps and staff, symbols of authority and power, were seized. In addition, native courthouses (symbols of colonial oppression), court messengers (colonial agents of coercion), and commercial establishments (i.e., European industries and shops) were attacked and looted.

In response, the British administration mobilized its soldiers and police to suppress what was described as the "women's riot." But although the colonial forces reportedly "thoroughly overawed" the women in some districts, the rebellion continued in ever-increasing intensity. As a matter of fact, the conflict spread even more widely. This, then, was the celebrated Women's War of 1929, aptly described by a historian as "the most massive and effective [women's] protest movement in [colonial] Nigeria."[41] Clearly, Madam Nwanyeruwa's resolve not to submit to colonial coercion had invariably catalyzed the women into a revolutionary action. Unfortunately, by the time the revolt was over, the colonial forces had inflicted heavy casualties on the women. About fifty-five women were reported dead, and several were wounded.

Significantly, by the early 1930s the political climate had changed dramatically. Among other things, the structure of the colonial administration had been dismantled. First, most of the corrupt and exploitative warrant chiefs were removed, and their caps and staff seized. (Parenthetically, this was part of the women's war aims.) More specifically, the indirect rule system, which was put in place by Frederick Lugard, the first governor-general of Nigeria, was now totally overhauled, having been found to have outlived its usefulness. Eastern Nigeria, therefore, witnessed a new era, characterized by frantic efforts to bring about political and social reforms. A new administrative structure, which now included women as active participants in the political affairs of the region, was now in place. Indeed, women hereafter "exercised considerable influence over the selection of new chiefs." The annual report on the political changes stated: "Practically no new chief has been selected without the consent of the women of the town, and he is in their hands if he wishes to keep their goodwill."[42] Perhaps even more revolutionary was the election of women as members of the newly constituted native courts. Clearly, Madam Nwanyeruwa's revolt had unleashed a revolution that, by all accounts, "affected the whole course of Southern Nigerian colonial history." But sadly, the women's vision of a new era proved elusive. They had, in fact, expected that the war would result in the departure of "all white men ... so that our country would remain as it was before the advent of the white man."[43]

MARY MUTHONI NYANJIRU

As in Nigeria, British colonial oppression catapulted Mary Muthoni Nyanjiru, a Kikuyu woman activist, into national prominence. Her courage and bravery came to the fore in 1922 during the Harry Thuku incident. Harry Thuku was a Kenyan nationalist and formerly the secretary of the Kikuyu Central Association. He was also an eloquent critic of British colonial policies in Kenya, especially the forced labor system. As an activist, he traveled from district to district and spoke forcefully against forced labor and the imposition of high taxes (hut tax) on the Kenyan people. He also criticized the pass law system (*kipande*), which required Kenyan males to carry identity cards. Particularly offensive to Thuku was the colonial forced labor policy on women, which proved to be too onerous and scandalous. Women and young girls were, in fact, forced to work for the European settlers and the colonial administration. Hence, Thuku campaigned for its abolition. This is how he described the forced labor system.

[Prior to 1915] only men had been made to work, but by about that time women and girls too were compelled to go out to work. [Hence] a settler who wanted labour for his farm would write to the D. C. [district commissioner] saying he required thirty young men, women or girls for work on his farm. The D. C. [then] sent a letter to the chief or headman to supply such and such a number, and the chief in turn had his ... retainers to carry out this business. They would simply go to the people's houses—very often where there were beautiful women and daughters—and point out which were to come to work. Sometimes they had to walk a distance from home, and the number of girls who got pregnant in this way was very great.[44]

A similar description is given in the British Church Missionary Society (CMS) report of 1921:

It is now the law that the people in the reserves can be compelled to do twenty-four days' work free as communal work, and able-bodied males at least two months work outside. Failure to accomplish this entails a penalty of being liable to do sixty days' work for the Government on public works at current rate of wage.... Just lately the people in the district have been put on communal labour to carry out the principle of inducing them to go out to work. The result is that hundreds of old men and girls have been put on the road work for ten or twelve days at a time away from their homes.[45]

The hardship involved in this forced labor system was further commented upon by a contemporary CMS missionary: "I was in a village a few weeks back, when a poor man just dragged himself in and threw himself down exhausted. I could see he was ill, and [I] gave him some medicine.... This poor man did not recover; in five days he was dead."[46]

Amazingly, CMS missionaries "endorsed" British labor policy in Kenya on the grounds that "compulsory labour [was] necessary ... if the country is to be developed as it should be." Besides, they argued, "such labour" would invariably result in "the prevention of idleness."[47] It is not surprising, therefore, that Harry Thuku's anticolonial rhetoric became "increasingly anti-chiefs, anti-missionaries, [anti-settlers], and anti-government." On the other hand, viewed by the missionaries as "an agitator [who] exercised a distinctly dangerous influence throughout the Colony" and by the colonial administration as being "dangerous to peace and good order,"[48] it was natural that Thuku would be declared a persona non grata, hence, his arrest and imprisonment in Nairobi on March 14, 1922.

British negative opinion of Thuku notwithstanding, Kenyan women saw him as their hero, since he was the one "who fought for us and stopped us from working as slaves."[49] Hence, on March 16, 1922, a mass demonstration was organized for the purpose of freeing Thuku from prison. This was the event that brought Mary Nyanjiru into political limelight.

As the agitated Kikuyu women demonstrators anxiously waited for the men to take the initiative to "get their leader free," and nothing seemed to happen, the women then seized the initiative. According to an eyewitness account, Mary Nyanjiru leaped to her feet, pulled her dress right up over her shoulders and shouted to the men: "you take my dress and give me your trousers. You men are cowards. What are you waiting for? Our leader is in there. Let's get him [out]." The hundreds of women [thereupon] thrilled their ngemi [Kikuyu ululation] in approbation.[50]

From here on, the crisis escalated, as Mary and the others felt compelled to "disengage," as it were, "from the politics of [male] dominance."[51] Specifically, Mary and her women cohorts took the matter into their own hands, that is, to release Thuku from prison. Under Mary's leadership, therefore, the women "made a rush for the prison door" and thereby confronted the fully armed police. Undaunted, the women "pushed on until the bayonets of the [police] rifles were pricking at their throats."[52] Suddenly, the police began to fire at the unarmed crowd, killing about twenty-eight people, including Mary. European settlers were also said to have joined in the shooting and were probably "responsible for most of the deaths."[53]

MARY'S LEGACY

Although Mary and her women compatriots failed to rescue Harry Thuku from prison (he was actually deported to Kismayu), Mary's name and the events of March 16, 1922 "lingered long in the general political consciousness" of Kenyan people. As a matter of fact, "the African version of what happened became part of the political education of new generations. The Kanyegenuri, for example, a famous political song, [still] commemorates the deeds of the Nairobi women on [that] day and in particular the bravery of Mary Muthoni Nyanjiru, who had taunted the men present with cowardice."[54] Also, the Harry Thuku incident definitely poisoned African-European relations, even within the church. "When I arrived [in Kenya] last year from furlough," wrote a CMS missionary in 1923, "I could see a marked difference in the demeanor of our senior teachers, and there now exists a decided line of demarcation between natives and non-natives, including men missionaries." Church "offertories" and even school attendance, we are told, "likewise suffered."[55] There seemed, in fact, to have been a general lack of confidence in the foreign missionaries, no doubt because of their open support of the settlers and the colonial administration. Again, to quote at some length from a missionary's report:

The majority of the native adherents at present do not seem to look upon us as their friends as in the days gone by. All the relief from their grievances in the shape of hut tax, forced labour, and the calling out of women and girls to work on the plantations and roads has been put down to the action of Thuku, their so-called saviour. Their love for spiritual things seems to have decreased. There is not the same willingness to give their substance to God's work, and strange to say many who were very diligent in learning to read, think that by abstention from school, etc., they are annoying the Government and, to use a common phrase, getting their own back. Whether this is only a passing phase time will show.[56]

Certainly, this growth of a new political consciousness was not "a passing phase," for memories of Mary Nyanjuri's and Thuku's patriotic endeavors continued to shape the character of Kenyan nationalist movements well into the 1950s. In any case, the Kikuyu women's mass protest had positive results. It finally induced the British administration to give serious attention "to the urgent need for colonial reform." In fact, African grievances could no longer be ignored. Hence, as in the Eastern Nigerian women's revolt, political and fiscal reforms followed in the wake of the Kukuyu women's uprising. Particularly noteworthy were the tax and forced labor reforms, which, as the anthropologist Audrey Wipper has observed, "signaled the end of [the colonial administration's] attempts to coerce more and more Africans into the labor force by increasing their tax rate. Never again were taxes raised for the sole purpose of filling labor needs."[57] In this context, Mary Muthoni Nyanjuri's death was not in vain.

WOMEN AND THE STRUGGLE AGAINST MARGINALIZATION

Finally, let us look at the women's struggles toward assuming, in the words of a feminist writer, "their rightful place as respected individuals and full citizens of their countries."[58] Here the focus is on two Nigerian women political activists, Mrs. Olufunmilayo Ransome-Kuti and Mrs. Margaret Ekpo. Both, as demonstrated later, were eloquent advocates of Nigerian women's rights. Mrs. Kuti, in particular, was perhaps the most articulate advocate of women's causes of her time. She was a remarkable woman, widely known for her charismatic leadership, political activism, and anticolonial ideology. Born in Abeokuta in

1900, Mrs. Kuti became involved in Nigerian politics from about the 1940s and remained politically active until her death in 1978.

Mrs. Kuti's political preoccupation seemed to be the promotion of women's political participation in Nigeria. As she once said of her mission, "[My desire is] to work for the improvement and liberation of Nigerian women."[59] Put differently, she actively sought to rescue Nigerian women from political marginalization. In fact, to this end she devoted most of her life to ensuring that Nigerian women participated actively in politics. Through this means, she evidently hoped, Nigerian politics would be freed from virtual male domination. Hence, Mrs. Kuti founded numerous women's organizations, which included the Abeokuta Women's Club (later renamed the Abeokuta Women's Union), the Nigerian Women's Union (with branches in most urban areas), and the Federation of Nigerian Women's Societies.

Essentially through these organizations Mrs. Kuti not only awakened Nigerian women's political consciousness but also served as avenues of social and political radicalization. Moreover, she effectively used these organizations as convenient forums for the articulation of woman's rights, above all, their representation in the political and economic institutions of the country. For example, the Federation of Nigerian Women's Societies (FNWS) became an effective organ for the articulation of women's political rights. Under Mrs. Kuti's leadership, for instance, the FNWS in 1958 demanded the granting of franchise to Northern Nigerian women, who, hitherto, had been denied voting rights in the Northern Region. The agitation, according to Dr. Mba, however, failed, essentially because of the Northern Nigerian political elites' "rigid attachment to an exclusively male franchise."[60] But as the pressure continued, Northern Nigerian women were finally able to vote in Nigerian elections, like their Southern women counterparts.

Mrs. Ransome-Kuti, to be sure, had political ambitions. She aspired, for example, in 1959 to enter the Federal House of Assembly under the auspices of her political party, the National Council of Nigeria and the Cameroons (NCNC). Her presence there, she hoped, would invariably enable her, on one hand, to break the virtual male domination of the House (there was only one women in the House then). On the other hand, the Federal Assembly would provide her a national platform to perhaps more vigorously advocate the rights of Nigerian women. Mrs. Kuti's candidacy was enthusiastically supported by Nigerian women, including Northern Nigerian women. For example, Northern Nigerian women members of the Northern Elements Progressive Union (NEPU), a party with NCNC sympathies, petitioned the NCNC authorities demanding Mrs. Kuti's nomination: "We Northern women have taken a decision on this matter and we have forwarded a letter to the National President to the effect that Mrs. Ransome-Kuti must be nominated for election; any decision by the N.E.C. [National Executive Council] to the contrary would be vehemently opposed."[61] Mrs. Kuti, however, failed to win the nomination. Yet her political activism remained undiminished.

As a political activist, Mrs. Kuti traveled widely in the country campaigning for the inclusion of women in politics. At the same time, she sharpened her criticism of British imperialism and, like her male compatriots, longed for the liberation of Nigeria from colonial rule. Her anticolonial ideology actually found expression during the shooting of the coal miners at Enugu in 1949. "When news of the shooting reached Mrs. Kuti at Abeokuta, she immediately announced that a delegation from Abeokuta branch of the NWU [Nigerian Women's Union] would visit Enugu. She wrote to Mrs. Ekpo [a political militant] in Aba to arrange for them to go to Enugu together.... Mrs. Kuti, Mrs. Ekpo, and other members of the NWU delegation arrived in Enugu on 17 December 1949."[62] While there, Mrs. Kuti strongly criticized the British administration for its callous treatment of Africans. Also, as a measure of women's solidarity, she and the NWU delegates visited the wives of the miners and offered solace and comfort to the injured miners at the hospital. Mrs. Kuti, as might be expected, used the occasion to appeal to her women compatriots not to relax in their political endeavors but to continue "to work for a patriotic national and all embracing women's movement in Nigeria."[63]

Mrs. Kuti's presence at Enugu was particularly significant in that the convergence of the NWU's delegates seemed symbolic of the "nationalist solidarity among women," as the national press described it. Second, Mrs. Kuti seems to have energized and inspired Eastern Nigerian women, who, according to the testimony of one of them, apparently showed little inclination "to probe into the affairs of [our] country. Mrs. Kuti on her arrival educated us." Equally noteworthy is the statement of Mrs. Ekpo, the militant feminist and nationalist from Aba: "I cannot explain to you," she wrote to Mrs. Kuti after the visit, "what new spirit you have poured into me. I am now 100 times stronger than before."[64]

MARGARET EKPO

Mrs. Margaret Ekpo was born in Creek Town, Calabar, in 1916. But she and her husband resided at Aba, now in Abia State. Her nationalism, according her own testimony, seems to have been rekindled during her visit to Ireland in 1944. There, we are told, she saw Irishwomen doing housework and other menial jobs. This was an important eye-opener; for European women in Africa hardly did housework. Of greater significance to Mrs. Ekpo was the fact that these Irishwomen "enjoyed civil rights" in their country. "These perceptions," according to her biographer, "radicalized Mrs. Ekpo's thinking about colonialism and feminism. She became a fierce opponent of colonialism and an advocate of the necessity for Nigerian women to demand the same civil rights that the European women had."[65]

Upon returning to Nigeria in 1948, Mrs. Ekpo became actively involved in sociopolitical movements that promoted Nigerian woman's rights. Like Mrs. Kuti, she formed women's organizations in Aba for the purpose of awakening the women's political consciousness. She joined the ranks of radical nationalists, whose political ideology centered on the end of British colonialism in Nigeria. For example, Mrs. Ekpo was a staunch member of the NCNC, and she was the leader of the NCNC Women's Association in Aba, as well as the national secretary of the Nigerian Women's Union, of which Mrs. Kuti was the national president. As a political activist and member of the Eastern House of Chiefs (she was appointed by Dr. Azikiwe), Mrs. Ekpo used her position to mobilize women to effect sociopolitical change. In 1954, for example, she formed the Aba Township Women's Association, which made it possible for women to have an effective voice in Aba politics. In the December 1955 elections for the Aba Urban District Council, for example, "the majority of voters were women." Besides, women for the first time were elected to the Aba Urban District Council.[66] Mrs. Ekpo herself played a vital role in the council. She was appointed in 1957 as a member of the Caretaker Committee of the council, and, in 1958, she was elected "unopposed" to the council. The era of male political monopoly seemed now over.

On the regional level, Mrs. Ekpo's political activism was equally quite significant. In 1953, for instance, she was nominated as a special member to the Eastern House of Assembly, thus becoming one of the three women in the House. As before, she used the House as a convenient platform to promote women's causes. In comparative terms, we are told, "she was far more articulate than her women counterparts in the Western House of Assembly, and was [particularly] eloquent in making demands on behalf of women."[67] Among other things, she Mrs. Ekpo utilized the legislature as an effective forum to criticize the employment of the wives of colonial officials, essentially because these European women "were taking jobs away from African women." Furthermore, she "criticized the voluntary agencies" [i.e., Christian missions] for not allowing married women to continue teaching. And she demanded from her male colleagues the inclusion of women in the region's political appointments, such as women's representation on the Eastern Regional Marketing Board."[68]

When, in 1961, Mrs. Ekpo won the election to the Eastern House of Assembly on her own right, she continued to concern herself with the advancement of women in both the political and economic spheres. Of particular interest to her, for example, was the improvement of rural roads. Improved transportation, she said, would enable women to more conveniently "carry their produce to market."[69] Like Mrs. Kuti, Mrs. Ekpo also agonized over the underrepresentation of women in politics. Increased female representation in the regional and federal assemblies, she reasoned, would, on one hand, improve the economic welfare of women, inasmuch as they would have their own spokeswomen there. On the other hand, to use a common jargon, "the more the merrier." In essence, increased female voice would enhance the economic position of women. On the political sphere, Mrs. Ekpo was particularly concerned with the 1963 census figures, which "inflated" the population of Northern Nigeria. If political representation had to be based on the figures, she feared, then Northern Nigeria would have a disproportionate representation in the Federal Assembly. The result would be the virtual exclusion of women from politics. Mrs. Ekpo thus raised an alarm.

We the women of the South wonder what is going to happen to us if the representation in the Federal House will be on the basis of the inflated census figures.... And then, I, Margaret Udo Ekpo, Mrs. Mokelu and Madam Young [in the Eastern House of Assembly] will leave the floor of this House because the women will not vote again.[70]

CONCLUSION

To sum up, it has been argued that African women, contrary to "uncritical speculations," to borrow an expression from Evans-Pritchard,[71] participated actively in the liberation struggle. As we have shown, the struggle took various forms and catapulted certain women into nationalist heroines. Attention has been drawn also to the efforts being made by women to liberalize politics. While much has been achieved in this sphere, a great deal remains to be done. For, as women themselves say, African women's struggle for liberation from male domination continues.

NOTES

1. Nina Emma Mba, *Nigerian Women Mobilized: Women's Political Activity in Southern Nigeria, 1900-1965* (Berkeley, CA: Institute of Interior National Studies, 1982), 295.

2. Susan Onyeche, "Rights of Women: An Address Delivered at Nwaooieubi Mbaitoli L. G. A. ..., 17th August 1992," 5-6.

3. See Molara Ogundipe-Leslie, *Re-Creating Ourselves: African Women and Critical Transformation* (Trenton, NJ: Africa World Press, 1994).

4. Ibid.; Jean Davison, *Voices from Mutira: Change in the Lives of Rural Gikuyu Women, 1910-1995*, 2d ed. (Boulder, CO, and London: Lynne Rienner, 1996).

5. Quoted in "Struggle for Change," *West Africa* (November 1-7, 1993): 1970.

6. See especially Toyin Falola, "Gender, Business, and Space Control: Yoruba Market Women and Power," in Bessie House-Midamba and Felix K. Ekechi, eds., *African Market Women: Women and Economic Power: The Role of Women in African Economic Development* (Westport, CT, and London: Greenwood Press, 1995); E. E. Evans-Pritchard, *The Position of Women in Primitive Societies and Other Essays in Social Anthropology* (New York: Free Press, 1965).

7. Falola, "Gender," 32.

8. See David Sweetman, *Queen Nzinga* (London: Longman, 1971); also "Nzinga of Angola" (c.1581-1663), in Sweetman, *Women Leaders in African History* (London: Heinemann, 1984), 39-47.

9. Oladipo Yemitan, *Madam Tinubu: Merchant and Kingmaker* (Ibadan: University Press, 1987); S. O. Biobaku, "Madam Tinubu," in K. O. Dike, ed.,

Eminent Nigerians of the Nineteenth Century (London: Oxford University Press, 1966), 33-41.

10. Sweetman, *Women Leaders*, 91-97.

11. The role of women revolutionaries in Guinea-Bissau and Zimbabwe has, however, been duly acknowledged in recent studies.

12. CMS, *The Church Missionary Review* 68 (1917): 210-11.

13. See John P. Jordan, *Bisop Shanahau of Southern Nigeria* (Dublin: Clonmore and Reynolds, 1949).

14. Hope M. Waddell, *Twenty-Nine Years in the West Indies and Central Africa ... 1829-1858* (London: Frank Cass, 1970), 483-84.

15. Ibid.

16. Ibid., 485.

17. CMS, Journal of Rev. J. C. Taylor, November 23, 1864. Also see F. K. Ekechi, *Missionary Enterprise and Rivalry in Igboland, 1857-1914* (London: Frank Cass, 1972), 23-24.

18. Mba, *Nigerian Women Mobuilized*, 117.

19. See Ekechi, *Missionary Enterprise*.

20. Edward Blyden, *African Life and Custom* (Baltimore and London: Black Classic Press, 1908); J. E. Casely Hayford, *Ethiopia Unbound: Studies in Race Emancipation*, 2d ed. (London: Frank Cass, 1969).

21. Patrick Cole, *Modern and Traditional Elites in the Politics of Lagos* (Cambridge: Cambridge University Press, 1975), 141.

22. Quoted in Chris Prouty, *Empress Taytu and Menelik II: Ethiopia 1883-1910* (London: Ravens Educational and Development Services, 1986), 137.

23. For the diplomatic wranglings, see Harold Marcus, *The Life and Times of Menilek II: Ethiopia 1844-1913* (Oxford: Clarendon Press, 1975).

24. Quoted in ibid., 126; Prouty, *Empress Taytu*, 89.

25. Prouty, *Empress Taytu*, 89.

26. Quoted in ibid., 91.

27. Ibid., 92.

28. Quoted in ibid., 90; Marcus, *Life and Times of Menilek II*, 130.

29. Prouty, *Express Taytu*, 160.

30. Ibid., 136.

31. Ibid., 142.

32. Ibid.

33. Rosa Parks was the brave African American woman from Montgomery, Alabama, who refused to sit at the back of the bus and thus unleashed the civil rights protests of the 1960s.

34. Cole, *Modern and Traditional Elites*, 191.

35. Nigerian National Archives, Enugu (NNAE) *Report of the Aba Commission of Inquiry 1930* (Lagos: Government Printer, 1930).

36. NNAE:OWDIST 9/13/47, Report by Major U.F.H. Ruxton, October 29, 1928.

37. Mba, *Nigerian Women Mobilized*, 77.

38. Cited in Adiele Eberechukwu Afigbo, *The Warrant Chiefs: Indirect Rule in Southeastern Nigeria, 1891-1929* (London: Longman, 1972).

39. Ibid., 237.

40. Ninna E. Mba, "Heroines of the Women's War," in Bolande Awe, ed., *Nigerian Women in Perspective* (Nigeria: Sankora, 1992), 81.

41. Mba, *Nigerian Women Mobilized*, 97.

42 . Quoted in ibid., 96.

43. Sylvia Leith-Ross, *African Women: A Study of the Ibo of Nigeria* (London: Faber and Faber, 1939), 38. But for a contrary view, see Mba, "Heroines," 85.

44. Quoted in Audrey Wipper, "Kikuyu Women and the Harry Thuku Disturbances: Some Uniformities of Female Militancy," *Africa*, 59(3) (1989): 302.

45. CMS, *The Church Missionary Review* 72 (1921): 88.

46. Ibid., 89.

47. CMS, *The Church Missionary Review* 71 (1920): 142.

48. CMS, *The Church Missionary Review* 74 (1923): 59; Wipper, "Kikuyu Women," 305.

49. Wipper, "Kukuyu Women," 305.

50. Carl G. Rosenberg and John Nottingham, *The Myth of "Mau Mau": Nationalism in Kenya* (New York: New American Library, 1966), 51-52.

51. This expression is borrowed from Ogundipe-Leslie, *Re-Creating Ourselves*, xv.

52. Rosenberg and Nottingham, *The Myth of "Mau Mau,"* 52.

53. Ibid., 54.

54. Ibid.

55. CMS, *The Church Missionary Review* 74 (1923): 59.

56. Ibid.

57. Wipper, "Kikuyu Women," 316.

58. Awuor Ayodo, review of *Re-Creating Ourselves*, in *Canadian Journal of African Studies* 30 (1) (1996): 142.

59. Mba, *Nigerian Women Mobilized*, 180.

60. Ibid., 178.

61. Quoted in ibid.

62. Ibid., 171-72.

63. Ibid., 172.

64. Ibid.

65. Ibid., 169.

66. Ibid., 117, note 2.

67. Ibid., 269.

68. Ibid.

69. Ibid., 270.

70. Quoted in ibid., 272.

71. Evans-Pritchard, *The Position of Women*, 39.

7

Gender-Based Discrimination in Housing and Urban Development Policies in Cameroon

Ambe J. Njoh

INTRODUCTION

In addition to national and international pronouncements manifesting interest in the status of women in developing nations, the literature on women in development (WID) has been growing and proliferating since the 1970s. The bulk of this literature has, however, focused on women as agents, rather than beneficiaries, of development (see, e.g., Swantz 1985; Boserup 1970). Questions on the differential impact of development policies on the well-being of women in these nations therefore remain largely unaddressed. Yet, a cursory observation of development policy outcomes in less developed countries (LDCs) suggests a systematic bias against women. The case of Honduras (World Bank 1995a) is illustrative. In 1974, Honduran authorities crafted a law, the Agrarian Modernization Law of 1974, as part of the country's land reform initiatives. A major provision of the law, on one hand, gives men sixteen or older the right to access to land without regard to any other qualification. On the other hand, the provision gives a woman access to land only if such a woman is an unmarried mother or widow with dependent children. In the event of the death or incapacitation of a beneficiary, the law further gives preference in inheritance rights to male offspring over their legally married mother. This situation, as intimated earlier, is not unique to Honduras. Rather, it is a ubiquitous characteristic of most developing societies.

In this chapter, we draw on the case of Cameroon to illuminate the most salient implications of such gender-biased housing and land development policies for the socioeconomic advancement of women. Our focus on one specific policy field as well as one developing country is in keeping with the recommendation of the WID Program Progress Report presented to the World Bank in February 1990.[1]

Initially, we examine the status of women within the larger context of national development in Cameroon (hereafter, the country). Then, we paint a vivid picture of the country's urban development policy. Next, we examine the policy to determine aspects thereof that impede the progress of women. Finally, we proffer some steps regarding how women in Cameroon in particular and the developing world in general can be empowered economically and otherwise. Hopefully, the information unearthed, and the analysis undertaken, as well as the suggestions proffered in this chapter, will be valuable not only to housing and urban planners but to all involved in efforts to ameliorate living conditions in developing countries.

BACKGROUND

The global economy has witnessed several shifts in the recent past. Prominent among these shifts are the breakdown of the socialist economies of Eastern Europe, the dissolution of the Soviet Union, and the attendant emergence of a new concept of division of labor at both the global and national levels. In Africa, these developments have, in large part, resulted in the further impoverishment of the people of an already penurious continent. Whatever small gains have been realized in the process have benefited only an insignificant stratum, namely, the elites. Thus, the rest, especially women, continue to bear the brunt of failed economic programs and projects.

Historically, the relatively underprivileged economic status of women in African countries is anything but indigenous to the continent. Rather, it is a product of an imported cultural and ideological socioeconomic system. The emergence of this system is coincidental with the visitation of colonialism and the concomitant introduction of capitalism as a preferred mode of economic production as well as the adoption of statehood as the dominant form of political organization on the continent in the late nineteenth century (Sudarkasa 1985). It bears noting that the colonial era coincided with a time (the nineteenth century) when Victorian England and other imperial societies had a rather myopic view of women's potentials. Thus, women's roles in society were seen as limited to the home. In fact, it was considered a status symbol for one's wife not to work away from home. Within this framework, work out of the home was accorded more in terms of prestige and economic rewards, while ostensibly economically rewarding activities undertaken within the confines of the home went unrecognized. Essentially, this model was transplanted to Africa during the colonial era.

Prior to that, people's status in society derived mainly from their role in the "domestic" and/or "public" spheres. Activities in either sphere commanded equal respect. With the introduction of capitalism, activities considered not directly rewarding in economic terms, such as domestic chores that are typically performed by women and children, were considered anything but productive. Among the myriad implications of these developments is the further accentuation in the gap between the economic power of African men and women. To be sure, the resulting gender-based socioeconomic disparities endemic to the continent in particular and the developing world in general have caught the attention of relevant authorities. Thus, for instance, since the 1970s, African leaders have, if only rhetorically and in principle, embarked on efforts to eliminate gender inequities in the distribution of economic power.

In Cameroon, activities in this connection not only have been far-reaching but have occasioned significant legislative reforms. In this vein, the country's Constitution provides for equal rights to men and women. The state's official position in relation to combating discrimination against women was adeptly summarized in the following statement to the United Nations General Assembly in November 1984 by William Etecki Mboumoua[2] (quoted in Azevedo et al. 1988: 164):

women must closely be linked with all types of the social and economic development, especially in the preparation of plans, formulation of policies and in the decision making. As a result of this human concept of development, the Government of Cameroon ... [has] established a Ministry dealing with the status of women, and a consultative committee to improve the status of women.

This statement conforms with the spirit of provisions of relevant United Nations (U.N.) Charters on Women in Development and is pursuant to the country's ratification of "the 1979 Convention on the Elimination of All Forms of Discrimination against Women."[3]

It is one thing for the leadership of African or other developing countries to issue official pronouncements attesting to their concerns with the issue of gender-based discriminatory practices. It is another thing to match such pronouncements with serious actions designed to combat these practices. It would appear that the authorities have thus far been strong on rhetoric but perturbingly weak on action. Yet, serious efforts to economically empower women are a sine qua non for any attempt to bring about sustainable development. This is because "sustainable development depends upon the full and productive participation of all members of society" (Blakeslee 1994: 7).

Certainly, the rhetoric on the part of the Cameroonian political leadership is yet to be matched with any significant action to economically empower women. Yet, the full and productive participation of the country's population cannot occur while its development policies continue to be systematically biased against, or fail to take into account, a majority of the population, namely, women.

URBAN DEVELOPMENT POLICY IN CAMEROON

One could hardly be more erroneous than by stating that European colonial powers initiated the practice of regulating and/or controlling the growth and development of geographic space in Cameroon. In fact, human settlement planning has a long and rich history in Africa in general and Cameroon in particular (see, e.g., Denyer 1978). Space in the present chapter prevents any attempt to further explore the tenor of this, albeit germane, thesis. Suffice, however, to state that precolonial human settlements in Cameroon exhibited a high level of sophisticated and careful planning grounded in sound practical principles and in some cases, religious beliefs. Our concern in this segment is, however, not with traditional human settlement policies. Rather, we are concerned with, for lack of a better descriptive scheme, modern town planning and housing policies.

Under the rubric of this scheme are rules and regulations designed to govern housing and spatial development dating back to the colonial era. An interesting aspect of the policies for the purpose of the present discussion is their goal. The contemporary town planning and housing policy of Cameroon, according to the country's Economic, Social and Cultural Development Plan, aims essentially at causing the public and private sectors to create a decent and healthy environment for every Cameroonian (Republic of Cameroon 1985a: 161). "Such an environment," the plan contends, "would be conducive to harmonious economic and social development" (Republic of Cameroon 1985a: 161). With no more than a superficial reading of the foregoing statement, one is wont to infer that the state is principally a facilitator in the urban development process. This is certainly not the case, as the picture emerging from a more scrupulous analysis of the state's actions, as opposed to its stated objectives, suggests otherwise. In fact, most state actions in the housing and urban development policy field in Cameroon can, for all practical purposes, be considered regulatory. Njoh's (1992) analysis of the country's "institutional framework for housing policy administration," which revealed that as many as 75 percent or six of the eight purely public housing policy institutional actors perform largely regulatory tasks, lends some credence to this assertion.

We contend that by assuming a regulatory, rather than a facilitating, role in the urban development policy field, the state effectively contributes to the economic problems of women in the country's urban centers. To shed some light on this point, we discuss how three important instruments typically employed by the government to control and regulate urban development activities negatively affect the economic status of Cameroonian women. The instruments include (1) the urban master development plan; (2) the land use decree, in particular, Decree No.76-165 of April 27, 1976; and (3) Ordinance No.73/20 of May 29, 1973, which stipulates the conditions for obtaining a building permit.

The Urban Master Development Plan. During the 1980s the government invested heavily in efforts to put together urban master development plans for the country's urban centers.[4] Currently, each major urban center in the country boasts an urban master development plan. The most important component of this plan for the purpose of the present discussion is the zoning ordinance. The ordinance contains rules and regulations guiding the use of urban land, water, and buildings (see, e.g., Republic of Cameroon 1985b). In this connection, each urban center is divided into four areas, with each area assigned a distinctively different use as follows (Njoh 1995): (1) residential, (2) business, (3) industrial, and (4) public. The residential areas are subdivided into three different parts consisting of low-income/high-density residences, middle-income/ medium-density residences, and high-income/low-density residences. Designated as public space are such functional areas as municipal cemeteries, green space, and miscellaneous public facilities.

Activities within each of these major areas are typically regulated and controlled by a set of meticulous and detailed articles, most of which stipulate the activities permitted in each district (Njoh 1995; Republic of Cameroon 1985b). One article, for instance, prohibits activities other than housing in residential districts. The article also stipulates the confinement of commercial activities to business districts. Similarly, it limits industrial activities to industrial districts, and so on. In addition, the article forbids the subdivision of any plot within low-income areas unless such a plot has an area equal to, or greater than, 150 square meters, and a minimum frontage of 8 meters. Another article makes it unlawful to use "centralized trading service zones or central business districts (CBDs) for other than commercial purposes." An important article of the ordinance requires buildings to be accessible from a roadway and stipulates that a right of way (ROW) measure at least 8 meters, with a pavement no less than 4.80 meters wide. Yet another important article prohibits the erection of more than four dwelling units on a single plot without a water main.

Some of the articles regulate plot size, building-to-plot area ratio, and building height in all the districts. Plots in low-income areas are required to have an area of 150 square meters with a depth of at least 10 meters. Buildings in such areas must occupy no more than 60 percent of the plot on which they are located. The floor area ratio (FAR)[5] is required to be no more than 0.70 in low-income residential areas and 0.40 in middle-income areas. The ordinance also places limitations on building height. The Building Ordinance for the City of Kumba, one of the country's largest urban centers, for instance, restricts building height to 12 meters in residential areas and 20 meters in commercial districts (Republic of Cameroon 1985b). The ordinance sets the minimum setback[6] at two meters in low-income districts. It further prohibits "the use of alternative building materials such as unrolled tin cans, old corrugated iron sheets, etc." (Njoh 1995). In fact, a perusal of Articles 11 and 12 of the ordinance reveals that it explicitly favors imported, as opposed to local, building materials. Additionally, the ordinance requires the provision of automobile parking lots as well as green space in all residential districts. In this latter regard, developers are required to plant one tree for every plot and every 200 square meters of surface area.

The Land Use Decree. The use of land in Cameroon is guided by one main piece of legislation, namely, Land Use Decree No.76-165 of April 27, 1976. This decree, which replaced earlier legislation including Statutory Decree No.

63-2 of 1963 and some portions of the Land Decree of (July 6) 1974, stipulates conditions for registering a land title as well as securing a land certificate. For instance, the decree allows any person to convert miscellaneous deeds or rights over a parcel of state land into a land certificate provided such a person was occupying or exploiting the parcel of land in question prior to August 5, 1974. Other deeds that can be converted into land certificates include (Njoh 1992: 26; Republic of Cameroon n.d.) deeds of acquisition of land registered in the "Grundbuch"[7]; deeds of lands acquired under the transcription system; final allocation orders for a grant of state land; land register books or certificates of occupancy; final judgments establishing or transferring real property; deeds of acquisition of freehold lands; and notarized agreements of land sale.

The process of actually converting the aforementioned deeds and/or documents into land certificates is both "cumbersome" and deliberately "slanted in favor of the economically powerful members of society," including civil servants, bureaucrats, and entrepreneurs (Pondi 1994; Njoh 1992; DeLancey 1989). The process includes the following steps. First, the parcel of land, which must be registered or whose deed must be converted to a land certificate, is demarcated with specially marked pillars[8] by a sworn surveyor. Then, a lengthy application for land certificate form is completed to include the following applicant identification information: (1) full name, (2) date and place of birth, (3) name of parents, (4) residential address, and (5) family status. Next, the following miscellaneous documents and/or information must be secured: (1) a cadastral plan showing reference points of the parcel of land in question, (2) all information pertaining to transfers, transactions, leases, mortgages, and other liabilities relating to the parcel of land, (3) a field report of the surveyed property boundaries, (4) all contracts and public and private deeds establishing the property rights, (5) a valuation report, which must be produced and/or endorsed by a sworn valuation surveyor, and (6) a receipt issued by the Department of Lands attesting to the payment of rents and other dues relating to the parcel of land in question. Finally, the applicant must submit the completed application dossier to the office of the local provincial chief of service for lands. This office is then required to transmit the application to the Central Lands Service in the national capital, Yaounde, where the parcel of land in question is ultimately registered in the National Land Registry, and the applicant, if unchallenged by any other party claiming rights to the same piece of property is then issued a land certificate.

The Building Permit Ordinance. Conditions for obtaining a building permit in Cameroon are stipulated in Ordinance No.73/20 of May 29, 1973. These conditions are summarized on the official "application for building permit" form and have been discussed in some detail by Njoh (1992). As Njoh (1992: 37) notes, "The building permit is the official document testifying that the plan of a proposed building or alterations to an existing building is not in contravention of building codes and land regulations in force."

The building permit is a prerequisite for all construction works, including the erection of new, and/or alteration of existing, buildings, fences, and embankments in the country.

The procedure for obtaining the building permit is as cumbersome as that for obtaining the land certificate. The building permit application process is further complicated by the fact that it entails completing three different files. Each file is required to contain the following documents and/or pieces of information (Njoh 1992: 28): (1) a site plan; (2) a block plan; (3) cost estimates of the intended construction works; (4) detailed building plans; (5) a town planning certificate, and (6) a land certificate or an attestation from the local Land Department, attesting to the applicant's ownership of the land intended for development.

IMPLICATIONS FOR THE SOCIOECONOMIC DEVELOPMENT OF WOMEN

The foregoing account contains only a minuscule portion of the myriad hurdles land developers, particularly housing developers, must contend with in Cameroon. We contend that these requirements are anything but an equal opportunity victimizer. More straightforwardly, the requirements harbor more negative implications for women than for their male counterparts in the housing policy field. What this means is that not only are women who are interested in undertaking residential development projects likely to encounter more difficulties than men, but they are also likely to bear the better weight of negative externalities associated with government housing and urban development regulatory measures. To buttress this assertion, we will explore some of the major implications of regulatory instruments in the following areas: (1) land use, (2) building materials, (3) land tenure, and (4) housing and urban design.

Land Use

The rigid compartmentalization of land use activities sustained by land use control legislation such as the zoning ordinance has negative implications for all residents of an impoverished country such as Cameroon, which lacks a well-developed and effective transportation system. However, these implications tend to be substantially magnified with respect to women. In Cameroon, the segregation of urban land use activities (1) directly inhibits the economic advancement of urban women, (2) facilitates crime against women, and (3) renders more difficult the domestic responsibilities of women.

Economic Advancement of Women. The formal sector in developing countries offers very few opportunities for women. Recognition of the widespread nature of this problem led the UN to make "economic growth, sound economic and productive employment" a central concern of its current women in development (WID) agenda (UN 1995: 2). While women constitute 51 percent of Cameroon's population, they make up only 33 percent of the country's formal sector labor force (Kurian 1992). The problem of joblessness among women is not limited to Cameroon. In fact, Kusow (1993) has observed that only a very small percentage of the women in developing countries have access to proper employment. The rest are employed or must seek employment in the informal sector. In India, for instance, as many as "43% of self-employed women work in their homes" (Kusow 1993: 221). Indian women, like women in other developing nations, are, in large part engaged in the informal sector, particularly, petty commodity production, such as preparing ready-to-eat food to sell in the streets.

However, the employment potential of the informal sector, hence, the potential of an important source of employment for women, is severely limited where urban policy seeks to rigidly segregate land use activities. To the extent that such segregation prohibits anything but living in residential areas, it effectively discourages activities such as home-based enterprises in the informal sector, which, as stated earlier, constitutes the most important source of economically productive employment for women in developing countries. The importance of the home as a place for productive economic activities in developing countries is underscored by Lisa Peattie (1987: 272) when she states that "in a part of the economy characterized by self-employment and by very small firms, involving, frequently, members of a single family, the house is often the factory, the shop, and the warehouse."

In cities of the developing world such as Bogota, Colombia, most businesses are known to function in rooms, garages, and sheds in, or attached to, residential units (Peattie 1987). In India (Mahajan 1993) and Malaysia (Selat 1993), women are actively involved in home-based, economically rewarding activities. It has been shown that the absence of opportunities in the informal sector in developing countries contributes to "the 'housewifization' process, isolation, and dependence" of women (Mahajan 1993: 252).

In the specific case of Cameroon, discouraging home-based enterprises through policies that strive to segregate land use activities has meant, for example, that women dealing in ready-to-eat food must travel long distances to organized marketplaces or other activity centers such as those offering formal employment in order to market their products. In one of the country's largest cities, for instance, some of the women trading in ready-to-eat food must carry the food on their heads and trek at least eight kilometers to the "Government Station, an area set aside for public and para-public offices, and located at the northwestern outskirts of the city" (Njoh 1995).

The importance of shelter location as a determinant of the economic condition of women in developing countries is acknowledged by Kusow (1993: 221-22) in the following statement: "Zoning laws which separate income activities from the residential sphere hinder women from engaging in income-generating activities in the home or around the neighborhood. For example, in Delhi, India, 700, 000 squatters were relocated to new settlements on the outskirts of the city between 1975 and 1977."

The relocation mentioned in the foregoing quotation, coupled with the absence of an efficient transportation system, made it difficult for women to combine domestic and income-generating activities. "Thus, the rate of female employment among the relocated fell five times more than that of men in the same area" (Kusow 1993: 222).

Crime against Women. The segregation of land use functions significantly increases the likelihood of women's becoming victims of criminal activities in the urban areas of a developing country such as Cameroon.[9] There are a lot of officially undocumented cases of Cameroonian women being attacked, mugged, assaulted, and raped on their way to and from activity centers such as industrial complexes and central business districts. In fact, there has been an unprecedented increase in the incidence of crimes against women, in particular since the mid-1980s, when the country's economic woes first emerged. A review of the crime records of some of the urban areas in the country reveals that most crimes in the residential areas take place during the day, while most of those in the central business districts occur at night (Njoh 1995). The explanation for this is simple. During the day, most people are away in activity centers. Thus, property and the few individuals, mostly women, left behind in residential areas fall prey to criminals ranging from thieves to rapists. Also, because of the long distances separating activity centers from residential areas and the absence of an efficient transportation system, women must sometimes leave behind leftover goods such as fresh food products for next-day sales. Often, however, the women return to find out that the products have been stolen. In one case, such goods were lost not to thieves but to a nighttime fire, which consumed a substantial portion of an urban market as well as portions of the surrounding central business district (Njoh 1995).[10]

Urban markets in Cameroon carry mostly household consumer domestic goods such as foodstuffs, cooking utensils, and clothing. The country's sexual division of labor has restricted women to the production and marketing of such goods. A similar division of labor has been recorded in other developing countries such as Kenya and Jamaica, where about 33 percent of the women employed in the informal sector are engaged in domestic activities (Kusow 1993). Thus, it is reasonable to deduce that women are likely to suffer a greater loss in comparison to men when an urban market in a developing country is victimized.

Domestic Responsibility of Women. Based on the gender division of labor in Cameroon, women have a greater responsibility for homemaking and child raising than men. In fact, this is true of other developing countries (Moser and Peake 1987; Chant 1987). Thus, any policy that inhibits the execution of domestic and related tasks makes life more difficult for women. Cameroon 5 urban development policy does just that. This policy, for instance, places limitations on building heights, stipulates large plot sizes, and prescribes a low floor area ratio (FAR). By so doing, it encourages a sparse physical development pattern for the country's urban centers. One result of this is an increase in the distances between important points such as the home and market, the home and school, and so on. Apart from this, the government, for obvious reasons, is often unable to provide adequate infrastructure such as water and streets in urban centers. This explains, in part, the fact that all urban centers in the country have only very few, sparsely distributed public water taps/fountains, few and poorly maintained streets, and an undersupply of other basic public facilities. In one city for instance, as few as seventy-seven public water fountains serve an urban area of 985 hectares (Njoh 1995).

Building Materials

As stated earlier, government policy concerned with the control and regulation of building activities in urban areas in Cameroon is explicitly biased against local and improvised building materials such as earth, wood, unrolled tin cans, and so on. In fact, as one commentator has observed, quality rather than scale of housing is at the heart of the country's housing policy (Njoh 1995). The negative implications of such a policy for the well-being of the country's women are plentiful.

For instance, the policy bears the potential to severely limit, if not totally eliminate, the direct participation of women in the shelter production process. This is because women are generally less likely to be skilled in the craft of building with such "sophisticated" materials as reinforced concrete, steel, ceramic tiles, and glass.[11] To limit the participation of women in the shelter production process is to exacerbate the gender-based functional differentiation problem that already exists in the country's labor market. Such a problem may result from the obvious differences between the wage entitlement of male construction workers skilled in modern building techniques and women construction workers whose skills are likely to be limited to traditional construction techniques.

Problems relating to biases in favor of imported materials and techniques in the building industry are not unique to Cameroon. Problems of this genre are said to have prompted single mothers in Kingston, Jamaica, to protest the actions of international aid organizations in their country's housing field (Basolo and Morlan 1993). Their protest was directed not only at problems relating to affordability, design, and attachment to location but, more importantly, at the use of inappropriate building technology, particularly imported building materials.

The fact that imported building materials are far more expensive than locally available ones is already well established in the relevant literature. In this regard, a study aimed at determining the relationship and consequences of technology choice in building construction in Pakistan revealed that the use of imported materials increased cost relative to traditional ones (Peattie 1987). Thus, given (1) that a rise in the cost of housing development triggers at least an identical rise in housing cost, and (2) the fact that women earn far less than men (see earlier), we therefore conclude that any attempt to discourage the use of improvised and/or locally available materials while promoting the use of imported ones, is tantamount to an effort to keep housing further out of the reach of people, especially women-headed households.

Furthermore, it is our position that the use of inappropriate technology, particularly, the excessive use of imported materials in the building development process, is one reason the participation of women in the construction industry in developing countries is, at best, marginal. In fact, some estimates put the involvement of women in this field as low as under 10 percent (Celik 1993: 199). Among other things, this means that women are yet to significantly benefit from employment opportunities in the construction industry—a sector well known for its employment-generating ability.

Land Tenure

Formalization of the process by which individuals gain access to land is of recent vintage in most developing countries. Prior to that, the process differed from one society to another. One important difference had to do with who (male or female) inherited land.

In Malaysia, on one hand, only women could inherit land. Men's access to land was guaranteed only through their wives or mothers (Stivens 1985 cited in Kusow 1993). In Cameroon, on the other hand, modern land laws, which had as one of their primary objectives improving women's access to land, have effectively guaranteed the direct opposite results. The country's customary land tenure systems in almost all cases prohibited individual landholdings in favor of group, particularly, familial, ownership. Thus, women and men alike, as members of extended families or communities, were guaranteed access to land and other real property. However, the modern Cameroonian state and the colonial state before it found such group ownership cumbersome, especially within the contemporary politicoeconomic and social sphere. Cognizant of this, the colonial administrators and, later, their indigenous successors have worked fervently to commodify land throughout the country. This effort culminated with the enactment in 1974 of a constellation of land ordinances. Foremost among these is Ordinance No.74-1 of July 6, 1974, which establishes rules governing land tenure in the country.

The complete modernization of the country's land tenure system in 1974 meant that thenceforth, access to land was no longer possible through membership in an extended family or any cognate body. The sole official factor that could determine one's access to land became one's ability to pay. Given that women, as argued earlier, are the least likely to be involved in economically rewarding activities, it follows that they are disproportionately affected by the new laws, which effectively make economic wherewithal the singular most important determinant of one's access to land. Thus, if women no longer have any access to land in Cameroon, it is because the country has been relentless in its effort to completely do away with the traditional land tenure system in favor of the European system.

This system, as intimated earlier, recognizes the individual, as opposed to the family, as a landowning entity. One of the major flaws of the system in the context of the present discussion relates to the fact that it accords individual entitlements to land almost exclusively to men. For one thing, land under government jurisdiction (which is most of the country's land inventory) has customarily been sold at below market value exclusively to individuals who not only have a verifiable source of income but are also prepared to develop the land with minimal delay. This eligibility standard inherently discriminates against women, who, as stated earlier, almost totally depend on the informal sector as a source of income. For another thing, state-owned land in Cameroon has been used as a source of political patronage (Njoh 1992; DeLancey 1989). The country's Land Decree of 1974 makes it possible for an individual to obtain a temporary grant of title to "unoccupied or unexploited" land[12] as long as such an individual could present a plan and possessed the funds to immediately develop the land. Taking advantage of this provision, the country's political leadership in the national capital is known to customarily give so-called "unoccupied and unexploited" land to regional bureaucratic and/or political leaders in exchange for political favors. Regional bureaucratic and/or political leaders are, of course, almost always men. In the rare event that this was not automatically the case, men's near monopoly of sources of cash income ensured them access to a lot more land through purchase than their women counterparts would ever dream of. In fact, empirical evidence suggests that since the 1974 landmark Land Reform Legislation was promulgated, only an insignificant segment of the female population has been successful in acquiring title to land.

In this regard, a recent World Bank study notes (World Bank 1995b: 38): "Only 3.2 percent of all land titles issued in the Northwest Province were given to women; in the Southwest Province the figure was 7.2 percent. For the country as a whole, it is estimated that women obtained under 10 percent of all land certificates." Women's access to land is further inhibited by the fact that the process for fulfilling the necessary land entitlement formalities is not only lengthy, cumbersome, and complicated but, also costly. For this reason, as Njoh (1992: 27) argues, "Although no hard evidence is available, cursory observation reveals that since the Decree establishing conditions for obtaining the land certificate went into effect on 27 April 1976, only very few applicants have successfully completed the entire process." Apart from being lengthy, cumbersome, complicated, and costly, the process involves visits to the national capital, where the final decision regarding land entitlement must be taken. For women, especially those with children, this tends to be prohibitively burdensome. This and other constraints to women's access to land have negative economic implications for Cameroonian women. For instance, women are often unable to secure loans "since banks demand collateral, as well as the returns which can be had from renting or selling land."[13]

The limited access of women to land as a problem has been acknowledged within a few circles in Cameroon. The National Association of Professional Women in the Media (NAPMEW) for instance, drew national attention to the problem recently when it urged the government of President Paul Biya to enact laws capable of significantly improving women's access to land in the country (Camnet 1995). In doing so, the association's secretary-general and journalist at the country's government-owned radio and television service (CRTV), Seraphine Tata, contends that by enacting such laws, the government will be living up to the commitment it made in 1994, when it ratified the (UN) Convention on the Elimination of all Forms of Discrimination against Women (Camnet 1995).

Housing and Urban Design

A prominent feature of Cameroon's urban development policy is an attempt to standardize housing and urban design schemes throughout the country. As Njoh (1992: 51) puts it:

the same rectangular cement block housing unit developed for low-income family in the south, where the vegetation comprises dense forests and the population, predominantly Christian, is built for a family of identical economic status based in the northern, grassland and predominantly Moslem region of the country. Yet there is little doubt that the northern Moslem would prefer a circular adobe (sun dried clay block) housing unit of Arabic architecture to a Western style, rectangular cement block unit.

Apart from the type of building and building material selected, the country's Muslim population in particular is likely to be concerned with the spatial configuration of dwelling units. While the country's urban development policy tends to encourage a gridiron spatial layout, in which buildings flank streets in a single file, a pattern wherein dwelling units are positioned around a courtyard is both indigenous to, and compatible with, the norms and customs of Muslim societies. In such societies, the seclusion of women is a common practice. Thus, courtyards may serve as the only outdoor space available to women. In fact, ignoring the importance of such space, as is currently the case under the country's standardized urban spatial development scheme, is likely to "cause severe psychological effects on women" (Kusow 1993: 226). In fact, this claim is buttressed by empirical evidence. For instance, as Kusow (1993: 226) reports, "A survey of two newly developed low-income housing projects in Tunis revealed that the design of small courtyards increased psychological depression, neuroses, and suicide among women residents."

RECOMMENDATIONS

At the heart of the discussion presented in this chapter is the contention that housing and urban development policy in Cameroon in particular and developing countries in general is inherently biased against women. Glaring examples of bias are located in facets of the policy dealing with land use, building standards and materials, land tenure, and housing and urban design. If the socioeconomic progress of Cameroonian women commands as much importance as the official position of the political leadership suggests (see earlier), meaningful efforts must be made to seriously revamp the laws. Heeding this, we make the following suggestions.

First and foremost, authorities must refrain from indiscriminately borrowing housing and urban development theories and concepts from advanced nations. In the area of land use control, the borrowed concept of zoning, which emphasizes the segregation of land use activities can be discarded in favor of a more pragmatic policy such as the promotion of a mixed land use system. A mixed land use system has been defined to include the following (Njoh 1995): "living and light home-based industries, wholesale and retail, vendours and hawkers, vehicular traffic and pedestrians and so on, all mix and mingle in ... merry confusion." Given its ability to encourage activities in the informal sector, a mixed land use system is more likely than any other system to contribute significantly to the economic empowerment of women. To the extent that such a mixed land use system permits the presence of people in all parts of the city at all times, it can be said to contribute to crime prevention. Furthermore, by reducing the distance between activity points, such a system is capable of facilitating the accomplishment of domestic chores on the part of women.

Second, we suggest the lowering of minimum standards for residential building development and the promotion of local building materials as strategies for (1) making housing more affordable to women, and (2) encouraging the participation of, hence, creating employment opportunities for, women in the building sector. Building construction cost typically amounts to as much as one-half to two-thirds the total cost of residential building development (Njoh 1995). Therefore, any strategy, such as the use of locally available building materials, that reduces construction cost automatically translates into a housing cost reduction strategy. As attested to in the following statement by Ferdinand Oyono, Cameroon's minister of town planning and housing (Oyono 1988: 7),[14] the Cameroonian government is well aware of this fact.

If there is any realistic approach in the search of solutions in reducing the building costs of low-cost housing in the Third World, it is undoubtedly the promotion of local construction materials. Cameroon understood this early enough and has made the use of local materials an essential component in its low-cost housing policy as the economic crisis lingers on.

To be sure, this statement attests to no more than the government's "official position" on the issue of building materials. Operationally or in practice, there continues to be an overt bias in favor of imported, hence, "sophisticated" materials.

Promoting the use of local building materials does more than simply reduce housing cost; it helps strengthen the informal sector, thereby aggrandizing employment opportunities for women in the construction sector as well as other nontraditional fields. As stated earlier, prior to the advent of modern housing and urban land use laws in Cameroon, women played a significant role in the construction sector. The employment-generating potential of the construction sector is well known. However, it must be pointed out that some of the factors that have traditionally mitigated against the participation of women in this sector have to do, in large part, with limited access to training and education (Celik 1993). Thus, programs to encourage the participation of women in this sector must encompass a training element if they are to succeed. Programs to endow women with construction and construction-related skills have proved successful in developing countries such as Honduras, where, thanks to such a program, a woman is reported to own and operate a floor-tile factory (Celik 1993). Similar programs account for the fact that a group of women in Mombassa, Kenya, on their own initiative were able to set up a concrete block-making factory (Celik 1993).[15]

Efforts to encourage the participation of women in the construction sector of Cameroon will require more than providing them with the skills necessary for gainful employment in this sector. With the disintegration of the extended family system in the country such efforts, to register any significant positive results, will necessarily include provisions for day care facilities for the children.

Finally, we suggest that authorities endeavor to adopt urban design schemes that are conscious of people's norms and culture. What this means is that there must be a retreat from the indiscriminate adoption of European and/or North American urban design schemes. The traditional practice of indiscriminately adopting such alien schemes fails to appreciate housing and urban form as products of their environment and elements of cultural expression. The contrast between European, North American, and African traditional urban design schemes is well articulated by Njoh (1995) in the following words: "While Europeans and North Americans may prefer arranging housing units in a row along straight motorable streets, African and Arabic designs dictate that units be arranged to form a circle, square, rectangle or similar enclosed design around a common area, the courtyard."

CONCLUDING REMARKS

Four overarching issues permeate the discussion in this chapter. First and foremost, there is the antiwomen, biased nature of housing and urban policy in Cameroon in particular and developing countries in general. Second and flowing from the first issue are questions on how to enhance women's access not only to housing but also to employment opportunities. Third, there is the inextricable link between the issue of women, housing, and urban development and the broader question of women in development. Finally, there is the issue relating to housing and urban design policy's instrumentality in efforts to empower women in developing countries.

It is not enough to simply frame urban and housing policy in social welfare terms or as an issue germane exclusively to minority groups, as has customarily been the practice. Authorities must adopt a gendered approach—one that seeks to empower women, thereby giving them an opportunity to contribute to national development in Cameroon in particular and the developing world in general.

NOTES

1. The report stressed the importance of a country-by-country assessment of specific legal and regulatory problems.

2. Etecki Mboumoua was, at the time, the country's ambassador to the United Nations.

3. This is an international, comprehensive treaty requiring parties to take the measures necessary to improve the status of women. As Blakeslee (1994) notes, this treaty received very little or no attention until more than six years later, following the World Conference on Women held in Nairobi, Kenya, in 1985.

4. By Cameroonian standards, any human settlement with a population of 5,000 or more is considered an urban center.

5. FAR is the maximum constructible floor area divided by the area of the plot.

6. The term "setback" refers to the distance from the street or roadway to the building line.

7. The "Grundbuch" was the official land register of the German colonial administration. This document remains an important part of the country's land administration system.

8. Specially marked property demarcation pillars are obtainable from the local Survey Department.

9. A penurious country such as Cameroon is unlikely to afford a police force equipped enough to guarantee the safety of the citizenry. Hence, there is the need for crime prevention through well-thought-out urban design schemes.

10. The market in question is the Kumba Main Market, and the fire was apparently the result of arson (Njoh 1995). We contend that the fire would not have done as much damage as it did were some living quarters authorized in the market and/or adjoining central business district.

11. To be sure, before the advent of policies that deliberately discourage the use of local and improvised building materials, Cameroonian women were actively involved in the shelter production process. In fact, such involvement remains a norm in the rural areas, where the phenomenon of self-building is alive, well, and strong.

12. The concept of "unoccupied and unexploited land" has its roots in that of "vacant and ownerless land," or *herres vacantes sans maitres*, which, by the way, is false within the African sense. In Africa, there was neither a piece of land nor body of water over which some African or African collectivity did not possess customary rights.

13. Personal correspondence via the electronic (Internet) network, Camnet.

14. The quotation originates in a speech by town planning and housing minister, Ferdinand Oyono on the occasion of the "World Housing Day" in Cameroon on Monday, October 3, 1988.

15. The task of training women as a means of increasing their participation in the construction industry has become a lot easier since the birth of the Women in Construction Advisory Group (WICAG) in 1984. WICAG is a professional group based in the U.K. whose main mission is to work in consultation with employers, trade unions, policymakers, and training bodies to increase jobs and training opportunities for women in the building industry.

REFERENCES

Azevedo, Mario, Gwendolyn Prater, and Margaret Dwight. 1988. "The Status of Women in Cameroon and Chad." In Mario Azevedo (ed.), *Cameroon and Chad in Historical and Contemporary Perspectives*. Lewiston, NY: Edwin Mellen Press.

Basolo, Victoria, and Michelle Morlan. 1993. "Women and the Production of Housing: An Overview." In Hemalata C. Dandekar (ed.), *Shelter, Women and Development: First and Third World Perspectives*. Ann Arbor, MI: George Wahr.

Blakeslee, Katherine. 1994. "Human Rights, Violence against Women, and Development." Remarks to Symposium on Violence and Human Rights.

Boserup, E. 1970. *Women's Role in Economic Development*. London: Allen and Unwin.

Camnet. 1995. "Women, Legal Reform and Development in Sub-Saharan Africa." A World Bank article posted on the electronic (Internet) network, "Camnet" (February 9, 1995).

Celik, Aliye Pekin. 1993. "Women's Participation in the Production of Shelter." In Hemalata C. Dandekar (ed.), *Shelter, Women and Development: First and Third World Perspectives*. Ann Arbor, MI: George Wahr.

Chant, Sylvia. 1987. "Domestic Labor, Decision-Making and Dwelling Construction: The Experience of Women in Queretaro, Mexico." In Caroline Moser and Linda Peake (eds.). *Women, Human Settlement and Housing*. London: Tavistock.

DeLancey, Mark W. 1989. *Cameroon: Dependence and Independence*. Boulder, CO: Westview Press.

Denyer, Susan. 1978. *African Traditional Architecture: An Historical and Geographical Perspective*. London: Heinemann.

Kurian, G. T. (ed.). 1992. *Encyclopedia of the Third World*, (4th ed.). New York/Oxford: Facts on File.

Kusow, Abdi M. 1993. "The Role of Shelter in Generating Income Opportunities for Poor Women in the Third World." In Hemalata C. Dandekar (ed.), *Shelter, Women and Development: First and Third World Perspectives*. Ann Arbor, MI: George Wahr.

Mahajan, Sulakshana. 1993. "Shelter and Income Opportunities for Women in India." In Hemalata C. Dandekar (ed.), *Shelter, Women and Development: First and Third World Perspectives*. Ann Arbor, MI: George Wahr.

Moser, Caroline, and Linda Peake (eds.). 1987. *Women, Human Settlement and Housing*. London: Tavistock.

Njoh, Ambe J. 1995. "Building and Urban Land Use Controls in Developing Countries: A Critical Appraisal of the Kumba (Cameroon) Zoning Ordinance." *Third World Planning Review* 17 (3): 337-55.

————. 1992. "The Institutional Framework for Housing Policy Administration in Cameroon." *Habitat International*, 46 (3): 43-57.

Oyono, Ferdinand L. 1988. "Priority to Locally-Made Construction Materials." *World Housing Day in Cameroon Monday, 3 October 1988. Ministry of Town Planning and Housing.* Yaounde, Cameroon: National Printing Press.

Peattie, Lisa. 1987. "Shelter, Development and the Poor." In Llyod Rodwin (ed.), *Shelter, Settlement and Development.* London: Allen and Unwin.

Pondi, Jean-Emmanuel. 1994. Review of *Power and Privilege in the Administration of Law: Land Law Reforms and Social Differentiation in Cameroon* by Cyprian Fisiy. Leiden: African Studies Centre, 1992. In *Journal of Modern African Studies* 32 (2)(June): 356-59.

Republic of Cameroon. 1985a. *VIth Five-Year Economic and Cultural Development Plan 1986-1991.* Yaounde: National Printing Press.

————. 1985b. *Kumba Master Plan: Zoning Ordinance.* Paris: BCEOM.

————. (n.d.). *Land Tenure and State Lands.* Yaounde: National Printing Press.

Selat, Norazit. 1993. "My Home Is My World: Women, Shelter, and Work in a Malaysian Town." In Hemalata C. Dandekar (ed.), *Shelter, Women and Development: First and Third World Perspectives.* Ann Arbor, MI: George Wahr.

Stivens, Maila. 1993. "The Fate of Women's Land Rights: Gender, Matrilinity, and Capitalism in Rembau, Negeri Sembilan, Malaysia." In Haleh Ashraf (ed.), *Women, Work, and Ideology in the Third World.* London and New York: Tavistock.

Sudarkasa, Niara. 1985. "Female Employment and Family Organization in West Africa." In Filomina C. Steady (ed.), *The Black Woman Cross-Culturally.* Rochester, VT: Schenkman Books.

Swantz, Marja-Liisa. 1985. *Women in Development: A Creative Role Denied?: The Case of Tanzania.* New York: St. Martin's Press.

United Nations (Commission on the Status of Women). 1995. "Preparations for the Fourth World Conference on Women: Action for Equality, Development and Peace: Review and Appraisal of the Implementation of the Nairobi Forward-Looking Strategies for the Advancement of Women: Report of the Secretary General" (New York, March 15-April 4).

World Bank. 1995a. *Toward Gender Equality: The Role of Public Policy.* Washington, DC: International Bank for Reconstruction and Development.

————. 1995b. *Cameroon: Diversity, Growth, and Poverty Reduction.* Washington, DC: Population and Human Resources Division, Central and Indian Ocean Department, Africa Regional Office. Rep. No. 13167-CM.

8

The State and Integration of Women in Ibo: Patriarchy and Gender Advancement

Ifeyinwa E. Umerah-Udezulu

INTRODUCTION

The Ibo are found in the southeastern part of Nigeria. Their origin is unknown and is subject to many speculations. Because of no written records on key historical facts, the Ibo rely heavily on oral traditions passed down from generation to generation.[1] Ibo people have a culture, but, unlike their historical counterparts, such as the Hausa and Yoruba, little or no chronological data existed from which to gather information. Therefore, my research relied heavily on my observations and interviews of my parents, relatives, elders of some communities, and intellectuals from the area. Nigeria is a patriarchal state, and Ibo women are coexisting with men within an androcentric system.

THE IMPACT OF TRADITIONAL LAWS AND CUSTOMS AND THE STATUS OF IBO WOMEN

Many researchers widely share the inclination that the Ibo society is egalitarian, in which everybody is assumed equal.[2] The egalitarian analogy relates to the fundamental belief among the Ibo that all individuals are endowed with the natural right to develop their maximum potentials. This shared conviction inculcates the hard work ethics that promotes individualism and acquisition of wealth.[3] Individualism encourages competition of one group against another and negates the idea of egalitarianism. The egalitarian standpoint, on the other hand, misrepresents the regional differences in the Ibo social structure and more frequently underestimates the implications of how groups are placed in the society. There is a remarkable difference in the political organizations of diverse Ibo village groups. For example, the practice of electing and divinely ordaining chiefs is widespread in several towns in Ibo society.[4] The positions of those chiefs suggest hierarchical ordering in the system. In some areas, the notion of *osu* (outcast) is still prevalent, and this idea negates egalitarianism. The *osus* became outcasts because of their parent(s)' violating certain sacred ordinances in the past. Such actions resulted in the family's being isolated by the rest of the society, and transcending the stigma is extremely tough for the family. They are ranked at the bottom of the social ladder and cannot intermarry with the so-called freeborn.

The egalitarian assumption and the regional differences camouflage gender integration in the system. The notion of status placement alludes to the roles people play, or the positions they hold in a given society. A system of social status connotes distinctive patterns of stratifications such as how people are ranked and hierarchical order of gender-based relations. The egalitarian ideology and regional differences affect integration in the system. Regional differences create a competitive edge among individuals because of the pressure to excel. As a result it pits one group against another, and this relationship creates gender adversaries. Women are a social class.[5] What differentiates women as a group is their gender, which is sociologically derived but not biologically given.[6] Because women form a group, a congruous segment, gender differences become compatible with gender-based interactions, a relationship in which power is vertically distributed in favor of men. Although individuals compete to achieve a high status, they are at a disadvantage in a society that values males over females.

The political organizations that uphold the two types of chieftaincy systems also encourage gender division. The elective system of chieftaincy in the Onitsha community traditionally nominates a man as the local chief. A ceremonial and political function is the responsibility of the chief. It is considered atrocious were women to hold such positions. The divinely ordained chief of, say, Nri-Agukwu town also precludes women from ever occupying such post. According to Ibo's traditional law and custom, chieftaincy is the highest rank in the social structure, and women cannot become chiefs because of the patriarchal nature of Ibo society. Therefore the egalitarian notion is gender-biased in favor of men, and Ibo women are yet to make headway in this context.

AGE GRADE AND KINSHIP STATUS AND THEIR IMPACT ON IBO WOMEN

Ibo society is stratified along gender line. The kinship system is a conglomeration of interconnected social statuses with gender-based implications. One dominant characteristic in Ibo custom comprises the special status accorded to male, birth order, the special emphasis on age grade, and the practice of polygamy. In any of these interactions, male power is sizable.[7]

Ibo society encourages gender division through emphasis of the seniority system. Birth order establishes the *okpara* status, which entrusts the first son or an "achievement-oriented" son with a special position in the family headship.

This sets him apart from others. Apart from his father, the *okpara* has the final say. The son's father also is a part of the *okpara* lineage system in his immediate family before marriage, and upon marriage the son establishes his own family, and the pattern continues.

Birth order essentially determines the role an individual plays, and the gender-based system endows the *okpara* with responsibility to act as head of the family. The Ibo society bestows the *okpara* with the *ofo*, which is a form of authority to perform ceremonial rites. One important Ibo tradition relates to the breaking of kola nut. This ritual is done to welcome guests. A male must carry out this function. If no male is around, then the oldest female would perform the kola ritual. The significance of the kola ritual suggests the gender favoritism in the system, since the males are preferred to carry out this key task. The *nzu* ritual relates to a visitor's action to reciprocate the hospitality of his host by being welcomed into such home. The males also carry out the *nzu* ritual solely.

The conventional Ibo society is hierarchical in nature. It consists of a number of states in the Federal Republic of Nigeria. Abatete is found in the Anambra state, near Onitsha. Abatete is in Idemmili Local government area. The town consists of four major villages, and these are partitioned into many subvillages. These subvillages are, in turn, segmented into *umunna*, or the kinship groups. Authority filters down from the elected chief, down to the *umunna* group commonly known as the patrilineage. The *umunna* represents a territorial unit subdivided into several *ezis*, or households. An *ezi* is distinguished by a large lounge *obu* where a family head resides and entertains his guests. Each *umunna* group is territorially marked from other groups, and power is hierarchically structured in the vicinity. In all these arrangements male power is sizable.

The leader or head of the *umunna* group is the *okpara*, who is the oldest ranking male. He wields the *ofo*, the special staff used in rituals and as a sign of authority. The different *ezis* or compounds found in a given *umunna* are also patriarchically structured, with males being the heads of households. The compounds compose many single homes or households that symbolize the economic achievements of the owners. Each unit appertains to members of several domestic classifications. The *umunnas* and members of the *ezi* have blood ties and cannot intermarry. The blood ties are stronger with the people in the *ezis*. The blood ties continue up the ladder, from *ezi* to *umunna* to subvillages, *ngo*, to villages and to the town, diminishing with each step of the family tree. The head of the domestic group exercises authority over its members. In any disagreement, the disputing member may appeal to the head of the compound for mediation. The head of the compound also handles external affairs ranging from the *umunnas*, to other groups, and Ibo women traditionally do not participate in such functions.

Seniority determines social status in a compound. The role of the *okpara* (the oldest or most influential male sibling) and *ada*, the oldest female sibling, reflects status accorded to the male or female kin. The *okpara* role is usually granted to the first son, whereas the *ada* role is assigned to the first daughter in the family. If any of these are disabled, his or her immediate sister or brother assumes the role. Each position has sets of expectations that the bearer must meet. While the *okpara* oversees the male-related concerns, *ada* regulates the female kinship. Sometimes the responsibilities overlap, but the male status antecedes that of the female's status. The precedence is given to the male, because of the perception that daughters get married and move away, while the sons are there to stay. Such idea connotes loss of influence by the daughters. The married daughters, including the *adas* and other female siblings, still maintain relationships with their blood relations, and their children are perceived as *nwadi anas*, or grandchildren. Just like their mothers, they do not inherit land from their maternal grandparents. Only the males can inherit land from their *umunna*. The privileges accorded to men, which are depicted in the diverse roles manifested by the *okpara*, *ofo*, *nzu*, and *umunna* systems, all reinforce the gender-based strategy by which Ibo women are vertically integrated into the society. The institution of marriage also serves as a backlash to Ibo women's status.

MARRIAGE AND SOCIAL POSITIONS AND IMPACT ON IBO WOMEN'S INTEGRATION

Marriage plays an important function in Ibo society. Marriage between the freeborn (*di ana*) and *osu* (outcasts) is prohibited.[8] Furthermore, marriage among blood relatives is forbidden. The traditional marriage in Ibo society must be validated by payment of a bride-price by the husband's family. The amount varies among families and areas depending on the background and education of the prospective bride.

Marriage in Ibo society is a union between two families. Marriages could be arranged by relatives or could occur through courtship. The process may take a long or short time to complete. Generally, the process is as follows: the man's family seeks marital consent from the woman's family. If the woman agrees, the marriage enters the second stage, negotiation of bride wealth through an intermediary, usually a man. When both parties are satisfied, the woman's character is tested when she visits her potential mother-in-law, and if she passes, then a marriage ceremony follows. I must emphasize that the woman officially undergoes all these scrutinies, while the male does not. Marriage is complemented by a church wedding, and the bride changes her last name, while the bridegroom does not. According to the Ibo's traditional law and custom, marriage is perceived as sacred and enhances a woman's status. A married woman has the respect of her peers and families. She is cordial, respectful, and congenial and can take on the responsibilities of establishing her own household.

Two kinds of marriage occur in Abatete: marriage between the bride and bridegroom and one between women.[9] The latter is rare but occurs mostly in circumstances where the wife is barren, *nwayi aga*, or has no male offspring, or her husband is deceased. Whatever is the case, the woman finds a new wife and, pays her dowry, and she resides with her. The new wife (not the barren woman) could have an outside relationship to produce a son. The woman's marriage benefits the older wife by neutralizing the adverse impacts of the inheritance law that discriminates against women with no sons by denying them property rights from their deceased husbands. In obtaining a spouse, the barren woman may be adopting a limited male function. Her situation never changes in the male-female arrangement. She is only taking action to secure her grounds in her husband's home. Abatete's traditional law prohibits women from inheriting landed properties from their father's lineage. Landed inheritance for women can occur only through marriage and goes to the males. In a circumstance where the woman has no son, the landed property is passed down to the nearest male relative. Therefore, one fundamental basis of female-female marriage is to produce a son to preserve the lineage and the subsequent inheritance.

Marriage, therefore, has gender-based implications. It is established to enhance the patriarchal traditions. Also, it safeguards male's interests, ensuring the continuity of his name and not the female's. Furthermore, it gives the men male offspring who would inherit their landed property, whereas the daughters inherit none of these lands. Furthermore, though it is a sign of prestige for the woman, she never attains the same status with her husband. She cannot assume the male's responsibilities unless he is deceased. A married woman is looked down upon (*onwero di*, she has no husband), and a divorced woman is criticized as having abandoned her husband (*osi be di ya gbapu*). A widow is called *nwanyi ajadu*, which suggests misfortune, though she had no role in her husband's death. She can remarry if she so wants or remain with her husband's family if she has some children. If she has no children, she either returns to her parents' house or could be taken in by the husband's oldest brother. The practice of a widow marriage can occur only when she is remarried by a male figure in her husband's family and is disappearing with the onset of modernization.

The process of modernization also affects the practice of polygamy, that is, the process of marrying two or more wives. Polygamy frequently occurs in cases where the woman has one or no sons. Some Ibo women may or may not support their husbands' marrying other wives. Nevertheless, there is no evidence to suggest that the wives seek annulment of their marriages because of their husbands' behaviors. She might be shocked and/or make threats. Nevertheless, she gets over that and normalizes relations with her husband and the new wife.

Some women who support the practice or who find themselves in this situation believe that the practice strengthens their position and eases their domestic obligations. The older wife has the opportunity to engage in trade or work outside the home. Power trickles down in a polygamous family from a husband, to the first wife, known as *nne ukwu*, or senior mother, to the second wife, who is called the *nne obele*, or junior mother, and so on. In case of any disagreement between the wives, the husband or *umunna* or the council of the elders would intervene to mediate between the disputing parties. The statuses of the wives depend on the number of children they have, their family backgrounds, and levels of their achievements—education and wealth—and the wives' abilities to talk with other people (i.e., personal relations).

A woman's status also depends on the status of her husband and her son. A wealthy husband's status enhances his wife's, and so does her son's or brothers'. Therefore, a woman acquires her husband's status from their mode of productions. A woman is highly ranked according to the successes of her son(s) in the public realm, such as a lawyer, doctor, or businessperson. If her male kin have low status, the woman is automatically categorized on such grounds. Her rank is also influenced by her achievement in the public sector—becoming a successful businesswoman, a lawyer, a doctor, a college professor, and so on. Even when she attains any of these career choices, and her husband is a laborer, she may be ranked high, but, according to the traditions, she is still under her husband.

The status of an Ibo woman relates also to whether she is unmarried, married, separated from her husband, or widowed. Single women have their associations in the villages known the *umu-okpu*. An *umu-okpu* could also be single or married. She simply retains that title after marriage. The associations mediate over family disputes and oversee burial ceremonies. They also carry out many diverse tasks such as imposing fines on any member or relatives who do not meet their expectations, such as neglecting his or her elderly parents, not attending meetings, or not making village contributions.

As stated, the married woman's or widow's position varies depending on her male kin's family background. The married women in the *ezi* and *umunna* also must struggle to get along with all the groups. They mediate disputes between quarreling wives and relatives and impose fines on any woman breaking the rules. They volunteer their services during marriage ceremonies, funerals, and other activities, cooking, cleaning up, and serving the quests. They also police one another's gardens against trespassing household animals and impose fines on any woman whose stray goats and sheep are causing havoc on another person's farms or homes.

These women, whether single, married, or widowed, are members of diverse associations ranging from the *umunna* level, to village, town, local government, and state and federal levels. For instance, the *Ugonwanne* and *Okwesilieze* women's associations have branches on the local and federal levels. They raise funds for building projects and scholarships and, provide financial support for their members during emergencies, wedding ceremonies, funeral arrangements, and so on. They also support political candidates during elections, campaigning for some candidates and registering voters. In spite of their support in this realm, very few Ibo women have become commissioners or ministers. Ibo men, on the other hand, have monopolized these offices. The institution of marriage augments the patriarchal differentiation in the society. Marriage is supposed to elevate women's status, but women are still subjugated to the intricacies of the androcentric stipulations. A woman is bought by bride wealth, a male serves as an intermediary during her marriage, she is expected to bear a son to consolidate her condition, and she inherits none of her father's lands. An Ibo man, on the other hand, is subject to none of these dictates. He enjoys inalienable rights because of his gender.

CHILDBEARING AND WOMEN'S STATUS

How much an Ibo woman is integrated into the system is determined by the number of children she has. Once a woman gets married, it is expected of her to have children, and the number of sons she has determines how well she fits into her husband's household. In spite of her academic achievements, she is under pressure to produce male children. A son ensures the continuity of the patrilineal arrangement. Consequently, this puts pressure on the woman to have children. In a special circumstance where the woman has one or no son or no children at all, she would be perceived as a failure; "she has not proven herself as a mother."

Such a woman's husband may marry with or without her consent. He would be under pressure by his relatives to take action. The phenomenon of a childless couple is virtually nonexistent because of societal expectations and the preference of sons to daughters. When she has some children, the woman is expected to raise them. Child raising is mostly the woman's responsibility, despite her qualifications and occupation. Implications of having many children are high maternal deaths in southeastern Nigeria.[10] Also, some woman cannot further their career objectives due to the amount of time devoted to raising children. The notion of the superwoman's syndrome is on the increase among some Ibo women, as many of these women combine their careers with raising their children. Some women may have house-servants and may place younger children in day care centers. They could also depend on co-wives to help with baby-sitting if they are available. Ibo society puts pressure on its women to reproduce, and multiple pregnancies are known to produce adverse consequences. In spite of Ibo women's career choices, they become victims of patriarchal demands that they must bear children and/or combine careers with child raising. Their dormant actions encourage polygamy in the system, which is another extension of androcentrism. Ibo women's educational attainment has little influence in such practices. Ibo women need to become aware of themselves and protect their interests. Their longevity is more important than losing their lives during the process of multiple childbirths.

EDUCATION AND STATUS OF IBO WOMEN

Before Nigeria became an independent country, the emphasis for many Ibo parents was to educate their sons instead of their daughters. Their preference was grounded on their perception that daughters get married and move away from home. Therefore, educating them would be a waste of assets since such benefits would accrue to their husbands' families. Such narrow perception gradually gave way in the 1970s. In the contemporary era, many Ibo young women are educated and make their career choices in fields of medicine, law, nursing, education, business, and so on. These women compete with their male counterparts in the public sector. However, the fact that these women have emerged into the public sphere later in the postcolonial era still means that they are vertically integrated instead of horizontally integrated.

Ibo women who are professionals are also a part of the brain-drain phenomenon. Many of them have left the country in search of better lives due to economic instabilities of the country. The brain-drain occurrence, combined with the career choices of some of these women, reinforced the superwoman's syndrome in the diaspora. Many Ibo women abroad cannot enjoy the luxury of having house-servants, and they therefore would have to combine their careers with raising their children. In spite of their achievements in the public realm, they are married and retain the "Mrs." title and are perceived as wives, mothers, and sisters. The Ibo woman's status depends on how she translates her education and wealth into personal relations and her ability to do some so-called prestigious acts. Such activities include joining different organizations, becoming active in community services, sponsoring relatives in schools and colleges, and caring for her parents and in-laws.

Because of the high incidence of educated Ibo women, there are generational differences between this group of women and their mothers. While the older generation (their mothers) upholds the traditional values and is more likely to practice them, women of the younger generation are more likely to adopt Western values. They would argue for equal rights, lobby to change laws that affect their status, and push for their spouses' involvement in the upbringing of their children. The gender implication of more women becoming educated is that this reduces the unequal distribution of resources among gender lines in the system. However, because these women emerge late into the political and economic realms, their integration would not be immediate but would become a gradual process.

PROPERTY RIGHTS AND THE STATUS OF IBO WOMEN

Property inheritances are traditionally conducted along gender lines, through their male kin. An Ibo woman's marriage unites her with her husband's household, but her identity is determined by the number of sons she has. The male child receives a higher ranking than the female, since males ensure the survival of the family name. The male child is also significant because of the property inheritance. His presence guarantees the continuity of the family tradition. The deceased father's property, especially land, is distributed by his sons, who, in turn, pass it down to another generation, and so on. The property is distributed by birth order, with the first son receiving preferential treatment. His younger brother receives other shares until the entire property is completely distributed by seniority.

A special daughter may inherit her father's property in the cities but not in the villages. Such inheritance must be explained in her father's will and may be contested by her full brothers, or stepbrothers. If a woman dies, her nontangible property, such as clothing, money, and jewelry, may go to her daughter(s). If she has landed property (tangible), it goes to the sons unless instructed otherwise. Many Ibo women have come to accept these traditional laws and do not challenge them, especially concerning land inheritance.

The divorce of an Ibo woman affects her status as opposed to her husband's. In case of divorce, which is normally granted by the courts, the husband has sole custody of the children. Also, in a rare circumstance where a woman gets custody, the children would later return to their paternal home to carry on the traditions. The dowry he paid may be returned to him, and the woman loses his last name.[11] Divorce is strongly discouraged among the Ibo but is granted because of irreconcilable differences. The woman returns to her ancestral home and can remarry if she so wishes. If she has sons, they can bring back their mother when they become older and successful. Property inheritances favor men instead of women. Such conditions enhance male status and undermine women's. Property inheritances support my standpoint that the Ibo society is patriarchal.

IBO WOMEN IN BUSINESS

The majority of Ibo women are involved in some form of small business. Because of the economic situation in Nigeria, government workers seldom get paid, and, if paid at all, they are paid in arrears. This forces these employees to have side businesses. Some have become self-trained contractors canvassing for contract jobs with the local, state, and federal governments. Ibo women's job descriptions vary, ranging from equipment and building suppliers, to supplying schools and universities with toiletries, books, and food, and so on.

The rate with which Ibo women are becoming involved in small businesses has led to the "cash madam" or "thick madam" syndrome (meaning filthy rich women). This notion suggests that women are becoming independent and self-employed and making enough money to earn a living. They therefore command respect due to how much income they generate from their businesses. Consequently, some of these women have small shops, beauty shops, restaurants, day care centers, sewing businesses, boutiques, and so on. Some midwives, nurses, doctors, and lawyers have established their own businesses in their various field of specialties, such as running private clinics, hospitals, or maternities (clinics for pregnant women for giving birth), and law firms, to become self-sufficient.

Women's involvement in the economic sector, though in inverse proportion to men's, holds promise for bridging the gender-barrier in this field. Nevertheless, Nigerian women, have not yet become major participants, in the workforce, such as being major entrepreneurs and having substantial contract work from the federal government and the multinational corporations. These kinds of joint ventures are still dominated by men.

MARKET WOMEN

Many Ibo women are involved in retail trade. They purchase and sell goods, such as rice, yams, kolanuts, palm oil, palm wine, gari, beans, cigarettes, matches, beer, bread, casava, clothing, soaps, body lotions, books, pencils, eggs, fruits and vegetables, salt peppers, melons, and so on. Sales could be carried out in small residential shops attached to the front of their homes, villages, or markets in the cities, depending on where these women reside. The marketplace is a special location where buyers and sellers converge to conduct commercial transactions. It is also a place to conduct noneconomic functions, such as social gatherings, meetings, and hearings, and to negotiate divorces and marriages, courtships, and so on.

The most notable feature in these markets is the zoning. Each product is designated in a specific area such as clothing markets, in which both genders are participants; meat markets are monopolized by men; fish markets are dominated by women; and food markets, such as gari and spices, are mostly dominated by women. These people have their small shops within the marketing zones. These shops could be either leased or owned by the occupants. They establish unions to oversee the operations and regulate the prices. The patriarchal divisions of labor occur in such markets as well. Men dominate in the spheres that generate more income as in the meat, as opposed to the fish, market. Women participate more in non-hard cash-yielding businesses, such as selling gari, spices, vegetables, and so on. Men, on the other hand, monopolize the electronic, construction, and tire businesses.

The proportion of the merchandise owned by these retailers shows the acute shortage of capital and spendable incomes. Petty traders may be selling rice, beans, pencils, soft drinks, or soda. They sell this merchandise on a small scale. For instance, soap is sold in separate cakes, and pencils are sold individually. This alone suggests the poor economic conditions of these market women and the consequences of this on their economic independence. These women have to support themselves and their families. Poor Ibo women cannot afford to pay their hospital bills when they or any members of their families become sick, nor can they afford to buy medications. They might borrow from close relatives, but such debts keep accumulating, and these relatives are poor as well. The lack of economic power is linked to malnutrition, inadequate access to health care facilities, and illiteracy. These factors affect Ibo women's status and their average life expectancy.[12] Nigeria needs to start acknowledging and confronting the problems and recognizing the important contributions of women to the system. The poor economic conditions challenge these women, endanger their lives, and threaten the systemic equilibrium that is necessary for sustainable development. These women lack substantial capital and technical know-how to engage in business. When compared with men, Ibo women trade in noncapital-intensive businesses.

IBO WOMEN FARMERS

Most Ibo women are farmers, particularly the ones who reside in the villages. The Ibo traditions of the land tenure system[13] rely on the following assumptions: land is people's possession; land belongs to lineage and cannot be passed down to another group of people other than to relatives; individuals within the lineage must be given land to build their homes and for cultivation; and every male kin must have access to his family land, though this might lead to partitioning of the plot into very small units.[14]

The principal means of acquiring land is through inheritance. According to Ibo traditional laws and customs, land is passed down from a father to his son. The patriarchal justification for such practice is based on the assumption that Ibo women get married and leave their parents' homes and consequently are not entitled to ancestral lands. Ibo women do not inherit lands from their parents, but they may get some lands through leasing or purchasing. They also have access to their husbands' lands, which they can use as farmlands. Nevertheless, these farms do not belong to them because of their gender.

During the farming seasons, these women farm alongside their husbands in a system known as intercropping. This notion occurs when two or more types of crops are grown on the farm. For instance, after the cultivation of yams, the principal crop, plots are allocated to the women individually. The women may elect to cultivate produce such as vegetables, corn, melon, and cocoa-yam beside their husbands' yam slopes. The yam is classified as a labor-intensive agricultural activity and, of course, would generate more income than the fruits and vegetables that fall into women's domain. Other crops that may be cultivated include bananas, breadfruit, oranges, pears, pawpaws, kolanuts, and plantain. These types of produce are planted and harvested separately in some smaller quantities to warrant gender-based analysis.

Women are also responsible for weeding these crops after the planting season, but harvesting is done by both genders. Following the harvest, Ibo women sell their produce in the villages or at the city markets. They form part of the marketing rings, establishing prices for their produce and trading in other commodities. The women are empowered through this avenue, because the majority of them manage the income generated through the trades. Nevertheless, the small-scale nature of the farming and businesses still perpetuates their impoverishment, illiteracy, and the general state of dependence. These are the women whom the state should try to help. The state should take the initiative to educate and train these women to become self-sufficient farmers. These women have to be taught how to preserve their harvests. Also, they have to learn how to market those commodities in the foreign and domestic markets.

CONCLUSIONS AND POLICY PRESCRIPTIONS

Although Ibo women's status seems to have improved, it is still low compared with men. The role of traditional laws and customs is gender-biased and presents a great deal of problem to the future stability of the Ibo society. On one hand, Ibo women are part of the system but have minimal or no rights. On the other hand, Ibo women have to support the system that plays a crucial part in alienating them. The *okpara*, the *nzu*, and the kola nut rituals enhance men's status by reinforcing the hierarchical gender ordering and simultaneously negate woman's rights.

The institution of marriage buttresses the gender dichotomy in the system by protecting men's interest, promotes the practice of polygamy, and encourages multiple childbirths at the expense of women's health. The childbearing and child-raising obligations are met by Ibo women, and this promulgates the superwoman syndrome, as many Ibo women combine their careers with raising children. Even though many Ibo women are educated, they are still subject to patriarchal dictates. Yet, Ibo women's education still holds promise for their liberation, because education creates awareness of women's conditions and helps these women to mobilize actions to combat the androcentral positions, by establishing laws to enhance their status.

Ibo women are not privileged to inherit their male kin's landed properties. Instead, their brothers are uniquely qualified to be bequeathed these lands. Therefore, the Ibo traditions of land inheritance are gender-subjective. The farming and marketing systems are gendered, with Ibo men dominating in the capital and labor-intensive businesses and agricultural activities. The state needs to revitalize the notion of women's essence and properly integrate the forgotten half of its population. Ibo women have positively contributed to the stability of the state system through their diverse capacities to produce and reproduce. The state needs to establish another set of social, political, and economic traditions and horizontally integrate women by harmonizing allocation of its resources. Special attention needs to be devoted to upgrading laws that discriminate against women and making those laws gender-neutral. Women have to become active participants with men. This tactic will revitalize the decaying social, political, and economic arrangements of the existing order and pave the way for the new millennium.

NOTES

1.   A. E. Afigbo, 1991, *The Image of Igbo* (Lagos, Nigeria: Vista Books, Ethnographic Series).

2.   Victor C. Uchendu, 1965, *The Igbo of Southeastern Nigeria* (Miami, FL: Harcourt Brace Jovanovich).

3.   Nnamdi A. Odoemene, 1993, *The Dynamics of Cultural Revitalization: A Case Study of the Igbos of Nigeria* (Enugu: Harris Print).

4.   Sylvester I. Nnoruka, 1995, *Personal Identity: A Philosophical Survey* (Uyo, Nigeria: Modern Business Press).

5.   Christine Delphy, 1984, *Closer to Home: A Materialist Analysis of Women's Oppression* (Amherst: University of Massachusetts Press).

6.   Chandra T. Mohanty, Ann Russo, and Lourdes Torres, 1991, *Third World Women and the Politics of Feminism* (Bloomington: Indiana University Press).

7.   Ifeyinwa E. Umerah-Udezulu, 1998, "The Interplay of Gender and Class in Policy Making: Women as Policy Makers in Developing Countries," in James Valentine, ed., *Capacity Building in the Third World* (Westport, CT: Praeger).

8.   This is based on interviews of some elders at Abatete.

9.   My Abatete contact.

10.   Ifeyinwa E. Umerah-Udezulu, "Health Care Crises and Women's Health: Maternal Mortality in Africa," *21st Century Policy Review* (Fall 1996-Winter 1997).

11.   Christopher C. Ndulue, 1993, *Abatete Political and Economic History and Some Aspects of Igbo Customs* (Aba: Abia State, Nigeria).

12.   Ibid.

13.   Ukamaka C. Asogwa, 1992, *A Manual for Working with Rural Women in Nigeria: A Study of Self-Help Promotion* (Enugu, Nigeria: Fourth Dimension).

14.   Ozoka U. Uchendu, 1994, *Women and National Development* (Lagos, Nigeria: Gong).

III

Educational, Economic, and Institutional Development

9

Women's Education in Nigeria: Improving Trends

James S. Etim

The Universal Declaration of Human Rights adopted by the General Assembly in 1948 in Article 26 states that "everyone has the right to education" and that this education should be directed to the full development of the human personality (United Nations 1997: 127). Other United Nations (UN) declarations have reaffirmed the rights of everyone to education irrespective of sex (see e.g., Document 22 of "The Report of the Secretary General to the Commission on the Status of Women [CSW] on the United Nations Educational, Scientific and Cultural Organization Study of Educational Opportunities for Women," May 1995). During the second United Nations Development Decade, beginning in 1970, some of the targets worldwide of the United Nations was that member states ensure "the progressive elimination of illiteracy, ensuring equality in literacy between sexes" and "equal access of boys and girls to education at the primary and secondary levels and at educational institutions of all types, including universities" (Document 39, December 1970). Since 1970, several United Nations conferences and documents have been produced on the status of women worldwide, and many show the dire need to improve the condition of women. The Convention on the Elimination of All Forms of Discrimination against Women adopted in 1979 obliges all governments to eliminate discrimination against women. The World Conference on Education for All "drew attention to the gender gap in educational opportunities and its consequences for human development. Article 3.3 emphasizes that the education of girls and women constitute a great priority" (UN Commission on the Status of Women 1995).

Education serves as the key to the development of both the individual and the nation. Nigerian educationist Ukeje speaks of education as an investment in people that pays untold dividends to society; if and when that investment is not made or is made inadequately, the society suffers a loss (Ukeje 1966: 155). According to Browne and Barrett (1991: 275), "Education is strongly associated with better health and nutrition, improved hygiene, higher child survival rates and lower fertility levels." The education of women is crucial to national development (UN 1995; Hill and King 1993). According to Ada Mere (1993), "Women are the most primary and constant agents of child socialization" (xix). The parent's education and early verbal interaction with the child have been shown to impact on the learner's reading achievement and overall educational attainment (Rubin 1993: 470; Hewison and Tizard 1980: 209-15). However, as Kathy Johnson (1989) pointed out, the home factor that emerged as most strongly related to reading achievement was "whether or not the mother regularly heard the child read" (353).

In Africa, several studies show that there is some relationship between a mother's educational level and the education of her children. Hyde (1993: 113) pointed out that mothers' "level of education and command of resources are important in their ability to keep their children in school," while Hill and King (1993: 12) posited that "a better educated mother has fewer and better educated children."

Nigeria is one of the signatories to the United Nations Declaration on Human Rights. Given the importance of women's education to personal and national development, it is worthwhile investigating and presenting recent data on the education of women. Specifically, this study reports on improvements in attendance at both primary and secondary schools; and presents and discusses data on women in the polytechnics and the universities and some of the policies the government has instituted to improve the lot of women. It also locates women's education in Nigeria within African and global perspectives and finally suggests what could be done to continue to improve the situation.

Over the last thirty years, there have been steady improvements in women's education. Universal primary education which began in the Western Region in the 1950s and continued nationwide in the 1970s, has been very helpful in improving the attendance rates for women in at least the primary level of education. Table 9.1 presents data on primary school education for 1990-1994. Data show that, over the period, there was growth in the number of girls attending primary school, from 5.8 million in 1990 to 7.1 million in 1994.

Table 9.1 shows that between 1990 and 1994, female teachers were on the increase in the primary schools. For example, in 1990, there were a little more than 142,000 female teachers; this increased to a little more than 201,000 in 1994, a 30 percent increase during the time period. Although there were still more male than female teachers, the gap is decreasing. In 1990, there were 47,000 more male teachers, while in 1994, the gap was merely 32,000. The presence of female teachers at the primary school in great numbers is of importance to pupils, especially girls. Research done in the United States and Britain shows that girls perform better when they are taught by female teachers.

Table 9.1
National Summary of Primary School Statistics

Total	1990	1991	1992	1993	1994
Schools	35,433	35,446	35,610	38,234	38,649
Enrollment	13,607,249	13,776,854	14,805,937	15,870,280	16,190,947
Male	7,729,677	7,741,897	8,273,824	8,930,650	9,056,367
Female	5,877,572	6,034,957	6,532,113	6,939,680	7,134,580
Teachers	331,915	353,600	384,212	428,097	435,210
Male	189,499	202,753	211,650	336,366	233,305
Female	142,416	150,847	172,562	191,831	201,905
Classrooms	376,611	377,439	407,987	447,859	444,985
Teacher: Pupil Ratio	1:36	1:37	1:39	1:27	1:37

Source: Adapted from Federal Government of Nigeria, *Annual Abstract of Statistics*, 1995 ed., 159.
Computer graphics: Melanie Marshall James.

Table 9.2 presents data on the situation at the postprimary school level between 1990 and 1994. Female enrollment improved from a little more than 1.4 million in 1990 to 2.03 million in 1994 at the secondary school level. The gap also between male and female enrollment was smaller over the time period, from 420,000 to 388,000, respectively. The number of female teachers also increased appreciably, from 46,074 to 54,949. The ratio of female to male teachers also decreased over the time period, from a little more than 1:2 in 1990 to less than 1:2 in 1994.

Table 9.3 presents data on education at the primary, secondary, and university levels from 1982 to 1990. At the primary school level in 1982, 6.31 million female pupils were registered. There was a slight increase in 1983 to 6.33 million pupils. However, there was a downward slide in terms of female pupils registered in primary school for the rest of the 1980s. Only in 1992 was the number of female pupils registered comparable to that in 1982. Two reasons can be offered for the cause of this slide in the 1980s. First of all, the structural adjustment program introduced in the 1980s and the consequent hardship and squeeze on funds may have caused many parents to withdraw their daughters from school or not to send them to school at all in the first place. Second, in the

Table   9.2
National   Summary   of   Postprimary   School   Statistics

Total	1990	1991	1992	1993	1994
Schools	35,433	35,446	35,610	38,234	38,649
Enrollment	13,607,249	13,776,854	14,805,937	15,870,280	16,190,947
Male	7,729,677	7,741,897	8,273,824	8,930,650	9,056,367
Female	5,877,572	6,034,957	6,532,113	6,939,680	7,134,580
Teachers	331,915	353,600	384,212	428,097	435,210
Male	189,499	202,753	211,650	336,366	233,305
Female	142,416	150,847	172,562	191,831	201,905
Classrooms	376,611	377,439	407,987	447,859	444,985
Teacher: Pupil Ratio	1:36	1:37	1:39	1:27	1:37

Source: Adapted from Federal Government of Nigeria, *Annual Abstract of Statistics*, 1995 ed., 162.
Computer graphics: Melanie Marshall James.

Table   9.3
Social   Statistics   and   Education   Students   Enrolled,   1982-1990

	1982	1983	1984	1985	1986	1987	1988	1989	1990
1st level									
T	14,655	14,383	13,025	12,195	11,870	11,540	12,691	12,721	13,607
F	6,307	6,332	5,471	5,732	5,160	5,020	5,383	5,724	5,878
2nd level									
T	3,393	3,561	3,503	3,850	4,191	4,561	4,965	5,404	5,882
F	867	905	945	987	1,086	1,195	1,315	1,447	1,593
General									
T	3,010	3,170	——	——	——	2,934	2,934	——	——
F	798	——	——	——	——	1,234	1,213	——	——
3rd level									
T	193,731	208,051	219,983	266,679	266,508	281,384	309,489	307,207	374,400
F	——	——	——	29,900	33,018	36,462	40,364	44,463	49,100

Source: Adapted from United Nations, *African Statistical Yearbook*, 1991, Vol. 1,
Table 41, 2.19-16.
Note: T = Total. F = Female.
Computer graphics: Melanie Marshall James.

LOBOO (Lagos, Ogun, Bendel, Ondo, and Oyo) states and some of the states in the East, levies and other costs were introduced into the system that may also have caused hardship on parents. The consequence would be to withdraw female pupils first. At the university level, data show yearly increases in the number of female students admitted into degree programs, from 29,900 in 1985 to 49,100 in 1990. The ratio between male and female students has, however, remained the same over the period, 8:1.

Although a lot of progress has been witnessed in primary education growth in Nigeria and the African region, more still needs to be done when the region is compared to other regions. Table 9.4 presents data from other regions for the average ratio of female to male enrollments.

Table 9.4 shows that in the African region, although there has been considerable progress in terms of the ratio of female enrollment, the region still has the lowest level of females enrolled in primary education. According to the UN Commission on the Status of Women (1995: 6), "Almost half of the children of primary school age are out of school, the majority of them girls."

Table 9.5 presents data on student enrollment in polytechnics by sex and level of study. During the time period, more female students were registered for various National Diploma (ND) programs than in the Higher National Diploma (HND) programs. For example, in 1987/1988, while 168 were in the agricultural engineering technology program at the ND level, only 15 were registered at the HND level. Except for mass communication, the ratio of males to females in the programs ranged from 6:1 to 4:1.

Table 9.4
Average Ratio of Girls to Boys in Primary Education by Region,   1970-1990

Region	1970	1980	1990
Africa	65	74	79
Asia and the Pacific	66	78	84
Eastern Europe	94	94	96
Latin America and the Caribbean	94	95	95
Western Europe and Other	95	95	95
World	77	84	87

Source: Adapted from Division of the Advancement of Women, United Nations Secretariat, based on information contained in Women's Indicators and Statistics Data Base (WISTAT), version 3, 1994, in *Commission on the Status of Women*, Table II.B.2, 5 Online.

Computer graphics: Melanie Marshall James.

Table 9.5
Student Enrollment in Polytechnics by Program, Sex, and Level of Study, 1987/1988 to 1990/1991

	1987 / 1988		1988 / 1989		1989 / 1990		1990 / 1991	
	ND	HND	ND	HND	ND	HND	ND	HND
Agric. Engr. Tech.								
male	1,822	339	296	82	324	216	419	162
female	168	15	57	13	79	43	110	29
Agric. Mechanization Tech.								
male	—	—	36	—	—	—	36	—
female	—	—	1	—	—	—	1	—
Agric. Tech.								
male	—	—	139	—	563	329	550	368
female	—	—	15	—	127	17	84	181
Animal Production Tech.								
male	41	62	38	69	—	—	167	—
female	10	11	18	15	—	—	52	—
Banking & Finance								
male	1,145	216	819	175	1,023	376	1,201	433
female	816	103	547	79	822	199	953	221
Cartography								
male	—	—	—	—	—	—	10	29
female	—	—	—	—	—	—	4	7
Chemical Engr. Tech.								
male	288	173	127	—	367	120	407	143
female	53	20	31	—	78	20	102	29
Co-op Studies								
male	182	8	44	—	28	3	35	3
female	54	6	7	—	48	5	49	5
Drug & Chemical Tech.								
male	—	—	—	—	—	—	—	—
female	—	—	—	—	—	—	—	—
Forestry Tech.								
male	—	36	24	—	—	—	—	—
female	—	—	—	—	—	—	—	—
Insurance								
male	271	68	59	66	144	92	324	23
female	261	27	75	21	137	51	234	16
Irrigation Eng. Tech.								
male	126	3	21	—	—	—	—	—
female	6	—	1	—	—	—	—	—
Library Science								
male	155	10	220	50	82	38	228	76
female	113	—	233	43	104	32	254	72
Marketing								
male	1,460	549	1,492	440	1,371	608	1,835	928
female	840	206	864	198	957	332	1,145	458

Table 9.5 continued

Mass Communication								
male	592	125	770	230	895	172	1,447	402
female	630	83	585	340	715	146	1,265	486
Metallurgy								
male	58	—	187	62	129	62	361	93
female	10	—	9	3	7	5	11	6
Mining Engr. Tech.								
male	117	86	135	16	232	126	140	142
female	42	2	13	—	10	4	17	9
Music								
male	32	6	—	—	—	—	32	6
female	35	5	—	—	—	—	35	6
Nutrition & Dietetics								
male	16	12	—	—	6	11	6	11
female	54	42	28	—	15	40	43	40
Photogrammetry								
male	—	—	—	—	23	8	23	8
female	—	—	—	—	5	—	5	—
Post Harvest Tech.								
male	—	27	—	67	—	—	—	67
female	—	4	—	10	—	—	—	10
Production Eng. Tech.								
male	—	—	—	—	—	—	—	—
female	—	—	—	—	—	—	—	—
Purchasing & Supply								
male	921	166	363	131	190	164	340	105
female	55	255	185	3	107	50	169	35
Rubber/Polymer Tech.								
male	32	—	40	—	—	—	—	—
female	22	—	28	—	—	—	—	—
Tourism								
male	52	31	30	—	24	—	29	—
female	29	27	12	—	7	—	12	—
Water Resources Tech.								
male	—	—	—	—	—	—	—	—
female	—	—	—	—	—	—	—	—
Wood/Paper Tech.								
male	17	5	16	7	—	—	21	7
female	14	5	11	2	—	—	14	2
Total								
male	31,719	10,586	23,278	8,339	26,422	12,468	38,935	16,800
female	14,009	4,102	12,011	4,362	13,968	5,295	21,396	7,817

Source: Adapted from Federal Government of Nigeria, *Annual Abstract of Statistics*, 1995 ed., Table 110, 172.

Computer graphics: Melanie Marshall James.

In Table 9.6, data for student enrollment by program, sex, and level of study are given for the years 1990/1991 to 1992/1993. More female than male students were registered in catering and hotel management, fashion and design, and secretarial studies. Female students were found in very large numbers in the areas of accountancy, business management, and science laboratory technology. Very few female students were registered in mechanical engineering compared to civil and electrical/electronics engineering. When Tables 9.5 and 9.6 are examined, the following points are observed:

1. In most of the areas, more female students registered in the ND program than the HND in each of the years.
2. Many female students were still in areas that are traditionally thought of as "female areas"—catering and hotel management, secretarial studies, and nutrition and dietetics. In these areas, more female than male students are registered for each of the years.
3. Between 1990 and 1993, the number of female students registered in mathematics/statistics kept getting less as the years progressed.
4. In areas where more male than female students were registered, the ratio of males to females ranged from 2:1 to more than 50:1.

There were still fewer females in science, technology, and mathematics areas than males. A closer analysis of the data in Table 9.6 shows the ratios between female and male students studying in different fields/disciplines.

Professor G. A. Williams, former vice chancellor at the University of Benin, has identified some of the barriers to the low numbers of female students in the areas of science, technology, and mathematics (STM). These include:

1. Irrelevance of curricular presentation in STM to girls' views and experiences of the world.
2. Masculine images of science projected in textbooks, media, and popular assumptions.
3. Poor facilities, including teacher supply, teacher quality, and equipment.
4. Nature of STM occupations, which are not easily combined with child raising and child care.
5. Lack of role models and career counseling (Williams 1995).

Table 9.7 shows the female/male ratios of students studying in the fields of science, engineering, and mathematics. Tables 9.8, 9.9, and 9.10 present data on academic staff in Nigerian universities between 1990/1991 and 1992/1993 school years. Table 9.8 (which presents data for 1990/1991) shows that a total of 10,779 male and 1,157 female faculty members were employed in Nigerian universities, giving a ratio of 1:10 (female to male). Further analysis shows that the University of Ibadan had more female faculty members than any other university for the year. In some of the universities, like Ahmadu Bello, Zaria (opened in the 1960s), and Sokoto (opened in the 1970s), there were no female

Table 9.6
Student Enrollment in Polytechnics by Program, Sex, and Level of Study, 1990/1991 to 1992/1993

	1990 / 1991		1991 / 1992		1992 / 1993	
	ND	HND	ND	HND	ND	HND
Accountancy						
male	5,494	2,222	4,220	1,893	5,313	3,278
female	2,822	796	2,204	882	2,724	1,573
Architectural Tech.						
male	698	251	349	153	607	281
female	86	29	113	22	128	35
Art and Design						
male	421	108	332	152	—	—
female	139	15	108	39	—	—
Building Tech.						
male	822	369	578	172	774	353
female	63	18	108	19	132	37
Bus. Admin. &						
Mgmt. Studies						
male	4,191	1,354	2,838	1,228	1,358	951
female	2,480	657	1,752	630	772	423
Catering &						
Hotel Mgmt.						
male	150	106	201	80	193	83
female	478	306	526	391	354	290
Civil Eng. Tech.						
male	1,217	759	910	466	989	598
female	183	55	142	114	131	83
Computer Studies						
male	—	—	381	42	1,024	83
female	—	—	150	20	486	35
Elect./Electronics						
Engr. Tech.						
male	2,711	782	2,094	547	2,342	1,110
female	178	22	144	34	159	61
Estate Mgmt.						
male	495	182	518	235	492	303
female	234	78	224	116	254	117
Fashion/Design						
male	27	11	11	7	13	12
female	75	19	30	23	142	17
Food Tech.						
male	458	190	389	141	420	214
female	452	193	349	208	433	305
Land Surveying						
male	729	256	33	—	360	128
female	105	35	2	—	48	8

Table 9.6 continued

Mech. Eng. Tech.						
male	2,489	576	1,335	361	1,389	685
female	46	16	63	17	74	30
Qty. Surveying						
male	396	149	378	172	354	224
female	57	11	102	30	96	34
Science Lab Tech.						
male	1189	335	1031	235	2023	360
female	583	172	489	131	1,412	201
Secretarial Studies						
male	1,412	287	640	356	1,191	410
female	2,543	686	2,447	739	2,628	918
Statistics/Maths						
male	920	165	648	198	886	288
female	228	55	183	71	357	86
Topographic Science						
male	41	62	—	—	33	37
female	10	11	—	—	9	9

Source: Adapted from Federal Government of Nigeria, *Annual Abstract of Statistics*, 1995 ed.,
     Table 110, 171.
Computer graphics: Melanie Marshall James.

Table 9.7
**Ratios between Female and Male Students in Various
Science/Technology and Mathematics Areas, 1990/1993**

AREA	RATIO RANGE FOR BOTH ND AND HND			
Building Technology	Between	1:6	and	1:8
Civil Engineering	Between	1:6	and	1:12
Computer Science		1:2		
Electronics / Electrical Engineering	Between	1:15	and	1:30
Mechanical Engineering	Between	1:20	and	1:50
Science Lab. Technology		1:2		
Statistics/Mathematics	Between	1:2	and	1:4

Computer graphics: Melanie Marshall James.

Table 9.8
Academic Staff by Institution, Sex, and Grade in Nigerian Universities,   1990/1991

Institution	G — Professors Associate Professors Readers M	F	R — Senior Lecturers Senior Res. Fellows M	F	A — Lecturers Research Fellows M	F	D — Assistant Lecturers & Junior Res. Fellows M	F	E — Others M	F	Total M	F	Grand Total M/F
Abeokuta	10	1	24	2	54	16	11	7	—	—	99	26	125
Abuja	10	—	2	—	25	2	11	5	—	—	66	7	73
ACE Ondo	4	—	11	—	32	—	34	—	11	—	92	—	92
Akure	17	1	28	—	51	7	19	4	16	3	131	15	146
Anambra	26	—	63	8	116	15	60	5	15	2	280	30	310
ATC Kano	—	—	12	1	17	4	15	12	—	—	44	17	61
ATC Zaria	—	—	10	2	25	10	9	6	26	10	70	28	98
Bauchi	16	1	20	—	33	3	35	5	25	8	129	17	146
Bendel	28	1	55	2	190	25	109	34	5	—	387	62	449
Benin	90	2	158	22	210	45	59	16	37	7	554	92	646
Cross River	14	0	34	1	98	18	85	18	40	21	271	58	329
DAC	—	—	—	—	—	—	—	—	60	—	60	0	60
Ibadan	250	17	284	56	334	80	90	26	—	—	958	179	1,137
Ife	147	2	256	3	308	24	149	13	—	—	860	52	912
Ilorin	76	2	132	4	150	13	55	11	5	—	418	30	448
Imo	27	2	55	5	127	30	38	8	26	9	273	54	327
Jos	46	3	101	10	174	40	81	11	45	8	447	72	519
Kano	26	—	82	2	151	9	58	8	59	8	376	27	403
Lagos (U. of)	170	13	201	45	154	59	17	4	48	5	590	126	716
Lagos (State)	13	2	17	3	73	23	16	10	0	0	119	38	157
Maiduguri	68	3	106	5	285	38	81	12	154	23	694	81	775
Makurdi	13	1	22	1	61	5	25	11	37	1	158	19	177
Minna	14	—	33	1	62	11	35	3	10	1	154	16	170
Nsukka	174	9	314	44	195	80	27	3	30	10	740	146	886
Ogbomoso	—	—	—	—	—	—	—	—	—	—	44	1	45
Ogun	20	3	52	4	114	14	41	8	34	2	261	31	292
Omlabar	51	2	90	10	160	34	88	20	38	9	427	75	502

Table 9.8 continued

Ondo	21	2	24	1	58	20	54	15	6	—	163	20	183
Owerri	15	—	48	4	77	8	29	5	18	3	187	20	207
Port Harcourt	57	1	111	15	164	38	30	5	8	1	370	60	430
Rivers	19	1	68	5	173	40	55	14	93	10	408	70	478
Sokoto	26	—	43	2	151	8	85	1	13	—	318	11	329
Uyo	22	—	34	2	111	20	82	31	38	15	287	68	355
Yola	14	—	18	1	70	8	38	2	22	—	162	11	173
Zaria	149	—	347	—	611	—	337	—	288	—	1,732	—	1,732

Total						11,936
male	1,068	1,628	2,777	952	4,354	10,779
female	56	206	533	202	160	1,157

Source: Adapted from Federal Government of Nigeria, *Annual Abstract of Statistics*, 1995 ed.,
     Table 127, 187.
Computer graphics: Melanie Marshall James.

associate or full professors. As a whole, most of the female faculty members were in the lecturer rank.

Table 9.9 presents data on academic staff by institutions by sex and grade levels for 1992/1993 school year.

At the professor/associate professor level, there were 71 female faculty members compared to 1,706 male members, giving a ratio of 1:20. At the senior lecturer level, the ratio is 1:9; at the lecturer level, the ratio is 1:6; and at the assistant lecturer level, the ratio is 1:5. Overall, the university system had 374 more female faculty members in 1991 than in 1990. In Table 9.10, data for academic staff in Nigerian universities for 1992/1993 are presented.

The University of Ibadan, Nigeria's oldest university, still has more female professors than any other university. At the professorial grade level, the ratio for male to female faculty members is about 1:10 at Ibadan and Lagos, 1:30 at Calabar, 1:40 at Ilorin, 1:22 at Port Harcourt, and 1:8 at Jos. In terms of first-tier university (including Ibadan, Ife, Lagos, Nsukka, and Zaria), although data are unavailable for some, it is safe to note that the ratio is 1:10 for females to males at the professorial level. For the second-tier universities (those opened in the late 1960s and 1970s) the University of Jos has the best record of 1:8. For the technological/agricultural universities that were opened mostly in the 1980s (Akure, Bauchi, Makurdi, Minna, Owerri, and Yola), the ratio at the professorial level is about 1:10 for each of the institutions except at Owerri, where the ratio was 1:43. At the senior lecturer level, overall, the ratio of female to male lecturers was about 1:8. However, there are variations ranging from a very high ratio of 1:4 at Imo State University, Ibadan, and Lagos to 1:50

at Maiduguri. Based on Tables 9.8, 9.9, and 9.10, certain observations can be made:

1. There were fewer female professors than male, the ratios ranging from 1:10 to 1:43 in some universities.
2. At the senior lecturer level, the ratio of female to male faculty was 1:9.
3. Most of the female faculty were found in the lecturer/assistant lecturer levels.

This situation is reminiscent of the report about the U.S. system in the 1980s by Ewell (1990: 45), who pointed out that "only a quarter of their professors were female, clustered in the lower ranks" At the regional level, Table 9.11 presents data on percentage of female faculty in selected African countries for 1990. When compared to other African countries, the percentage of female faculty in Nigerian universities is very low, as seen in Table 9.11; Comoros has 31 percent, while Algeria has 20 percent.

CONCLUSIONS

Although there has been great progress in the education of women in Nigeria, problems still abound. The following, listed in the *Report of the Fourth World Conference on Women* (UN 1995) as problem areas to the overall education of women, are applicable to Nigeria:

1. Customary attitudes.
2. Early marriages and pregnancies.
3. Gender-biased teaching.
4. Lack of accessible school facilities.

Regarding technical and technological studies, Evans (1995 online) pointed out the following as barriers to women's education in the area:

1. Lack of female teachers and assumptions and attitudes of male teachers;
2. Inflexible selection and entry requirements.
3. Often has large attendance requirement for practical skills/laboratory-based work.
4. Male-oriented language and male images in teaching materials.
5. Instrumental pedagogies and curriculum content that ignores the social context of technology.

Some of the reasons indicated support some of the findings by Williams (1995) of the problems women encounter as they forge ahead in science, technological, and mathematics education in Africa.

Educational, Economic, and Institutional Development

Table 9.9
Academic Staff by Institution, Sex, and Grade in Nigerian Universities, 1991/1992

	Professors Associate Professors Readers		Senior Lecturers Senior Res. Fellows		Lecturers Research Fellows		Assistant Lecturers & Junior Res. Fellows		Others		Total		Grand Total
Institution	M	F	M	F	M	F	M	F	M	F	M	F	M/F
Abeokuta	10	1	24	2	54	16	11	7	—	—	99	26	125
Abuja	9	—	20	1	32	5	10	9	—	—	71	15	86
Akure	19	1	32	2	60	6	25	7	28	3	164	19	183
Anambra	39	4	61	9	118	29	14	14	—	—	232	56	270
Bauchi	19	1	28	—	53	1	43	4	63	17	206	23	229
Bendel	28	1	36	1	109	14	60	13	22	9	255	38	225
Benin	94	4	161	27	184	45	71	36	66	16	576	128	704
Calabar	58	1	84	17	136	35	83	23	32	10	393	86	479
Enugu	26	—	64	6	96	12	50	10	5	1	241	29	494
Ibadan	247	17	274	66	306	84	74	15	1	—	902	182	1,084
Ife	147	2	256	13	308	24	149	13	—	—	860	52	912
Ilorin	81	1	125	4	151	9	70	7	1	—	428	21	449
Imo	30	2	70	9	136	27	34	7	24	10	294	55	293
Jos	63	5	105	9	170	38	68	21	56	15	462	88	550
Kano	26	—	82	2	151	9	58	8	59	8	376	27	403
Lagos (U. of)	170	13	201	45	154	59	17	4	48	5	590	126	716
Lagos (State)	26	—	39	—	102	—	25	—	18	—	210	—	210
Maiduguri	81	2	116	3	295	44	80	3	128	23	700	75	775
Makurdi	13	1	22	1	61	5	25	11	37	1	158	19	177
Minna	12	—	38	2	54	10	41	3	10	—	155	15	170
Nsukka	145	7	296	47	215	74	25	4	30	11	711	143	854
Ogbomoso	19	—	8	—	11	3	26	3	16	1	80	7	87
Ogun	20	3	52	4	114	14	41	8	34	2	261	31	335
Ondo	21	2	33	1	61	4	78	19	6	—	199	26	292
Owerri	18	—	41	5	35	9	18	5	—	—	112	19	131

Table 9.9 continued

Port													
Harcourt	57	1	120	5	170	42	31	5	8	1	386	64	450
Rivers	27	2	66	11	166	39	53	14	106	10	418	76	349
Sokoto	16	—	35	3	128	5	60	3	57	1	296	12	308
Uyo	17	—	34	1	104	22	87	32	29	9	271	64	288
Yola	15	—	22	1	83	7	50	2	48	4	218	14	232
Zaria	143	—	230	—	352	—	210	—	116	—	1,051	—	1,051

Total						12,912
male	1,706	2,774	4,186	1,711	1,004	1,531
female	71	306	690	308	156	11,381

Source: Adapted from Federal Government of Nigeria, *Annual Abstract of Statistics*, 1995 ed., Table 128, 188.

Computer graphics: Melanie Marshall James.

Both the federal and state governments have through the programs instituted been instrumental in improving women's education. This has been done in three areas:

1. Federal Government Girls Colleges.
2. Federal Government College of Education for Girls.
3. Laws against early marriages.

In the 1970s, the federal government decided that every state will have two federal government colleges, one coeducational and the other, solely for girls. Often referred to as "unity schools," these colleges have not only helped in fostering national unity but also aided in allowing more girls to receive high-quality secondary school education. These schools are some of the best in the nation in terms of quality of students, staff, and equipment and therefore ensure that many of the students who graduate stand a better chance of furthering their education.

At the state level, many of the states, especially those in the north, have two types of secondary schools—single-sex and coeducational. Although this has happened because Islam (predominant in the north) favored this kind of arrangement, the process has also allowed more women to go to school. In the south, many of the Christian missions had single-sex schools, while state governments tended to build coeducational schools. These single-sex schools ensured that more girls began and completed their studies.

In the quest to produce more teachers for the primary schools and junior secondary schools (in the wake of the universal primary education scheme of the 1970s), the federal and state governments have established several colleges of

Table 9.10
Academic Staff by Institution, Sex, and Grade in Nigerian Universities, 1992/1993

Institution	G Professors Associate Professors Readers M	F	R Senior Lecturers Senior Res. Fellows M	F	A Lecturers Research Fellows M	F	D Assistant Lecturers & Junior Res. Fellows M	F	E Others M	F	Total M	F	Grand Total M/F
Abeokuta	na	na	na	na	na	na	na	na	na	na	na	na	na
Abia	30	2	70	9	137	27	34	7	24	10	295	55	360
Akure	20	1	31	3	71	4	30	10	28	—	180	18	198
Bauchi	19	1	28	—	53	1	43	4	63	17	206	23	229
Bendel	na	na	na	na	na	na	na	na	na	na	na	na	na
Benin	107	4	176	27	191	59	51	24	48	9	573	123	696
Benue	11	—	8	1	33	4	30	5	—	—	82	10	92
Calabar	63	2	92	15	155	36	82	27	68	22	460	102	562
Enugu	29	—	84	1	98	12	34	7	15	1	260	21	281
Ibadan	247	21	306	74	405	110	123	38	—	—	1,091	243	1,334
Ife	na	na	na	na	na	na	na	na	na	na	na	na	na
Ilorin	84	2	129	4	140	18	54	14	9	—	416	38	454
Imo	9	—	8	2	12	1	11	7	—	—	40	10	50
Jos	63	8	112	11	195	11	77	17	58	15	505	62	567
Kano	34	—	106	3	153	9	134	11	44	9	471	32	503
Lagos (U. of)	156	13	185	50	143	59	29	9	26	15	539	146	685
Lagos (State)	na	na	na	na	na	na	na	na	na	na	na	na	na
Maiduguri	73	6	111	2	258	29	129	21	11	1	582	59	641
Makurdi	na	na	na	na	na	na	na	na	na	na	na	na	na
Minna	14	—	39	2	55	11	42	4	11	—	161	17	178
Nsukka	144	7	294	60	211	71	37	7	34	14	720	159	879
Ogbomoso	23	—	14	2	23	3	54	8	—	—	114	13	127
Ogun	23	6	45	4	110	17	83	11	—	—	261	38	299
Ondo	na	na	na	na	na	na	na	na	na	na	na	na	na
Owerri	43	1	51	4	68	10	30	5	—	1	192	21	213

Table 9.10 continued

Port													
Harcourt	44	2	132	8	174	10	59	7	7	—	416	27	443
Rivers	na	na	na	na	na	na	na	na	na	na	na	na	na
Sokoto	22	1	43	2	139	7	56	1	38	1	298	12	310
Uyo	24	1	56	4	124	27	75	24	36	13	315	69	384
Yola	23	2	21	—	131	6	62	7	40	5	277	20	297
Zaria	na	na	na	na	na	na	na	na	na	na	na	na	na

Total						12,912
male	1,706	2,774	4,186	1,711	1,004	11,381
female	71	306	690	308	156	1,531

Source: Adapted from Federal Government of Nigeria, *Annual Abstract of Statistics*, 1995 ed.,
Table 129, 189.

Computer graphics: Melanie Marshall James.

Table 9.11
Percentage of Women among University Teachers, 1990

Algeria	20%
Benin	10%
Burundi	11%
Central African Republic	11%
Comoros	31%
Nigeria	10%

Source: Adapted from Women in Development Network, "Education and Training
Statistics—Africa," 1998, Online.
Computer graphics: Melanie Marshall James.

education. This has opened more avenues for women to obtain postsecondary
education. Recently, to encourage female teachers in the technical areas, the
federal government established the Federal College of Education (technical) at
Gusau, which is solely for women.

In 1995, the federal government established the Ministry of Women Affairs
and in 1997 directed that this ministry should be established in all thirty-six
states (Ejime 1997). This is, in essence, government's continued efforts to give
voice to women's issues and to ensure that the welfare of women is catered to.
However, government and institutions could still do more to improve the lot of
women in the educational sphere:

1. *Science and Technology*. At the secondary school level, more states may need to establish scholarship funds for girls pursuing these subjects. At the university level, more women could be encouraged to study science and technology disciplines through:
   a. Admitting more via the remedial programs.
   b. Providing some incentive allowances for students in the area.
   c. Reviewing the curricula and textbooks to remove the gender bias.

2. *Funding for Students in Polytechnics and State Universities*. Education is not free in the state universities and the polytechnics. Many students, although qualified, may not be able to attend these levels of education. Given the fact that many parents have the attitude that it is better to send a boy to school than a girl, many female students may not be able to attend these institutions. It may therefore be necessary for government to provide some funds to enable women to obtain scholarships or loan schemes at low percentage rates so as to be able to attend these institutions.

3. *Female faculty in these institutions should increase*. There are several ways to achieve this—for example more female graduate assistants should be recruited so that eventually they will be trained.

4. *Teaching Strategies*. There is the constant need for faculty to review teaching strategies to ensure that the learning styles of women are taken into consideration as instruction is delivered. In an interview (1997) with Katherine S. Mangan , Professor Lani Guinier, in the case of law, argues that "women generally learn better through cooperative approaches than through adversarial ones." Furthermore, Guinier points out that aggressive teaching styles force women to be more like men, thereby damaging their self-esteem. In her own study at the University of Pennsylvania Law School, she found out that "women underwent more stress, received lower grades and fewer honors than their male classmates, despite entering with identical credentials" (A 12-13). She ascribes the problem to the Socratic method of instruction, and, as a result of this, she calls for a review of teaching methods in law schools. In a related study, Ewell (1990) reported that in most classrooms, "professors call on women students less frequently, ask them less probing questions and interrupt or ignore their comments more often. Moreover, the aggressive, competitive 'masculine' style of classroom exchange disadvantages ... women" (52). As a result, she calls for classroom environments that encourage small group collaboration (discussion, group projects and group grades), action project and journal writing (55). All these are suggestions that university faculty in Nigeria (and, indeed, anywhere) can use to revise and define instruction so that women can benefit more in the process.

REFERENCES

Anselmo, Sandra. 1978."Improving Home and Preschool Influences on Early Language Development." *Reading Teacher* 32(2).

Browne, Angela W., and Hazel R. Barrett. 1991. "Female Education in Sub-Saharan Africa: The Key to Development." *Comparative Education* 27(3).

Ejime, P. 1997. "Nigeria Gets More Women Ministers." *Panafrican News Agency.* Online: http://www. (Posted March 8, 1997).

Evans, Karen. 1995. "Barriers to Participation of Women in Technological Education and the Role of Distance Education." Online: http://www.col.org/O/html/barriers.htm

Ewell, Barbara C. 1990. "Empowering Otherness: Feminist Criticism and the Academy." In Bruce Henricksen and Thais E. Morgan, eds., *Reorientations: Critical Theories and Pedagogies*. Chicago: University of Illinois Press.

Federal Government of Nigeria. 1995. *Annual Abstract of Statistics*. Lagos, Nigeria: Federal Government Printer.

Hewison, Jenny, and Jack Tizard. 1980. "Parental Involvement and Reading Attainment." *British Journal of Educational Psychology* 50(3): 209-15.

Hill, M. Anne, and Elizabeth M. King. 1993. "Women's Education in Developing Countries: An Overview." In Elizabeth M. King and M. Anne Hill, eds., *Women's Education in Developing Countries: Barriers, Benefits and Policies*. Baltimore and London: Johns Hopkins University Press for World Bank.

Hyde, Karin A. L. 1993. "Sub-Saharan Africa." In Elizabethe M. King and M. Anne Hill, eds., *Women's Education in Developing Countries: Barriers, Benefits and Policies*. Baltimore and London: Johns Hopkins University Press for World Bank.

Johnson, Kathy. 1989. "Parents and Reading: A U.K. Perspective." *Reading Teacher* 42(6): 353.

Mangan, Katherine S. 1997. "Lani Guinier Starts Campaign to Curb Use of Socratic Method." *The Chronicle of Higher Education* (April 11): 10-11.

Mere, Ada. 1993. "The Unique Role of Women in Nation Building." In Gay Wilentz, *Binding Cultures: Black Women Writers in Africa and the Diaspora*. Bloomington: Indiana University Press.

Rubin, Dorothy. 1993. *A Practical Approach to Teaching Reading*. 2d ed. Boston: Allyn and Bacon.

Tripp, A. M. 1988. *Women and the Changing Urban Household Economy in Tanzania*. Evanston, IL: Northwestern University Press.

Ukeje, B. O. 1966. *Education for Social Reconstruction*. Lagos, Nigeria: Macmillan.

United Nations. 1991. *African Statistical Yearbook*. Vol. 1. New York: United Nations.

———. 1995. *Commission on the Status of Women*. "Monitoring the Implementation of the Nairobi Forward-Looking Strategies for the Advancement of Women." Online: gopher://gopher.un.org:70/00/esc/cn6/1995/1995-3.en2

———. 1995. *Report of the Fourth World Conference on Women*. Beijing, Sept. 4-15, 1995. Online: gopher//gopher.undp.org:70/00/unconfs/women/off/a-20.en

———. 1997. *The United Nations and the Advancement of Women 1945-1996*. New York: United Nations.

Williams, G. A. 1987. "Science, Technology and Mathematics Education for All, including Women and Girls in Africa." Keynote at the Commonwealth Africa Workshop on Gender Stereotyping in Science, Technology and Mathematics Education. Report of a Commonwealth Regional Workshop, Accra, Ghana. In Karen Evans, "Barriers to Participation of Women in Technological Education and the Role of Distance Education." Online.

Women in Development Network. 1998. "Education and Training Statistics—Africa." Online http://www.focusintl.com/statrla3.htm

10

African Women in the Development Process: Business and Computer Technology Issues

Alice Etim

INTRODUCTION

The main objective of this chapter is to examine business and computer technology issues that affect African women. The approaches presently utilized by various governments in the development processes have not helped African women. Many of them are economically very poor, even though they are working much harder than ever.

This chapter raises questions about the educational structures and discusses the barriers to building substantial businesses by women. These include inadequacy of funds provided through government-backed lending institutions and commercial banks, women's lack of managerial skills, and their inability to incorporate computer technology into their businesses.

Some African countries have experimented with various programs. In Nigeria for example, the government has implemented the structural adjustment program (SAP), and Work-for-Yourself (WFY) and opened the rural areas for development through the Directorate of Food, Roads, and Rural Infrastructure (DFFRI). This chapter reviews how women have been negatively affected by SAP.

Meaningful development cannot occur without women. Therefore, both the federal and state governments (and the appropriate agencies), together with nongovernmental organizations, should support women in the developmental process. The government should provide funds and training. Banks should reevaluate their lending policies to enable women to have access to bank funds. Banks should move into areas such as participatory equity shares, equipment leasing, specially guaranteed development stock, venture capital, and so on in order to empower women. Women should also use alternative ways such as partnership and cooperatives to generate funds and bring in other people's ideas and computing skills to build their businesses. They should also seek training to build on, and develop, their managerial skills so that their businesses can prosper.

Many African countries are facing critical changes in the political, economic, or social realms. Some have implemented the structural adjustment programs (SAPs) based on the conditions stipulated by such lenders as the International Monetary Fund (IMF), World Bank, and others. These changes affect all facets of women's lives. This chapter examines issues affecting women in the development process in relation to business. In the last twenty years, as a result of the developmental processes that many African countries are going through, the condition for African women has been deteriorating. The chapter begins with a background discussion on education and training as a means of showing that women are not adequately prepared to enter and contribute effectively in these fields of endeavor. It also presents various strategies that women can use to build their businesses. Finally, suggestions are made to help African women incorporate computer technology in their small businesses.

Education and Training

Many social and cultural factors have adversely affected African women's education and training. The fact that a girl is going to be married makes parents very unwilling to spend lots of money in educating her. In many rural areas, traditions favor the girl to sit home and learn from the mother how she can make a good wife. However, it should be noted that, in a changing world, women need formal education so that they can best take care of themselves and their families and contribute to society.

Very few women participate in higher levels of the school system as students, lecturers, and administrators because of the increasing rate of teenage pregnancy, attitude toward women's education, early marriages, parents' literacy level, and parents' income level. Table 10.1 presents data on the distribution of female and male enrollment at the tertiary level of education in 1965 and 1988 based on country group or region in Africa.

Research shows that a growing body of Africans believe that a better-educated mother has fewer and better-educated children. She is productive not only at home but also in the workplace. Education holds the key to women's empowerment because many benefits can come from educating women in all fields. Closing the gender gap in education will equip more women with the skills to succeed in the workplace and build better businesses.

COMPUTING AND TECHNOLOGY

Evans (1995 online) pointed out several barriers to women's technological education:

Table 10.1
Enrollment Rates at the Tertiary Level of Education,
1965 and 1988 (percent)

Country group or region	Females		Males	
	1965	1988	1965	1988
Low-income	0.2	1.1	0.7	2.8
Lower-middle-income	2.1	10.3	3.6	14.1
Upper-middle-income	3.1	15.6	5.9	18.3
Sub-Saharan Africa	0.1	1.1	0.6	3.3
Middle East / North Africa	2.1	11.8	5.6	16.2

Source: Adapted from UNESCO data as presented in King and Hill (1993, 12).
Computer graphics: Melanie Marshall James.

1. Lack of female teachers/assumptions and attitudes of male teachers.
2. Inflexible selection and entry requirements.
3. Often, the student/teacher ratio is large and as such individualized attention is missing for practical skills/laboratory-based work.
4. Male-oriented language and male images in teaching materials.
5. Instrumental pedagogies and curriculum content that ignore the social context of technology.

Based on how society perceives male and female roles, the home, and the family, enormous motivation is given to men to major in computing, science, and technology courses. The few women who go into these fields face excessive pressure from peers, family members, school systems, and the general public. Some of the reasons given earlier support many of the findings by Evans (1995, online: 4) of the problems women encounter as they forge ahead in science and technology. According to Evans: "The 'world wide' problem of low participation in Science Technology (ST) education is compounded by low enrollment rates of girls in formal education, when compared with boys, with the gap widening at the higher level of education."

G. A. Williams, former vice chancellor of the University of Benin, Nigeria, in a paper presented at the Commonwealth conference in 1987 (as reported in Evans 1995) identifies other barriers:

1. Relegation of women to the home;
2. Parental perceptions of costs/benefits of educating girls (affecting mainly low-income families);
3. Double and conflicting demands on girls of traditional and school learning;

4. Masculine image of science and technology as projected by teachers and textbooks; and
5. Poor facilities, including teacher supply, teacher quality, and equipment.

Women's Involvement with Computing and New Technology

It is critical that women get involved in all aspects of computing, if they are not to be left out of the information age. The number of African women in computing and information technology both as students and as workers is small (Table 10.2).

This example of polytechnic enrollment of female students shows very few female students in critical fields such as computer studies, math/statistics, and electrical/electronic engineering when compared to male enrollment in such fields. I revisit this issue after the next section on business to suggest possible ways of incorporating computer technology into women-owned businesses.

BUSINESS

For many Africans, women have the primary role for home management; they raise children, care for elderly family members, and perform household chores. Any economic activity such as owning and managing a business is performed as additional responsibility necessitated by mostly economic survival. Forced to enter the workforce or manage a business, women have less time to spend on developing an idea or a new business when compared to African men.

Despite this primary role for home management, they are economically very active. Iweriebor (1996) sums this by saying that Nigerian and most African women, from time immemorial, have been known to be, first and foremost, economically active. Westernized forms of education, business/managerial training, entrepreneurship development, and so forth have widened opportunities for these women to generate reasonable income.

The general poor economic situation in many African countries has hindered African women's progress in their various economic activities. There have been cutbacks on food subsidies, health care services, and other social services/infrastructures. Women's economic productivity will have to increase to cater to these needs. According to the United Nations (UNICEF 1993):

As Africa sputters through the 1990s, its women will struggle hardest to do more with less: Africa's women have been and continue to be the invisible agents of structural adjustment, doing with less so that others may have more and working harder so that others may profit. Economic planners cannot continue to ignore the needs and concerns of these silent sufferers. (51)

The many structural adjustment programs that have been implemented by almost all African countries have further compounded women's economic problems. Most of these countries have instituted programs that were part and parcel of lending institutions' (e.g., International Monetary Fund [IMF]

Table 10.2
Student Enrollment in Polytechnics by Program, Sex, and Level of Study in Nigeria, 1991/1992 to 1993/1994

FIELD	1991/1992		1992/1993		1993/1994	
	ND	HND	ND	HND	ND	HND
Computer Studies						
male	381	42	1,024	83	1,257	130
female	150	20	486	35	606	63
Elect./Electronics Engr. Technology						
male	2,094	547	2,342	1,100	1,389	329
female	144	34	159	61	132	87
Statistics/Math.						
male	643	198	886	288	1,396	388
female	183	71	357	84	540	125

Source: Adapted from the Federal Government of Nigeria, *Annual Abstract of Statistics* 1995 ed., 172.
Note: ND = national diploma and HND = higher national diploma.
Computer graphics: Melanie Marshall James.

and World Bank) stipulations for advancement of funds to these nations. Nigeria and some other African countries have implemented the structural adjustment program (SAP), which bears the government flag of helping to establish the policy of liberalizing trade so that local producers would compete in the world market. These local producers include women who own small, indigenous businesses. The key question is, How can these small, indigenous business owners (especially women-owned businesses) effectively compete with large producers at home and abroad? Many small, indigenous producers have trades that range from blacksmithing to a small sewing factory. Since these are very small-scale businesses, it has become difficult for them to compete with larger firms. SAP has, therefore, been viewed by many as a destructive tool to the local entrepreneurship.

Ogundipe-Leslie (1996) criticizes SAP on the basis of negative effects that local businesses have experienced, especially women-owned businesses. According to her, SAP has brought about economic impoverishment of Nigerian women because of loss of businesses, and jobs and inaccessibility of education for many girls (192). One major effect has been the devaluation of the Nigerian currency, the naira. Local businesses that depended on foreign experts or materials had to close down because they could no longer afford to pay salaries or raw materials' expenses. Inadvertently, SAP has led to loss of many businesses and unemployment for women.

The structural adjustment program has been a dismal failure primarily because it is a foreign tool that is being implemented in entirely different cultural systems. James (1997, 132) states: "African countries are required by the World Bank to implement structural adjustment programs (SAPs) without careful consideration of the prevailing cultural systems in these countries. The result is that SAPs related conditionalities exacerbate social, economic, and environmental problems." For sustainable development, African countries should modify SAPs to suit their economic, social, political, and cultural conditions. Women and small business owners should have a critical say in the redrafting of policies and procedures for implementing SAPs.

SMALL BUSINESS DEVELOPMENT

In different countries and regions, the term "small business" carries different meanings. Multiple criteria are used to define any small business based on the prevalent conditions in any given country's economy at a specific time period. Variables usually taken into account include number of employees, total assets, annual sales volume the business generates, initial capital outlay, ownership, management styles, and type of industry or trades.

In many parts of Africa, number of employees, type of ownership, and initial capital outlay are usually the key variables used in categorizing a business. Businesses that have 1 to 100 employees are defined as small businesses (First Bank of Nigeria 1986; Lektu 1987; Philip 1987). The types of businesses include peasant farming, poultry, retail trade, fishing, ceramics, metal- and woodwork, handcraft and weaving, tailoring and dressmaking, auto mechanics and repairs, and small-scale subcontracting. These businesses span both rural and urban African communities. With the exception of a few, such as auto mechanics and metalwork, women are deeply involved in all categories of these businesses.

Small-scale businesses perform a significant role in emerging economies. A young economy leaves open doors and bountiful opportunities for small businesses. Increased awareness of this importance, education, and per capita income generally lead to a high demand for goods and services that are better serviced by small business units.

The importance of small businesses includes:

1. Rapid employment generation;
2. Maintaining a means of entry for new, indigenous entrepreneurship, especially in the countryside;
3. Accelerating rural development and contributing to stemming urban immigration;
4. Establishing links between agricultural and other industrial sectors;
5. Improving the welfare and economic lives of women and their families;
6. Production of raw materials or semifinished goods and essential source of specialists to larger firms; and

7. Providing assistance toward the development of local technology and innovation.

THE CASE OF NIGERIA

In Nigeria, Ihyiambe (1986) explained that the greatest landmark achievement the government of Nigeria has made lay in the establishment of the Nigerian Bank for Commerce and Industry (NBCI). This government-owned financial institution has a main objective of catering to the financing needs of small businesses.

Nigerian women are core participants in small businesses such as trading, farming, contracting, cloth making, and so on. These women face a common problem: they lack finances to build their businesses to satisfactory levels that will allow them to compete effectively with one another or with foreign-owned businesses. Although the federal government of Nigeria and various state governments have allotted large sums of money in the successive national development plans and other loan schemes for the development of small businesses, participation of women in obtaining such funds has been negligible.

Commercial banks could have been the alternative source of funds for women loan applicants. However, in my work in the Lion Bank of Jos, Nigeria, I observed that most women who applied for loans never got beyond the first screening. In a study at the University of Jos in 1987, I found out that the women business owners who had applied for bank loans, when interviewed, perceived that they were not given loans for the following reasons:

1. Failure to produce a good feasibility project.
2. Lack of managerial skills.
3. Lack of collateral.

Failure to Produce a Good Feasibility Project

Many African women entrepreneurs usually start small. They often start on the frontage of their homes or in kiosks usually located at the market square. Their businesses lack proper organizational structure and forecast projection that commercial banks and other creditors require in order to provide funds. Since many of these women entrepreneurs lack adequate accounting/managerial skills, it is difficult for them to write good project proposals and feasibility studies. With little or no funds, it is also hard to employ the services of professionals such as accountants or business consultants to write the feasibility studies that will enable them to obtain commercial bank loans. Creditors view them as poor credit risks and candidates likely to default on their loans.

Lack of Managerial Skills

Many women do not have the essential skills to manage their businesses because of limited education and lack of managerial training. For any entrepreneurial success, one has to learn basic skills of managing the human and physical resources at her disposal. Since many of the women business owners/managers have less formal business education, they rely mainly on trial-and-error methods of management, gut feeling, and advice from family members and friends. The consequence of this is that there are no proper planning, organizing, coordinating, and controlling of the business enterprise. Moreover, many of these women lack computer skills that could be used to help manage the business. Financial analysis, forecasting, and record keeping on the computer are a few of the processes that small businesses can utilize to assist in effective decision making. Improper record keeping jeopardizes their ability to obtain credit facilities from financial institutions or to disburse them judiciously and profitably.

Lack of Collateral

Commercial banks in Nigeria require that a loan applicant present some assets that will be used as guaranty for any funds advanced to the applicant. Many of these women-owned businesses are unable to provide adequate collateral. They are denied credit by commercial and merchant banks despite the fact that the Central Bank of Nigeria's credit guidelines to these banks since 1980 stipulate that at least 16 percent of bank loans and advances should be reserved exclusively for small businesses and women-owned businesses. These commercial and merchant banks still prefer to pay penalties for noncompliance rather than incur what they regard as high losses or bad and doubtful debts as a result of funding these small businesses. Table 10.3 shows the relative low level of credit granted to small businesses, including women-owned businesses.

Table 10.3
Loans and Advances to Small Businesses, Including Women-Owned Businesses by the Banking Sector (in millions of Naira)

	1980	1981	1982	1983	1984	1985	1986
I. Aggregate Loans and Advances to All Businesses	64	86	100	110	115	121	57
II. Aggregate Loans and Advances to Small-Scale Businesses	1.13	1.85	2.06	3.51	7.05	9.72	1.45

Source: Adapted from Central Bank of Nigeria in Philip (1987, 3).
Computer graphics: Melanie Marshall James.

Lack of Major Infrastructure

Even though this is not one of the conditions commercial banks use to deny credit to women-owned businesses, it is a major problem that continues to affect small businesses, especially those located in rural areas. Lack of facilities and infrastructure such as regular power supply, motorable roads, constant water supply, buildings, and so on have contributed to the slow pace of business development, especially women-owned businesses. Inadequate continuing education facilities, poor medical facilities/services, and lack of communication tools have also hampered the effectiveness of women-owned businesses.

SOURCES OF FINANCE FOR AFRICAN WOMEN-OWNED BUSINESSES

Following from the last section and the information provided in Table 10.3, it is clear that women-owned businesses receive very little financial assistance or loans from the government and banks. This section explains three other alternative sources of funding for these businesses.

1. *Personal and family funds.* Many African women-owned businesses rely on personal savings and gifts from family members. Some women will work for other people, government, and larger businesses and build savings through them. As soon as they have enough capital, they open their businesses.
2. *Cooperative Thrift Society (Etibe or Esusu Contributions).* Many women have an alternative source of funds using local cooperative thrift societies. These thrift societies bear different names depending on what part of Africa one is considering. In southeastern Nigeria, among the Ibibio, it is called *Etibe* or *Nka-Iban-Utom.* Among the Igbo it is called *Esusu.* Most of these thrift societies share common goals, generate funds, share business ideas, build business acumen, build a network, and market their goods/services. The women may have different backgrounds, but most of them in a particular society will have a similar background. They meet weekly in either a set location or in a member's house to discuss issues and pay their weekly dues. At the end of the meeting, all the funds collected for that day are given to one of the members.

   Such funds can be used for new start-ups, renovation, business expansion, purchase of equipment, and so on. Rarely will such funds be used for direct purchase of food. These women recognize such funds as set-aside funds or savings. If the money a member gets is not enough, she will save it until it's her turn again. Every time a member "carries the funds," it is an add-on capital for major business investments. In addition to catering to their business/economic needs, these thrift societies provide social responsibilities such as helping members' families in crisis situations and assisting in community projects.
3. *Credit from local moneylenders.* A few individuals provide loans to highly enterprising women to assist them to start their businesses. These lenders are substitutes for commercial lenders such as banks; their interest charges are very low.

RECOMMENDATIONS

Education and Training

African women should be viewed as active participants in the development process. They are economically very active. Many African women are petty traders usually nicknamed "market women." These women must do more than petty trading to make an impact in this technology and information era. From the outset, girls should be encouraged like boys to appreciate technical fields and major in computer science or related fields. Both private and public schools should provide facilities for computer and technology education from the elementary school level to colleges and universities.

Government development projects should target women to train and retrain them to become more effective as business owners and as workers. Providing training and access to resources for self-employment and entrepreneurship will enable women to achieve economic progress.

Mentoring

Women who are already in technical fields should work with those who are new entrants. These mentors play a significant role to increase the number of women who remain in such fields as computer science, engineering, and other technological areas. College and university students in technology education should be allowed to participate as mentors in the local elementary and secondary schools.

Finance

Government Support. Though the various African governments have supported the small business sector, many women in this sector operate with little or no government support. Government should target women-owned businesses and provide adequate funding to assist them. In Nigeria, for example, the apex lending institution to small businesses, National Bank for Credit and Industry (NBCI), should ensure that funds distribution is equitable for businesses owned and operated by both men and women. Modalities should also be developed to prevent bureaucratic red tape, fraud, and abuse of the funds disbursed.

Bank Lending to Women-Owned Businesses. Women who already own businesses and those aspiring to own one should be supported financially by banks. This will help to build businesses that can compete effectively and generate employment opportunities. As discussed in the business section of this chapter, there are several hindrances to women-owned businesses. Finance is a major impediment to business development. Banks need to review their lending policies so that women can have access to bank funds to develop their businesses.

Participatory equity shares, equipment leasing, specially guaranteed development stocks, and venture capital are some options that banks can use to extend funds to women-owned businesses. Given the fact that some women have no collateral and are new in business, there are risks involved in lending money to them. Banks and other lenders can monitor funds usage and repayment by developing a repayment plan for each creditor, providing free supervision, workshops, and ideas to assist women in the effective financial management of the business. Banks should be willing to establish branches in rural communities in order to reach the women whose businesses are located in these areas.

Computer Usage

Computer usage is in its infancy in Africa. Women-owned businesses fit into such categories as peasant farming, poultry, retail trade, fishing, ceramics, metal- and woodworking, handicraft and weaving, tailoring and dressmaking, auto mechanics and repairs, and small-scale subcontracting. Owners and personnel of these businesses can use computers for inputting and processing daily financial transactions, record keeping, forecasting trends, building models, communication, information retrieval, monitoring market forces, and so on.

Computer usage may seem unattainable to these businesses. They face the high cost of computers, lack of trained computer personnel, erratic electricity supply, and a wide spectrum of other problems. Certainly, it will take commitment of major funds to embark on computer usage. Some options for these women-owned businesses might include:

1. Bank loans and government financial packages to include adequate funds for purchasing computers, and training personnel to use these computers in the businesses.
2. Government to open small business development centers in the universities or polytechnics. Such centers will provide training needs, including how to incorporate technology in the daily operation of these businesses.
3. Government agencies such as NBCI and the small business development centers to train personnel who will serve as consultants to small businesses, including women-owned businesses, particularly in computer technology issues. Government should make it mandatory that any small business will provide at least one person to be trained and supervised in computer usage.

Women Need to Embrace Joint Business Ownership

Partnerships and cooperative societies hold great potential for African women in business. African businesswomen need to embark on partnerships/ cooperatives with family members or friends who can contribute to building equity capital or bringing in managerial, computing, or some other crucial skills to the business. Currently, some of the women-owned businesses use the services provided by family members. Women should go beyond just employing additional unskilled or semiskilled family members to building businesses with partners who can help such businesses to grow. With the help of a legal professional or the local court, the partners can have the articles of partnership carefully written to protect each partner and to clearly define such sensitive issues as equity capital contribution, profit sharing, limited liability, management, death or illhealth of a partner, and so on.

CONCLUSION

African women have made very significant contributions to the continent's economic, social, and political development through different avenues and channels. In this chapter, we have emphasized the fact that they can contribute using their business acumen and entrepreneurship skills. Computer technology, if incorporated into African women-owned businesses, will not only enhance these women's skills but allow for better generation of information. There are different ways of using computers to generate and manage information. I recommend that women could lease with the libraries, banks, university centers for economic development, and other resource institutions available in their community, which could help them learn about computer systems, retrieving information, storing information, and managing files in the computer. The American Association for the Advancement of Science (1992) in a study on Computer and CD-ROM capability in Africa recommended that CD-ROM technology be used by libraries in Africa to store large amounts of data/information for use by scholars and researchers. Libraries should ensure that some of the CD-ROM have information tailored to small businesses so that women entrepreneurs could access such information. This way, the women business owners and managers will have quick access to accurate, timely, and organized data for efficient business management. Moreover, where possible, women entrepreneurs should lease with the resource institutions mentioned before for training through classes, workshops, and technical assistance to develop their computer and business skills. This way, women can continue to grow in skills development, which will enable them to continue to contribute to the development of the continent. The feminization of the development process in Africa is, indeed, a task that will help build a stronger Africa.

REFERENCES

American Association for the Advancement of Science. 1992. *Computer and CD-ROM Capability in Sub-Saharan African University and Research Libraries.* Washington D.C. American Association for the Advancement of Science (AAAS).

Cottrell, Janet. 1992. "I'm a Stranger Here Myself: A Consideration of Women in Computing." In *Learning from the Past, Stepping into the Future,* the Proceedings of the 1992 ACM SIGUCCS User Services Conference, November 8-11, 1992, Cleveland, OH. New York: Association for Computing Machinery, 71-76.

Etim, Alice. 1988. "Bank Financing of Small Scale Industries: The Experience of First Bank of Nigeria, Jos Metropolis and Its Environs." Unpublished thesis, University of Jos, Nigeria, 45-49.

Evans, Karen. 1995. "The Commonwealth of Learning: Barriers to Participation of Women in Technology Education and the Role of Distance Education." Online (Internet) http://www.col.org/O/html.barriers.htm, 1-5.

Federal Government of Nigeria. 1995. *Annual Abstract of Statistics*. Lagos, Nigeria: Federal Government Printer.

First Bank of Nigeria. 1986. "The Impact of the Second Tier Foreign Exchange Market on Small Business." *First Bank of Nigeria Business and Economic Report*. Lagos, Nigeria: First Bank of Nigeria, 4.

Ihyiambe, R. H. 1986. "Problems of Small Scale Industrial Development in Nigeria—Can Solutions Be Found?" Workshop on Entrepreneurship Development, National Bank of Commerce and Industry (NBCI), Lagos, Nigeria, 10-15.

Iweriebor, Ifeyinwa. 1996. "Boosting Female Education." *West Africa* (March 4-10): 349.

James, Valentine U. 1997. "Operationalizing Concepts of Sustainable Development in Africa." *21st Century Policy Review: An American, Caribbean and African Forum* (Fall 1996-Winter 1997): 132-33.

King, Elizabeth M., and M. Anne Hill. 1993. "Women's Education in Developing Countries: An Overview." *Women's Education in Developing Countries: Barriers, Benefits and Policies*. Baltimore: Johns Hopkins University Press for World Bank, 11-13.

Lektu, J. D. 1987. "The Role of Small Businesses in Economic Development." Workshop paper on Small Scale Industries, University of Jos, Nigeria, 14.

Ogundipe-Leslie, Molara. 1996. *Recreating Ourselves: African Women and Critical Transformations*. Trenton, NJ: Africa World Press, 190-92.

Philip, O. 1987. "Promoting Small Scale Industries through Government Policies." Conference Paper on Small Scale Industries and the Development of Nigeria, Nigeria Institute of Social and Economic Research, Ibadan, 2-5.

Shade, Leslie R. 1993. "Gender Issues in Computer Networking." Online (Internet) Community. Networking: International Free-Net Conference, August 17-19, 1-14. http://www.mit.edu:8001/people/sorokin/women/lrs.html

UNICEF. 1993. "Challenges for Children and Women in the 1990s: Eastern and Southern Africa" in *Profile*. Nairobi, Kenya: UNICEF Eastern and Southern African Regional Office, 51.

11

Women in the Mobilization and Allocation of Household Savings in Developing Countries: Promoting Interlinks between Women's Indigenous Savings Groups and Community Banks in Nigeria

Noble J. Nweze

INTRODUCTION

Women in developing countries play vital and evolving roles as food producers, processors, and marketers. As men migrate off the farm due to mounting demographic pressure on land, decreasing soil fertility, and increasing rural poverty, agricultural activities are becoming increasingly "feminized." Yet, statistics from studies in developing countries in general and Nigeria in particular indicate that, in spite of growing recognition of the effect of improved inputs and new technology on output levels, which have given rise to increased demand for credit, women still have little access to formal finance. Erroneously, leaders of institutional credit assume that rural producers are men and that the rural household is always a single economic unit with common production goals, resources, and benefits (Saito and Spurling 1992).

As an alternative, therefore, there is an increasing tendency for women to depend on informal credit sources, which abound in rural areas. They are popular with rural women (Nweze 1991) and demonstrate women's propensity to save (Geertz 1962; March and Taggo 1986). However, most forms of informal credit are fraught with problems. They also tend to be distant from the more modern and larger financial markets and have only a limited capacity to provide credit (Saito and Spurling 1992). It has also been observed that as long as women rely solely on informal markets, they will continue to remain outside the economic mainstream (Berger 1989).

This chapter attempts to highlight the credit problems of women in Nigeria in light of the substantial upswing in rural financial services. It critically examines the functioning of women's traditional savings groups and the prospects of establishing a link between them and the formal financial sector.

AGRICULTURAL CREDIT IN NIGERIA

Credit is a scarce commodity in rural areas of Nigeria. This is evidenced by the fact that moneylenders in the informal sector charge about 90 percent or more in interest, leading to chronic indebtedness of the small farmers (Miller 1977; Ihimodu 1986). To ameliorate this situation, successive Nigerian governments have attempted to bridge the credit gap in the rural sector. This ambition is indicated in successive national development plans and other official documents and encapsulated in the following specific objectives:

1. To facilitate the flow of credit to farmers to enable them to adopt improved farming techniques;
2. To internalize some activities in informal credit markets to minimize exploitation of farmers while sourcing credit;
3. To ensure flow of adequate funds from banks and other financial institutions; and
4. To assist banks to aggressively support agriculture through minimization of some risks and moderate costs involved in lending.

To accomplish these stated objectives, government has focused on the following policy measures: (1) credit allocation and rationing, (2) establishment of new financial institutions, and (3) special credit schemes and funds.

Credit Allocation and Rationing

This is a "supply-led" strategy based on the assumption that rapid expansion in the supply of financial resources to the "preferred" sector, combined with concessionary interest rates and credit rationing, can be employed to accelerate the pace of rural development. By this approach the federal government requires commercial banks to lend a prescribed percentage of their loan portfolio to the farmers and agroindustrialists. For instance, in 1980, commercial banks and merchant banks were directed to lend a minimum of 44 and 46 percent of their total loan portfolio to agricultural production and manufacturing (including agro-allied industries), respectively. This rose to 47 and 50 percent in 1985 and 1990, respectively. In 1994, the two banks were required to lend a minimum of 60 and 58 percent of their total loan portfolio to agricultural and industrial production, respectively (Evbuomwan et al. 1993).

Concessionary interest rate granted to the agricultural sector was another credit policy measure adopted by the federal government prior to interest rate deregulation in 1987. For instance, in 1980, the rate of lending to the agricultural sector was 7.5 percent, while in 1985 it stood at between 8 and 9 percent.

Establishment of New Financial Institutions

During the past three decades or more, a variety of rural banking has been promoted by the federal government as a reaction to the fundamental inadequacy of banking facilities in the rural areas. For instance, the first of its kind, the rural banking scheme, was based on a financial review committee report that recommended that the government compel commercial banks to open branches in rural areas (Okigbo 1976). As of June 1992, 765 of the 766 branches stipulated by the Central Bank of Nigeria (CBN) had been opened. An additional directive was that not less than 60 percent of the deposits mobilized from the rural areas was to be advanced as credit to rural borrowers.

In spite of the laudable objectives of the rural banking scheme, it is on record that nearly two decades after its establishment, there are clear indications that the problems and issues that led to the plan's being put in place are still prevalent. These include a low level of rural savings mobilization, inadequate use of banking services, and the lack of credit for rural people (Okorie 1986, 1990; Ewulu 1986).

Government also established the Nigerian Agricultural and Cooperative Bank (NACB) in 1972 to provide loans to agricultural enterprises. Available data show a quantum leap in the amount disbursed by the bank, from N28.6 million in 1980 to about N4,715.5 million in 1992. Correspondingly, the number of projects financed rose from 66 in 1980 to 463,526 in 1993. According to the CBN "Annual Report and Statement of Accounts" (1993), credit disbursed for on-lending purposes continued to account for about a third of the total, with on-lending for production taking the highest share of 27.3 percent in 1993. In the same year under review, the dominance of direct credit with respect to projects under the smallholder scheme was sustained.

The on-lending schemes of NACB are expected to channel credit to small farmers who cannot borrow directly from the bank. However, such schemes have not been successful with the smallholder farmers in general and women in particular, as is evident from the fact that less than 30 percent of the total NACB loans are in favor of such schemes.

The Agricultural Credit Guarantee Scheme (ACGSF)

In response to the commercial banks' lack of interest in financing agriculture, CBN established in 1977 the ACGSF for the purpose of providing guarantees for loans granted by commercial banks to the agricultural sector. The objective was to increase the level of bank credit to the sector by reducing commercial banks' fear of indebtedness of farmers (Ihimodu 1986).

The extent of liability of the fund in regard to guaranteed loans was 75 percent of the value of principal and interest outstanding, to a maximum of Naira (N) 100,000.00 to an individual farmer and N1.0 million to a cooperative society (corporate body). The number and value of loans guaranteed in the first three years (1978-1980) of its operation were 3,686 loans amounting to about N111.47 million, in all the states. Between 1980 and 1993, the number and value of loans guaranteed under the scheme stood at 180,782 in number of loans and 975.1 million naira, respectively.

A critical appraisal of the ACGSF has revealed the inherent weakness of the program—concentration on the recovery aspect of agricultural advances and less emphasis on the intractable difficulties encountered in reaching numerous smallholders scattered all over the agricultural scene.

AGRICULTURAL CREDIT: HOW DO WOMEN COUNT?

The observance of 1975 as International Women's Year and the period 1976 to 1985 as the United Nations' Decade for Women have generated a high level of interest in all aspects of the condition of women and their role in the economic upliftment of rural life (Okonjo 1991). Yet agricultural programs in developing countries are still being designed and implemented on the assumption that every farm manager and decision maker is a man. This is no longer a valid assumption. Available evidence reveals that women constitute a vital force in agriculture in the developing world and account for 70 to 80 percent of household food production in Sub-Saharan Africa, 65 percent in Asia, and 45 percent in Latin America and the Caribbean. As men continuously migrate to urban centers in search of greener pastures, women's role as agricultural decision makers is being strengthened (Saito and Spurling 1992).

In Nigeria, women constitute about 70 percent of the rural dwellers and about 50.4 percent of the population. Although statistics on women's participation in various types of economic activity are difficult to quantify, it is obvious that in addition to household management and care, rural women are engaged in agricultural production, processing, and marketing. Women are also engaged in small-scale animal production. Contrary to traditional views that smallholder agriculture is dominated by male farmers, while women (wives) serve as helping hands, it is now known that some women function as farmers in their own right, as well as heads of their respective households (Adeyokunnu 1975). Women in this category include

1. Widows (especially the relatively younger ones) who have lost their husbands and are therefore left with the responsibility of caring for their children. Statistics are not available with respect to the number of widows residing in rural areas. Past and current (1991) censuses categorized population figures based on sex and age, thereby ignoring the vital statistics on widowhood.
2. Divorced mothers who have been granted custody of the children by law courts. There is also no documentation concerning this category.
3. Women abandoned by their husbands and now bearing the responsibility of child care.
4. Single mothers who bear children out of wedlock. It is expected that this category of women will constitute the least in number due to traditional sanctions and family opprobrium.
5. Unmarried women living among kinsmen, who have lost any hope of marriage.

The farm characteristics of these categories of women (including those living with their husbands) are of significance to agricultural credit and extension. They almost always share the same production characteristics as the men but have limited access to land, production credit, and other farm inputs such as fertilizer and agrochemicals. Whatever usufruct right may have been in any part of the country, the customary land rights do not allow women to own land. Since, in most cases, title to land is the required collateral for obtaining credit from formal lending institutions, the lack of title discourages women's participation in agricultural credit services.

Smith and Stevens (1988) note, with reference to Tanzania, that "control over adequate land is the basis for food security and for the accumulation of capital through farm expansion and cash crop production" and that "female household heads, because of land deprivation, are able to secure neither a truly reliable food supply nor the expansion of their productive capacity."

A recent study that appraised the farm characteristics and economic status of female-headed households in Nigeria (Nweze 1991) also highlights the smallness of holdings cultivated by female-headed households, which averaged less than one hectare (1 ha). In the case of widows, customary laws give preference for land inheritance rights to their adult male children, who may wish to use land for purposes other than farming.

The study cites land restrictions as a major constraint in providing credit to female farmers, especially those who do not have husbands to stand for them. This leaves the women with inadequate capital with which to invest in food production, expand their enterprises, or take full advantage of seasonal price variation and better bargaining power.

Women smallholders are constrained by credit problems from both formal and informal sources. From the informal sources, the problems relate to scarce, unreliable, and expensive loans (Ihimodu 1986). Even village moneylenders are reluctant to lend to women for the simple reason that they do not have land tenure or title to land that could be pledged as collateral. In some places, widows were found to borrow by proxy. This is likely to be a common cause of double indebtedness and extortion. Since women's credit needs are not necessarily high, most moneylenders prefer to lend higher sums to male farmers in order to ensure higher interest rates and to cover costs.

From the formal or institutional sources, the problems have to do with the insensitivity of commercial banks and allied institutions to the plight of women producers. In spite of the emergence of many rural credit programs and other cosmetic and ephemeral women's programs, the de facto situation is that women have little or no access to formal credit. The terms and conditions for advances both for the NACB and commercial banks under the ACGSF are not in favor of women smallholder farmers. Both place undue significance on the security that a borrower can offer and thereby support the traditional form of security-oriented banking. Since women smallholder farmers find it difficult to obtain certificates of occupancy, and many do not hold titles to land and may have no other movable assets to charge in favor of banks, they rarely succeed in getting loans (Ijere 1986).

With respect to NACB in particular, Ijere notes that

the farmers who have tasted the bureaucratic procedures of the Bank have not found the experience pleasant and hence they regard the NACB as a poor substitute for commercial banks. Their experience can be said to be justified having regard to the fact that, so far, most of the loans advanced by NACB have been in favour of the big borrowers who alone can offer good security. (11)

The fact remains that neither the NACB nor any other institutional source has simplified lending procedures to suit women small holder farmers at their present literacy level.

Evidence abounds that point to many innovative credit programs that have demonstrated that institutional credit can still be made to reach the poor, including women farmers, without compromising the source's financial discipline or institutional viability. Specifically, rural credit programs such as the Grameen Bank of Bangladesh, SEWA in India, and Badan Kredit Kecamatan in Indonesia are relevant reference points. Local authorities may have to study these success stories for possible adaptations or search for some alternative methods of agricultural finance that will take care of the special needs of the various categories of women smallholders.

THE INFORMAL CREDIT MARKET

Because rural women do not have access to institutional credit, they tend to rely increasingly on a myriad of noninstitutional sources. By noninstitutional sources is meant the whole array of informal savings and credit arrangements and traditional institutions, which may differ in structure, organization, and management, and are not usually registered but occupy a preeminent position by filling the gap created by the near absence of a formal financial market in rural areas.

The noninstitutional financial market in Nigeria can be broadly categorized into two major sectors: (1) traditional moneylenders and (2) traditional systems of group savings and credit administration. We now consider the second category, focusing our attention on the forms that are most widespread and popular among rural women.

Traditional Savings and Credit Groups

In further classification of traditional savings and credit groups, it is necessary to apply the methodology that identifies traditional groups according to what they do rather than what they are called. This is because in Nigeria in particular and Africa in general, evidence abounds to show that traditional associations with nominally different appellations perform similar functions

(Ardener 1964; Bratton 1986). Following this procedure, therefore, we can pinpoint the following four major types of women's traditional associations with savings and credit functions:

1. *Rotating savings groups.* Rotating savings groups are popular among rural women. In this variant of financial self-help, each participant contributes to a common fund, which is then handed over to each member in rotation. The cycle ends when every member has taken a turn. By affording participants the opportunity to save, it functions like a bank.
2. *Rotating savings and credit groups.* Rotating savings and credit groups differ from rotating savings groups because part of the fund (never all), is put in a general fund for loans to needy members.
3. *Nonrotating savings groups.* Nonrotating savings groups function like a savings bank, with each member contributing a predetermined or variable amount at regular intervals, and the total sum is kept with the treasurer or, in a few cases, deposited in a bank, At the end of the cycle, the fund is paid back to each participant. Lending is not apparent in this type.
4. *Nonrotating savings and credit groups.* These function like nonrotating savings groups but with an additional function: the funds generated from other sources like fees, fines, and levies are put into a fund that may be utilized for purposes of loans and other financial services to members.

How Women's Traditional Savings and Credit Groups Function

A typical women's traditional savings and credit group is made up of participants united by ties of family and marriage, by residing in the same location, by belonging to the same religious or ethnic group, or by the same age grade, farming system, or trade, for the purpose of contributing fixed or variable sums of money at regular intervals to meet members' various needs.

Two types of membership are normally found among the women's groups investigated: *open* and *restricted* membership. Membership of a restricted group may be based on one or more criteria, of which the following have been found: age, sex, kinship, occupation, and marital and social status. Open or unrestricted groups usually have larger membership of up to 200 participants.

The leadership committee comprises the chairperson, or president, a secretary, and a treasurer. In others, financial secretaries are required to assist the treasurer, while the less formal groups usually have a president and another leader who doubles as a treasurer and a financial secretary.

A typical group meets weekly or monthly, especially on Sundays (exceptionally, on Saturdays). Attendance at meetings is mandatory. On the occasion of the meetings every member is expected to deposit some amount, which varies from group to group (from N5 to N200) and may even be higher in urban-based groups patronized by traders. Compulsory regular contribution of cash is a permanent feature of all the associations. In some associations, members could make multiple contributions that would permit such members to receive the funds accordingly. There is usually a positive correlation between the amount of group savings, membership size, and economic status of members.

The importance of savings in these financial self-help groups could be gleaned from the level of savings generated from their activities. The savings potential of twenty-three women's financial self-help groups was investigated in Nigeria. The findings reveal that for the twenty-three groups surveyed, there were over 5,800 members with a total monthly contribution of N69,600. The average woman/month contribution amounted to N12. Interestingly enough, there was a yearly increase in the amount of savings accumulated by the surveyed groups due to yearly increases in membership size and the amount of contributions per participant.

Interestingly also, the total turnover of funds over the life of the twenty-three groups amounted to N4,176,000, which is an average saving of N18,1565.2 per group in a span of five years. These estimates could exceed the average savings generated by newly established community banks in some rural communities of Nigeria.

The survey revealed, with reference to the sources of members' cash payments, an overwhelming reliance on farm sales, which points to the significance of the savings and credit associations in mobilizing excess cash from productive sources. A noteworthy consideration is the belief by the participants that they save more than they would if they saved in a solitary fashion. This has to do with the discipline of having to meet regularly with the rest of the group and making a compulsory deposit (Miracle et al. 1980).

The groups have bylaws (usually written) establishing penalties for lateness, stealing, fighting, gossiping, and default in payment which attracts the highest fine of up to fifty naira (N50). This is so because regular contributions by all are the foundation of all financial self-help activities. Ardener (1964) wrote that fulfilling this financial commitment is a solemn duty that must be performed, even at the expense of other obligations.

The rules by which groups with rotating funds operate may vary in some cases, while in others they are found to be similar. In most groups studied, the contributions rotate at each monthly meeting, implying that each participant contributes to a fund that is handed over to one member each time the group meets. The right to the fund rotates until every participant has received her turn. In some cases, the order of rotation is determined by the leader or president, who is usually given the privilege of being the first to collect. In a few others, members who are adjudged financial risks usually attract fewer contributions from members. Such less creditworthy participants will, in turn, reciprocate in each case with the exact amount. The decision about the order of rotation could be reached on the basis of individual needs or by age, in which case the oldest member receives first, and the youngest, last. To obviate the problem of infighting, the order in which individuals receive the collective deposit is sometimes altered at the beginning of a new cycle. In such a situation, participants expect, in the long run, to have an average favorable position in the orders of rotation.

It is also possible for a member to arrange for her right to receive a fund in the future to be transferred to another person. This concession is common in associations with large membership, with the result that a participant may have to wait a long time before her turn comes. A participant who needs money for an urgent purpose may have to swap positions with another whose turn is imminent. It is also possible for a needy member to borrow from someone (not necessarily a member) to whom she transfers her right to her fund in settlement. Such a borrower continues to pay her contributions to the group only to allow the lender to collect the fund when her fund becomes due.

Generally, providing credit is a significant function of women's traditional savings groups. This is so because the lack of funds has been identified as a common problem to most of the groups. Thus, a considerable proportion of the funds generated is neither hoarded nor lodged in the bank but lent out to needy members. With respect to loans, our survey revealed that 83 loans were made by twenty-six associations totaling N9,420 or an average of N111.3, while in 1987, 143 loans were made totaling N12,790 or an average of N89.4. The corresponding data for 1988 were 201 loans totaling N19,498 or an average of N97.

In evaluating the performance of a credit system, it is not enough merely to know whether or not credit is available. We must also inquire into the terms and conditions to which the borrower is subjected before she obtains credit. The rate of interest charged is of major concern. So are length of time of loan, repayment plan, security required, timeliness of loan in relation to purpose, and adequacy of loan.

With respect to cost of borrowing, our data showed that the rates are high compared with the ongoing market rate of 18-20 percent and reflect the general scarcity of funds. When compared with private moneylenders' rates of 100 percent or more, the rates could, however, be considered moderate. Loans were for durations ranging from one month to twelve months or slightly more, pointing to the general short-term nature of the loans from the informal source. The majority of the loans were received during the months of January to June, which correspond with the planting season. As expected, too, the due dates for the majority of the loans came after the peak harvest period of September to December, when cash is available from sales of most crops. This period also corresponds with the end of a cycle in most groups, with the result that borrowers strive to repay their loans before the end of cycle. Apparently, such loans made early in the year and due later in the year often lead to inadequacy of loanable funds in women's traditional savings groups.

Deserving attention, too, is the seasonality of production loan demand and repayment in groups with "rotating" funds. Since the position of a participant in the order of rotation in associations with rotating funds determines the month of the year one receives the fund, it is possible that one's position may be such that she gets the fund "off-season" unless she intends to use the money for purposes other than agriculture. As shown earlier in this chapter, participants who need the fund before their turn could pay a specific amount for the privilege and could therefore use the fund when needed.

Repayment of the entire loan amount along with the interest when the loan is due is provided for in many instances, while in others, interest payments on loans were collected at different times. In a few others, provision is made for monthly installment payments.

The security for loans is usually the savings of the borrower plus those of at least one member whom she can persuade to act as a guarantor.

Use of Informal Credit

From an investigation concerning the use to which the fund is put by the beneficiary, the following emerged. A large proportion of informal credit is probably put to productive uses (farm and nonfarm), while part is spent on consumption and durable goods. Farm-related expenditure accounted for more than one-third of the total expenditure. Particularly noteworthy in farm-related expenditure is the use of funds to hire farm labor. This constituted the largest single use, judged by either the proportion of savings spent on it or either the average amount or the number of respondents who used the funds for farm labor.

Nonfarm use probably accounts for a smaller proportion of the total fund received by beneficiaries. Out of this, investment in human capital (children's school fees) topped the list, indicating the value members placed on their children's education. Following this is the use of funds to pay medical expenses and trading.

Consumer orientation cannot be ignored regarding use of informal credit as a considerable proportion of funds accumulated by members through their associations and probably channeled into consumables and durables. In this category, food and clothes top the list, while social expenses are also significant. Although household items such as sewing machines and bicycles are classified as consumption and household durables, it is common knowledge that these items could be used partially or entirely to earn income.

An important observation concerning the use of credit is that the major part of the fund is usually invested in the member's professional activity. For instance, a test of the relation of farming status to the proportion of funds used for agricultural purposes lent credence to this. Cases are also reported of winnings being used to start a business (e.g., start a shop, purchase a grinding machine). The reason for this is not far-fetched: these financial self-help groups are predominant in areas (mostly rural) with severe scarcity of credit. It follows that savings are channeled not only into consumables but also into productive activities.

Distinguishing Factors

We shall now examine what seem to be the distinguishing factors behind the popularity among rural women of these self-help groups and why preference is given to them with regard to the formal financial system.

These appear to be:

1. The ease with which participants could borrow funds rather than travel far to seek loans;
2. Absence of complex loan transactions.
3. Opportunities to save more than would have been possible if participants saved privately.
4. Possibility of making small deposits in a manner not acceptable to most formal institutions, thus making it possible to accumulate lump sums.
5. Timeliness in granting loans.
6. Low transaction costs compared to formal sector financial institutions.
7. Low default rate due to the application of effective rules and regulations within a sociocultural frame.
8. Less rigid, more flexible than institutional financial system and usually adapted to prevailing socioeconomic conditions in each locality where they are practiced. Flexibility is very evident from the way in which savings and credit are combined with other activities, as in labor exchange, work groups, and group investments.
9. Represent a multifaceted institution where the socioeconomic functions, the traditional and the modern, are tightly linked and interdependent. The organization and member initiative of such associations are well grounded in the indigenous culture, with the result that economic functions revolve around the traditional social structure, and the high standard of morality in economic activities is accounted for by the well-integrated norms of the social reality (Soen and de Comarmond 1972).
10. The invocation of traditional sanctions to discipline erring members and the expulsion of dubious participants through recognized traditional procedures.
11. Based on common ownership and mutual aid, they are usually set up with a goal and strategy for achieving the established objectives for the mutual benefits of members.
12. Through the strong sense of fellowship they engender, each member realizes the immediate benefit by the joint effort.
13. Exceedingly ubiquitous and favored by all classes of rural workers, age grades, and professions, thus making a greater impact than has been possible through modern forms of credit cooperatives that satisfy the requirements of a comparatively few members.

It follows from the preceding that the possibilities of growth and expansion of the women's savings groups are immense, as they can still develop into more beneficial economic ventures that will further enhance the welfare of members. They leave no one in doubt as to their capability to further tap the savings of their members and the desire for utilizing additional savings and credit for investment in agriculture and other productive activities.

Of relevance also is the eagerness of the women to receive additional loans from their groups, which they considered the most convenient source of credit. An obstacle to these, however, is that, although these traditional savings and credit associations are veritable sources of financial relief to members, the volume of savings and credit does not yield large sums of money to afford sufficient credit to participants. This implies that for these groups to be relied upon in far-reaching development processes, they must not be allowed to operate completely outside the formal financial sector.

INTERLINKS BETWEEN FORMAL AND INFORMAL FINANCIAL INSTITUTIONS

There is an emerging groundswell of opinion about linking formal and informal institutions in developing countries. This is based on the premise that informal credit institutions cannot cope with realities of contemporary societies if they function apart from formal institutions. For instance, in 1984, the Third International Symposium on the Mobilization of Personal Savings in Developing Countries, organized by United Nations, agreed, inter alia, (1) that linkages between formal and informal financial institutions seem to be more promising than separate development and (2) that the means of improving the performance of the noninstitutional sector were policies directed to enhancing its links with the institutional financial sector (UN 1986: 13). Also apropos at the international level are the activities of such agencies as the World Bank, Food and Agricultural Organization (FAO), Deutsche Gesellschaft fur Technische Zusammenarbelt (GTZ) of the Federal Republic of Germany, and others that brought to light the need to promote linkages for rural savings mobilization and credit delivery to the poor in developing countries (Kropp et al. 1989).

In Nigeria, there is no doubt that in the past, during the introduction of modern cooperatives in the country, the public authorities attempted to suppress the traditional credit associations. For instance, while the European-type cooperatives were being introduced into Nigeria, the indigenous credit associations were ignored because they were regarded as unsatisfactory and irreformable (Strickland 1934). As awareness grows of the need to explore their suitability and potential in fostering socioeconomic development in rural areas, the attitude of public authorities toward the traditional associations is changing. They are no longer considered fraudulent and irreformable organizations; rather, they are now accepted as a means of mobilizing household savings and promoting rapid economic development. The clearest expression of the intentions of the authorities in this regard could be gleaned from the statement of the executive chairman of the National Board for Community Banks: "Community Bank is a way of formalizing traditional and informal systems of credit provision in the country, based on a well-known and honoured practice of community self-help and self-reliance. It is a means of promoting serious economic development at the grassroots."

One therefore envisages a close link between community banks (CBs) and women's indigenous savings groups in the design to formalize traditional and informal systems of credit provision—a partnership that will obviate the constraints hindering women's access to credit. In this section, we try to appraise the feasibility of such a partnership and analyze the problems needed to be tackled in the process.

Community Banking in Nigeria

The federal government of Nigeria in the 1990 Budget Speech approved the community banking system as an adjunct to its grassroots economic development. A community bank was conceived as a self-sustaining financial institution owned and managed by a community or a group of communities for the purpose of providing credit, deposit, banking, and other financial services to its members, largely on the basis of their self-recognition and credit worthiness (CBIC 1990). It is a kind of bank serving only a community, defined by the Nigerian authorities as "a group of people who possess a common bond arising from residence, occupation, profession or other similar attributes and who interact fairly frequently in the pursuit of economic or social goals."

Community banks are expected to fill the financial gap arising from the absence of orthodox banks, which rely on viable and negotiable collaterals as the basis for giving credit. The central focus of the community banks is the rapid enhancement of the development of productive activities in the rural areas and thus the improvement of the economic status of both the rural people and the rural areas.

The inclusion of cooperatives, development associations, farmers' groups, clubs, trade unions, age grades, and so on, in the ownership structure of community banks is seen by experts as an ample opportunity to involve all and sundry in the operations of the banks, including rural women. It is also a strategy to enable community banks to retain their local focus and concentrate on community service.

The number of community banks established within a relatively short time is quite impressive. As of July 31, 1991, the total number of applications received by the board was 1,055, while only ten banks had started operation. By December 1993, 402 out of the total 879 community banks in the country had operated for nearly two calendar years. There are today at least 1,500 community banks in Nigeria, most of which are well managed. It is therefore timely to look at the prospects of a partnership between women's traditional savings groups and already established community banks.

Partnership Prospects

A successful implementation of partnership between savings groups and community banks in Nigeria depends on several factors: current level of banking awareness by the women; women's willingness to deal collectively with the banks; leadership structure of the groups; mobilization and use of funds; evidence of rules/regulations and record keeping; and the structure and orientation of banks.

1. *Level of awareness and familiarity with banks.* It is widely believed that, since most rural women are illiterate, they are unaware of the benefits of dealing with the banks. Contrary to this belief, our study shows that most rural women are aware of the usefulness of bank savings irrespective of the fact that only few had dealt with the banks in the past. The women's grouse about banks in general revolved around nonavailability, complex transactions, emphasis on collaterals, and high-handedness on the part of bank officials.

   Although the community banks are in a unique position to serve the women's needs, further institutional and "behavioral" adjustments are necessary if community banks are to provide appropriate services to rural women. Specifically, community banks should involve rural women in conceiving, planning, and evaluating programs designed to engender savings habits among them. Customer-oriented banking procedures must evolve to increase ease and spread of transactions (Kropp et al. 1989).

2. *Willingness to deal with banks as a group.* The normative response of most women's groups indicates their willingness to patronize community banks if and when they become available in their communities. This is so because the women are aware of the limitations of their own associations. They recognize that although group savings are potent instruments for solving small credit problems, they cannot be compared with banks in terms of quantity and quality of service. However, it must be stressed that for community banks to succeed in mobilizing the savings of women's traditional groups, they should incorporate those features that make informal savings schemes attractive to the rural women.

3. *Leadership structure.* There is much evidence of a high degree of organizational efficiency among women's traditional savings groups. From this structure emanate the leadership, stability, and discipline that could be successfully utilized in fostering a lasting partnership with community banks. Any functional adjustment could be worked out jointly; it must not be imposed from without or from bank management. In any case, the groups should not be made to lose their indigenous features.

4. *Unity of purpose in the mobilization and use of savings.* Several studies have attested to the ability of traditional savings groups to mobilize members' savings and extend credit to those who need it (Okorie and Miller 1976; Miracle, et al. 1980; Mauri 1987; Nweze 1991). The proven discipline and regularity of savings and the time-honored practice of credit extension to needy members could provide the basis for a lasting and beneficial relationship with community banks.

5. *Adherence to rules, regulations, and proper record keeping.* Most traditional savings associations studied showed evidence of record keeping, especially pertaining to savings and credit; and minutes and attendance. Written bylaws, evident in a majority of those studied, are with respect to admission, registration, leadership, withdrawal, savings, and credit. Written bylaws also provide for sanctions against stealing, absenteeism, and default in meeting financial obligations. Cases of default and embezzlement are few and far

between. Therefore, the reproach of absence of records/bylaws, embezzlement, and fraud should no longer be upheld against interlinks between the informal and formal financial sectors.

6. *Ownership structure, orientation, and spread.* Statutorily, community banks are better suited to promote rural development than commercial banks. In terms of ownership structure, community banks reflect their rural or community orientation. More than 80 percent of the banks investigated are jointly owned by community development associations (CDAs) and individuals within the community, while, in a few others, cooperative societies, social clubs, and age grades are shareholders, directly or indirectly.

Functionally, since community banks do not engage in such sophisticated banking services as foreign exchange transactions and corporate finance, they should be able to concentrate on some of their nonbanking functions that promote cooperative and group formation, assisting clients in agricultural marketing and other services defined in the community bank prospectus.

The spread of community banks has been remarkable. In less than four years, more than 1,500 community banks began operation all over the country. A strategy adopted to ensure this spread was the proviso that each application be backed specifically by the CDA of each community. This, in turn, ensures that all members of a community have unimpeded access to a bank (NACB 1994).

Constraints to Partnership

There are practical problems in promoting partnership between women's traditional savings groups and community banks in Nigeria. These have to do with constraints to actual implementation of any linkage program once it has been conceived and planned. Some of the following constraints derive from the structure and attitude of community banks, while others could emanate from traditional women's groups.

1. *Insufficient orientation.* Most community banks are not adequately equipped for statutory nonbanking functions as stipulated in the Community Bank Decree, 1992. Obviously, the banks have begun operations fully aware of their primary role as financial institutions. Therefore, it is not surprising that most community banks have not engaged in nonbanking services such as supporting cooperative and group formation activities. Perhaps it is still early to evaluate community banks in the light of these nonbanking functions. However, the reason for concern is that they have neither the facilities nor the personnel for this important role.

2. *A dearth of trained personnel.* The community bank authorities are more interested in employing bank personnel who are experienced and skilled in orthodox banking. As expected, too, a significant proportion of community bank personnel comprises retrenched staff from distressed and merchant banks in the country. Against this background, therefore, it is doubtful if this crop of personnel is really familiar with the needs and potential of women's traditional groups and has the aptitude and orientation needed for banking with the poor.

Surprisingly, the revised community bank prospectus of 1992 is silent on the issue of recommending a community development officer on the staff of each community bank.

3. *Noninclusion of financial self-help associations in development plans.* Although the attitude of public authorities toward the traditional groups is changing, their noninclusion in development plans and the absence of an enabling environment for their growth point to the reality that successful Nigerian authorities have not really appreciated the need to enable the rural poor to develop their own system for mobilizing local funds. Clearly, community banks cannot achieve the objectives of savings mobilization and credit to members if they act independently without official recognition and inclusion in public plans.

4. *Unsuitability of some traditional women's savings groups.* Some women's savings groups are unsuitable for any link with community banks on account of their orientation and attitude toward savings. Included in this category are those groups that do not normally engage in building up internal funds but that distribute their proceeds and do not yet engage in regular savings collection. For such groups there is hardly any basis for any financial or institutional relationship with a bank.

5. *Lack of legality.* Also noteworthy is the banks' insistence that an account cannot be opened and administered in the name of a traditional savings group because of its lack of official recognition and legality. In fact, it has been revealed that many community banks regard the lack of possibilities to sue a traditional savings group as the major hindrance to any kind of business relationship.

CONCLUSIONS AND RECOMMENDATIONS

In spite of possible implementation constraints, several indications point to the prospects of financial and institutional links between community banks and women's traditional savings groups. Such a link between the two sectors requires high priority in government strategies. It has to be supported by policy changes encourage institution and behavioral adjustment in both women's traditional savings groups and community banks. Whatever changes are necessary, the important point is that interlinks between the informal and formal financial markets have the potential to improve the lot of women. The following measures may be necessary:

1. Since a major problem of traditional groups from the viewpoint of public authorities and banks is their lack of legal status, it is necessary to start by according some of them official recognition using some eligibility criteria. Obviously, this will facilitate the required links with the community banks and inclusion in development plans.

2. To facilitate links between the two sectors, each community bank and women's group should work out a specific, mutually beneficial, and symbiotic relationship. For instance, both can work out a scheme in which credit becomes

the objective of savings. A significant level of success could be achieved through training.

3. There is an urgent need to regulate the operations of the informal financial sector. Any control will have to be done with great caution in order not to compromise those indigenous features that are their source of sustenance. Suggested action could include requiring them to register with local government authorities and enactment by government of special savings association legislation that could streamline their operations.

4. The activities of viable savings associations need to be vertically integrated. This will require the creation of coordinating central organizations at the village and local government levels, the establishment of higher associations at the state level, and the creation of an apex organization at the national level. Such an organizational structure for each type of association will facilitate the free flow of information, including investment opportunities, better use of resources, and training.

REFERENCES

Adeyokunnu, T. O. 1975. "Agricultural Development, Education and Rural Women in Nigeria." Ibadan, Nigeria: Department of Agricultural Economics, University of Ibadan.

Ardener, S. 1964. "The Comparative Study of Rotating Credit Associations." *Journal of the Royal Anthropological Institute of Great Britain and Ireland* 94 (2): 201-29.

Berger, M. 1989. "Giving Women Credit: The Strengths and Limitations of Credit as a Tool for Alleviating Poverty." *World Development* 17: 14-29.

Bratton, M. 1986. "Farmer Organization and Food Production in Zimbabwe." *World Development* 14 (3): 367-84.

CBIC. 1990. "Community Bank Prospectus." Lagos, Nigeria: Community Bank Implementation Committee.

Central Bank of Nigeria. 1993. "Annual Report and Statement of Accounts (for the year ending 31st December 1993)." Lagos, Nigeria: Central Bank of Nigeria.

Evbuomwan, G. O., E. U. Ukeje, and F. A. Afelumo. 1993. "Review of Policy and Developmental Objectives in Agricultural and Agro-Based Industrial Financing." *Bullion* 17 (4): 41-56.

Ewulu, J.N.J. 1986. "Problems of Rural Banking: Funding and Investment." Paper presented at Financial Institutions Training Center's Course on effective rural board management, Enugu, Nigeria.

Geertz, C. 1962. "The Rotating Credit Association: A Middle Rung in Development?" *Economic Development and Cultural Change* 10 (21): 241-63.

Ihimodu, I. I. 1986. "Bridging the Agricultural Credit Gap in Nigeria: The Role of Credit Institutions and the Agricultural Credit Guarantee Scheme Fund." In A. Osuntogun, and R. Uqorji (eds), *Financing Agricultural Development in Nigeria*. Lagos, Nigeria: ARMTI.

Ijere, M. O. 1986. *New Perspectives in Financing Nigerian Agriculture*. Enugu, Nigeria: Fourth Dimension.

Kropp, E., M. T. Marx, B. Pramod, B. R. Quinones, and H. D. Seibel. 1989. *Linking Self-Help Groups and Banks in Developing Countries*. Bankok: Asian and Pacific Regional Agricultural Credit Association.

March, K. S., and R. L. Taggo. 1986. *Women's Informal Associations in Developing Countries: Catalysts for Change?* Boulder, CO: Westview Press.

Mauri, A. 1987. "The Role of Financial Intermediation in the Mobilization and Allocation of Household Savings in Developing Countries: Interlinks between Organised and Informal Credits—The Case of Ethiopia." A paper presented at International Experts' Meetings on Domestic Savings Mobilization through Formal and Informal Sectors, East-West Centre, Honolulu, June 2-4.

Miller, F. 1977. "Agricultural Credit and Finance in Africa." Rockefeller Foundation.

Miracle, M. P., D. S. Miracle, and L. Cohen. 1980. "Informal Savings Mobilization in Africa." *Economic Development and Cultural Change* 28 (4): 701-24.

National Board for Community Banks (NBCB). 1994. *Community Banks Newsletter*. Abuja, Nigeria: National Board for Community Banks.

Nweze, N. J. 1991. "The Role of Women's Traditional Savings and Credit Cooperatives in Small-Farm Development." In C. K. Doss, and C. Olson (eds.), *Issues in African Rural Development*. Little Rock, AK: Winrock International Institute for Agricultural Development.

Okigbo, P. 1976. *Report of the Committee on the Nigerian Financial Systems*. Lagos, Nigeria: Department of Customs and Excise.

Okonjo, K. 1991. "Rural Development in Nigeria: How do Women Count?" In M. O. Ijere (ed.), *Women in Nigerian Economy*. Enugu, Nigeria: Acena Publishers.

Okorie, A. 1986. "The Extent of Risk in Commercial Banks' Lending to Agriculture in Nigeria: Some Empirical Evidence." *Savings and Development* (4): 409-18.

———. 1990. "Rural Banking in Nigeria: Determining Appropriate Policy Variables." *African Rural Social Science Series*. Research Report No. 9. Little Rock, AK: Winrock International Institute for Agricultural Development.

Okorie, F. A., and L. F. Miller. 1976. "Esusu Clubs and Their Performance in Mobilizing Rural Savings and Extending Credits in Chaozara Sub-Division, East Central State, Nigeria." *Technical Report* AETR/76.1. Ibadan, Nigeria: University of Ibadan, Department of Agricultural Economics.

Saito, K. A., and D. Spurling. 1992. *Developing Agricultural Extension for Women Farmers*. World Bank Discussion Paper No. 156. Washington, DC: World Bank.

Smith, C. D., and L. Stevens. 1988. "Farming and Income-Generation in the Female-Headed Smallholder Household: The Case of a Haya Village in Tanzania." *Canadian Journal of African Studies* (CJAS) 22 (3): 552-66.

Soen, D., and P. de Comarmond. 1972. "Savings Associations among the Baileke: Traditional and Modern Cooperation in Southwest Cameroon." *American Anthropologist* 74 (5): 1170-79.

Strickland, F. C. 1934. *Introduction of Cooperative Societies into Nigeria*. Lagos, Nigeria: Government Printer.

United Nations. 1986. "Savings for Development: Report on the Third International Symposium on the Mobilization of Personal Savings in Developing Countries." New York: United Nations.

12

Women and Development in West Africa: Traditional Views in Contemporary Literature

Anthonia C. Kalu

Most analysts of development tend to focus explanation on traditional Western conception, the stages, the sequences, or the structural imperatives that enhance or constrain development within the international capitalist economic system (Chilcote and Johnson 1983; Frank 1969; Mittelman 1988; Rodney 1982; Rostow 1960). Whether such focus is on the system's theory emphasis or on the macrostructural dynamics, that is, organizational and technological dimensions of social systems, or on the neoclassical emphasis on the institutional structures, the overwhelming tendencies seem to ignore the role of individuals and therefore community-based mechanisms for political and economic development. This remains true for Africans in general and for African women in particular. Frequently making unsuccessful attempts to straddle contemporary, Western-oriented African realities and African traditional worldviews, the Western-educated African writer has tended to escape into the world of literature as a strategy for facilitating self and community reflection and reevaluation.

A persisting problem for Africanists in general and African scholars in particular is that most of the records that they must use are based on anthropological and historical accounts that are either too expensive or not readily available. Lacking access to expensive anthropological excavations and historical research, most of these scholars have tended to use memory and what I call *intellectual anthropology* to excavate African histories, thought, and values from a wealth of resources available within the lived African world. This work defines intellectual anthropology as the exploration of a system of thought (in this case, African),[1] the core that informs, directs, and affects societal action and its creative efforts to establish and maintain institutions and technologies that support advancement in all aspects of life and experience. Used objectively, this approach asserts African action as a logical outcome of African thought systems emanating from African life and experiences. This means that researchers engaged in efforts to reclaim and maintain African rights, dignity, and privilege from colonization and enslavement to the present will undertake the infusion of African memory, creativity, and initiative as primary to the premise of an African development enterprise. Perceptive engagement of the internal dynamics of the African worldview will facilitate the creation of African support systems in the service of African development.

This chapter examines African development from the point of view of African women writers' efforts to reclaim a neglected Africa from the colonizer, using the colonizers' languages. Exploring African development from the African woman's point of view, it focuses on works written in the postcolonial period about Africa and Africans from precolonial through the postcolonial experience. The works of selected African women writers and personal interviews with Nigeria's Flora Nwapa[2] and Ghana's Ama Ata Aidoo[3] provide the background for the claim that specific uses of woman-as-female-and-principle in the works of African women writers portray and maintain Africa's knowledge bases on issues and strategies inherent in African traditional thought about development. Some of these issues and applicable strategies in the lives of identifiable groups of African women and their communities are briefly examined. Although the groups of women identified in these works do not fit generally accepted feminist modes, prevailing scholarship tends to analyze African women's experiences using conclusions and predictions from Western feminist thought. This situation places some African women writers who do not see themselves as writing from or against a Western feminist viewpoint on their guard.

Discussions with the late Flora Nwapa about feminism and the use of feminist strategies in her works invariably produced this response. Consistently identifying feminism as a Western-based project, she insisted that it was not a preferred reference point. She chose to discuss African women's issues and problems from an African experiential base, which, essentially separate from the West's, engages dialogues different from those significant to Western feminist viewpoints. Her insistence in this regard continues to pose some basic questions for feminist-oriented scholars who engage her works.

There is no inherent conflict in Nwapa's refusal to accept an intrinsic relationship between Western feminisms and the work she accomplishes. Explicitly Igbo and participatory from within an Igbo traditional narrative mode, Nwapa's work is not subversive (Stratton 1994: 87-93) in the Western feminists' sense of the term. Ogunyemi also refers to a Nwapa "ideology [that] is integrative rather than adversarial, as it is child directed and community centered rather than self oriented or solely woman centered" (1966: 5). Rather than assigning Nwapa the authority of integrating and democratizing Igbo (African?) narrative tradition and practice, this chapter asserts that Nwapa's work derives from an Igbo conception of woman and her relevance within a given and identifiable ethos. Her knowledge of Oguta[4] Igbo traditions authorizes her facility for working within its boundaries and engaging its capacity for innovative thought and action. Nwapa is purposefully involved in the presentation of a system of thought that is uniquely Igbo (Nigerian and/or African) even when it sometimes expresses ideas that are significant to Western feminism. This point is important, given the various attempts to impute Western feminist viewpoints and strategies into her work (Andrade 1990; Ogunyemi 1966; Stratton 1994). Such extrapolations make it difficult to access the wealth of African ways of knowing in the works of African women who, interested in providing viewpoints similar to, different from, and/or opposed to Western feminisms, use core African constructs in their delineation of African women's experiences. Purposeful and successful deployment of African narrative traditions and worldview does not here imply that these women writers find all African traditions and customs advantageous, supportive, or oppressive of Africans. Additionally, the successes or failures of these attempts do not indicate alliances between African thought and Western feminist theoretical frameworks such that these theories will subsume African views of the world.

Ogunyemi addresses this apparently inherent conflict in her different levels of exploration of Nwapa the Oguta woman and Nwapa the artist. She finds that Nwapa can be misread or "partially" read as "feminist" (1966: 134) even though Nwapa refuses to be labeled as such (133). Given that a significant number of African-descended women scholars remain cautious about associations with this label (Walker 1983), the most plausible strategy employs an African experience-based approach in the exploration and analysis of African women's contributions, autonomy, and liberation such that both the works and their authors maintain significance in areas not coextensive with received Western feminist thought. Asserting the relevance of this essential difference is necessary to initiating the process of giving full credence to the vision and creativity of continental and diaspora African women writers. In this regard, for example, it is necessary to formulate conclusions that do not derive the impetus for the Aba Women's War of 1929 from a latent Western feminist imperative, as this invariably calls for a research agenda that ignores and/or erases the capabilities for uniqueness and creativity that African women scholars claim for African womanhood.

Ama Ata Aidoo addresses this difference and uniqueness in her works. In conversations with her about writing and African traditions she asserts, "I don't think we are alien to writing. Orality does not preclude writing. Among the Akan, Adinkra cloth is full of writing.... The fact that we are writing in the Roman script does not mean that we never wrote" (1962: 21). Although African writing cannot be confused with others, what is not so obvious is that Africans may not be writing from the same exigencies and purposes as Westerners or people of other cultures. The certainty with which African women writers speak about the uniqueness of African experience and intellectual life makes this chapter's assumptions necessary and plausible.

CULTURE, TRADITION, AND MODERNITY

Social, political, economic, and religious traditions unique to the African experience continue to exist and manifest in the postcolonial state. Consequent conflicts and contradictions between the demands of postcolonial existence and development and traditional African expectations of the same continue to pose problems for Africa's development endeavors. This situation necessitates objective deployment of the advantages and limitations of postcolonial technology and memory for the provision of detailed discussions of African traditions and thought. This proposal is based on the assumption that African archives exist whose contents can be excavated using intellectual anthropology. Given the complex relationships between society, language, and culture and their impact on development projects in the postcolonial state and experience, it is necessary to reevaluate knowledge bases grounded in (1) African languages and cultures and (2) the intersections between the colonizers' languages and cultures and the Africans'.

Deprived of meaningful advancement in the political and military domains during colonial interference, colonized Africans engaged issues of disfranchisement through exploration and rearticulation of African languages and culture. Most African responses to colonization begin within the folk arts and narrative traditions, and, after African admission to formal Western education, literature assumed some of the archival function. This method of reengagement of African thought is also observable in the case of African enslavement in the New World. The history of Africans written in Roman script had to wait for anthropologists, archaeologists, oral historians, and other scholars with innovative ideas about retrieval systems. In the meantime, the verbal arts, intrinsic to pre-European interference in African life, continued to observe, comment on, modify, and (reconstruct) African experience.

Though the African woman's activities and participation did not gain recognition, acclaim, and relevance in the predominantly male-oriented new order, the African woman remained visible in traditional arenas. It is not coincidental that efforts at the retrieval of the African essence relevant to this period have discourses of the African woman at their core. In contemporary African literature, works like Achebe's *Things Fall Apart*, Okot p'Bitek's *Song of Lawino*, Ngugi wa Thiong'o's *Weep Not Child*, and, later, Flora Nwapa's *Efuru*, Mariama Ba's *So Long a Letter*, and Bessie Head's *The Collector of Treasures* explore aspects of a disfranchised Africa in which the African female, the female principle, or both are ignored, maimed, shelved, or deleted. Most of these works maintain that a dynamic female principle is essential to the core of African survival and advancement. Writing Africa's essence in a new and foreign script has required that African writers employ either the African woman to speak of/and her silence in the new language (p'Bitek, Ba, Nwapa, Head) or the female principle to retrieve an estranged male order in an alienated homeland (Achebe, wa Thiong'o).

Consequently, it is difficult to ignore the obvious impact of the African woman writer's use of this tool of Africa's self-regeneration. It is possible that, having appropriated Christianity from another culture, the colonizing European may not have recognized the use of the female principle in the regeneration of male power in the birth of the Christ. The difference on the African scene is that the woman and the female principle, rather than being confined to the home, are ubiquitous. The point here is not about a return to precolonial African traditions anymore than it is about another crucifixion. As an organizing principle, the public execution of male corporeality (in the Christ) that is later returned to essential, creative principle convinces because of humanity's continuing search for meaning and control. Although mob executions are no longer acceptable, the rule of law insists that balance, harmony, and order are indispensable to nonlinear progress. As such, gender equity is a sine qua non to advancement. What is at issue here is global advancement. If it is accepted that women do not have to become men in order for progress to be made, then it cannot be true that Africans should become Europeans for global advancement to continue.

Consequently, this is an argument for a reexamination of the African idea of the nature of liberation and liberated spaces as perceived in and lived by the African woman. The major problem for Africans since colonization is that this idea of woman-as-female-and-principle was not recognized, reharnessed, or incorporated (ideas like Christianity, taken from other cultures, were incorporated through war and conquest) by the colonizer. Its influences therefore remain unacknowledged and unrecognizable in contemporary technological advances, making its utility difficult to claim in any society, including colonized African societies. Further, unlike the idea of science as a male domain, for example, this concept was not used to claim exclusive rights or access for any group. Instead, it continues to be used to create and maintain a balance of opportunities and access in the constant quest for harmony in community.

Reducing the power and impact of the female principle in the public arena during colonization diminished the overall power and impact of African thought in African life. Within the development discourse, closer observation reveals that European progress at home has relied heavily on the concept of male power and dominance. This route to dominance and power tended to erase African male power, which most of precolonial African thought harnessed to female power using a complementary set of relationships grounded in a complex network of abstract associations that were constantly under revision. The capacity for creativity and revision of this system is evidenced, for instance, in the flexibility of the outer boundaries of the extended family system where fictive kins are created. Understanding the level of abstraction that leads to the establishment of fictive kins allows in-depth examination of an important aspect of African thought that caters exclusively to development through extension of the family, the basic social unit. Lack of understanding at this level, for example, leads Okonkwo (*Things Fall Apart*) to kill the child Ikemefuna, who called him "father." By killing Ikemefuna, Okonkwo, intent on concealing the female principle in his life, put a knife on one of the things that held Umuofia together.

TRADITIONAL COMMUNAL STRUCTURES AND DEVELOPMENT

Although other African writers do not respond directly to the abomination that is Ikemefuna's death, those who do, especially the women, address African communities' positions on this aspect of Africa's development agenda. In Nwapa's *Efuru*, Nwosu and Nwabata seek out Efuru, who not only undertakes the training and nurturing of their daughter, Ogea, but also eventually begins to take care of them. Within the development discourse that this work explores, it is important to note that Nwosu is Efuru's cousin (37). Existing norms allow them to re-create Ogea as Efuru's *maid* as a way to alleviating misery[5] and suffering for Nwosu, who has lost his yams to flood. Basing her project on Igbo thought and practice of conversation and rhetoric, Nwapa revisits the issue of male death as an accepted form of payment for other kinds of death by asserting the predominance of a dynamic for a mutual search for life. Nwapa's style, premises, and assertions of the argument, like Achebe's, are derived from Igbo narrative traditions. She insists on the extent to which Ikemefuna's death by Okonkwo's hand is inconsistent with both Umuofia thought underlying Okonkwo's admission into the group of elders and Oguta-Igbo thought supporting Efuru's nurturing of Ogea. Ogea is introduced using the following frame, which for its comparative structure with the arrival of Ikemefuna to Okonkwo's household insists on Nwapa's purposeful use of Igbo rhetorical modes:

That is how Ogea came to live with Efuru and her husband. She was a mere child, only ten years old. How could she look after a baby? Ogea cried and cried when her parents left her. She refused to eat and refused to do anything in the house. She was so uncooperative that Efuru did not know what to do with her. At first she was soft with her. But when she saw that this did not work, she became very firm and flogged her when she was naughty. Once or twice, she *threatened* to put pepper in her eyes. (40; emphasis added)

Like Ikemefuna, Ogea brings folktales, songs, and dance with her to her new home. Collectively, the women in Efuru's life nurture Ogea into mature Oguta womanhood. Together with Efuru, Ogea learns about loss and grief, industry, and success. With Efuru, she moves from one home to another, observing and absorbing Oguta life and thought through Efuru's experiences in her marriages, life in her father's compound, and, later, her relationship with Uhamiri, the Woman of the Lake.

Starting with the same narrative frame that introduces Ikemefuna to contemporary Africa's (re-)presentations of precolonial thought and life, Nwapa explores negotiable progress despite previously noted logical contradictions, deficiencies, accidents of history, and individual incapacity within that experience. Ogea's social growth to eligibility for marriage to the same man as Efuru (rather than death by her hand!) refers to the amplitude of the structure of Igbo thought on the applicability of the concept of woman-as-female-and-principle to development strategies used to impact the individual and the community. Rather than advocating polygamy, the point here is the potential for cooperation that women adapted and/or reworked for individual and group advancement. Apprenticed to Efuru, Ogea can never be lost to Oguta womanhood, and her family will not starve. From this point of view, Nwapa's refusal to be labeled "feminist" makes sense, for she is not arguing for equality between the male and female principle. That is already a given. Her writing project is grounded in the (re)-presentation of traditionally established strategies for the exploration of routes to personal and group advancement, the sum of which should lead to communal development. Since simultaneity in existence between the corporeal and the intangible is the expected norm, violence and violent deaths, when they occur, are not acceptable conclusions within this structure.

Maintenance of harmony between the ancestral world and the world of the living remains a worldview that all agree is universal to Africa and Africans. Creating or maintaining rifts between these two worlds is considered an abomination in most African cultures. Those perceived as posing such threats are openly ostracized with words, actions, or both. In this regard, Ama Ata Aidoo, responding to a question about the kind of writer she is, states,

[I am] an African writer. I think that's what I am. Apart from the overlay that I was born into Christianity, my conception of human relations is couched in ideas of generosity, kindness and reciprocity. When I permit myself to be spiritual, it's very comforting to think that life is a continuum. That others were here before us. We are part of both the past and the future. Death is not all. You cannot divide life anymore than you can divide water; it is passing as it is coming in. Someone who I cannot remember says, "Life is a spiral." (1996)

Aidoo's fictional and analytical works continue to examine these ideas. In *The Dilemma of a Ghost*, she explores some of these concepts through the portrayal of complications arising from Ato Yawson's return home from the United States after graduation from college. Ato's return is further complicated by his introduction of Eulalie, his Afro-American wife. Like most African women in contemporary African literature, Eulalie is portrayed in the complex environment of the African family and marriage. Eulalie's arrival to the new Ghana as Ato Yawson's wife poses the question, How do those who stayed behind explain African expectations about society and family to those who went away and have become, in significant ways, part of the Western norm? To all the characters in *The Dilemma*, Aidoo's Ghana is new. This point is made in the structure of the Odumna Clan house: "The action takes place in the courtyard of the Odumna Clan house. It is enclosed on the right by a wall of the old building *and both at*

*the center and on the left by the walls of the new wing... in the middle of the left
wall there is a door leading into the new rooms*" (31; emphasis added). Later, in
the "Prelude," we hear that "it is only to be expected that they should reserve the
new addition to the house for the exclusive use of the One Scholar. Not that they
expect him to make his home there. No ... he will certainly have to live in the
city when he arrives from the white man's land. But they all expect him to come
down now and then, at the week-end and on festive occasions" (34). This Ghana
that Eulalie and Ato return to is already under reconstruction. The Odumna Clan
house with its new wing for the One Scholar, Ato, is no longer under the
complete control or supervision of "the vanguard" referred to in the "Prelude." In
addition, Ato has become unsure of his roles as son, brother, and nephew. His
apparent indifference to the need to pay the debts incurred to sponsor his
education abroad is remarked by family members and villagers alike. He has to
be reminded of other customary activities by his uncle, Petu.

Petu: We have killed the goats and chickens. The women will send you and your wife
some of the Oto and then you can eat a proper breakfast. *But do you not think you and
your wife should come near the Stool Rooms?* (77; emphasis added)

The Dilemma presents some issues about the utilization of resources at the
beginning stages of development in the postcolonial state. The services of all
family members have been mobilized for Ato, the One Scholar whose new
achievements resemble those of traditional elders. This results in social status
reversals and the displacement and misplacement of authority and power. Further,
the reduction of the statuses of the women of the house to potential servants for
the Western-educated African man incorporates them as a normal part of the
postcolonial experience. Petu, the traditional elder, assumes the new role of
"messenger" for the new elite, making full utilization of his expertise
unnecessary during this time of transition. The net result is one of wasted
resources, as everyone in the old section of the Clan House as well as Eulalie in
the new wing wait for Ato to take charge of a changing Ghana. Much later,
family members realize that Ato cannot become a viable leader without help
from identified members of "the vanguard" who perceive both office workers and
office work as inherently unproductive (62).

Ato's education and postcolonial Ghana parallel the construction of the new
wing to the Clan house. Esi Kom invests all her family's wealth in the
possibilities of the new dispensation only to find that those debts may never be
repaid as her son introduces another new and alien concept for her sponsor. Ato's
inadequate knowledge of the Clan house's expectations for advancement is
evidenced in his inaction (not inadequate or wrong action) in times of crises.

Without liquidating the financial and emotional obligations she incurred
during his education abroad, Ato expects his mother to understand, without
discussion, his new family planning scheme in a culture where marriage is
inextricably tied to childbearing. This is not to say that either viewpoint is good

or bad. However, it is necessary to look at the implications of the frequent and consistent return to the question of childbearing in African women's lives. What, beyond the number of pregnancies, its inherent perils for the woman's body, the number and preferred gender of children, the fact that men do not become pregnant, and a host of other ills attributable to this much-maligned but natural activity of the female being, is at issue for Africa and the African woman? What does this issue have to do with African development? For this particular discussion, why would Ato's grandmother want a great-grandchild when she already has grandchildren? Why should Esi Kom want a grandchild? Should Eulalie Rush-Yawson, born and raised in Harlem, New York, become responsible for the fulfillment of any of these women's desires for continuance?

Research and analyses of some of these questions have focused on the African woman's dilemma regarding traditional expectations to grow up, get married, and have a houseful of potentially useless male and oppressed female children (Andrade; Ogunyemi; Stratton; Umeh). Buchi Emecheta's intertextual reading of Nwapa's *Efuru*, using Nnuego in *The Joys of Motherhood*, has been well noted and documented among feminist and other scholars (Ogunyemi; Stratton; Umeh). Further, African societies' use of the idea of large households to maintain subsistence agricultural economies is well known and documented. These ideas remain problematic and have been cited for their oppressive tendencies, for all involved, and in what appears to be unnecessary adherence to primitive African traditions and customs. The question for the development strategists remains, What should Africans and Africa do, given the conflicts posed by these seemingly inappropriate behaviors springing from inadequate worldviews? What should Aidoo's Esi Kom do and/or expect at this time, the evening of her life? More to the point: What should Ghana do, given the dilemma of all the Atos of Africa whose education necessitated the transfer of family wealth, acquired through the implementation of subsistence economies, to Western educational institutions? Ato's family's concern is that its vision for advancement not end with him. This may sound like a cliché until one looks at the problem a little differently. During my conversations with Aidoo, I thanked her for her contributions to African literature; she responded,

I didn't even know that I was making a contribution. I am an imaginative writer. I have resisted the idea of becoming a publisher. I used to say to my colleagues in Ghana, "Why don't you all write?" And they would say, "Ama, don't bring that here. Writing is your business." Writing was not for me a putting down of ideas. It was about writing a poem about something, writing a play. The impulse to express yourself. The impulse itself. It is important that people understand that in Africa. It becomes prohibitive and inhibitive ... an impulse to just express yourself. When you write, you do one or two things. You delight ... it's entertainment. It can supply information. At its very best, writing entertains, informs and inspires others. The least you can do is to give pleasure to people. In order to give pleasure to young people it becomes prohibitive. It took me two plays, two volumes of poetry, one novel ... for me to be able to say I was a writer. Otherwise it is too big. Not as many young people are writing, but they need to be encouraged.

Though standard in its references, Aidoo's response here is more to the point for African development and vision than one would like to admit. Like all writers, she insists that writing entertains and informs. But, as an African writer, she asserts that young people should be encouraged to write. What becomes clear is that Africa will not have young writers if there are no African children; and African women bear African children. This is Esi Kom's family's dilemma: Who will she entertain with stories of ancestral hopes and achievements or teach how to write Adinkra script if Ato and his wife decide not to have children? Who will add newer wings to the Odumna Clan house and/or maintain and rebuild the old section should Ato and his wife die childless? Does Esi Kom's family or Ghana have the choice to not produce future writers at this point? Given that Ato finds it easier to show Eulalie "the new Methodist School" (63) rather than encourage her to visit with his family members, is it more appropriate for the Western-educated African to ignore the non-Western-educated and their expectations while advancing Western educational structures and programs on the continent? Does it matter for Odumna Clan house members, Ghana, or Africa what choices the Atos in our communities make? What are the implications of their choices at the international level? Succinctly stated, what does the African feminist who advocates prohibitive ideologies for the traditional visionary/strategist (Efuru, Esi Kom) suggest when Africa's current debts were incurred to provide the means to advancement and increased productivity, and projects that have already been paid for return little or no profit in a capitalist-oriented international market?

Returning to the question of marriage, family, and birth control, the issue is not whether or not African women invariably get married and have countless children but that too many African women can no longer provide the guidance and support that Esi Kom gives Eulalie when she "supports Eulalie through the door that leads into the old house" (93). In most traditional African societies, birth control was so ingrained that women who had children too close together were often ostracized. Even in societies where women were expected to have many children, pregnancies were spaced far enough apart to allow each child to grow, and nursing mothers were usually sexually inactive, with some nursing their children for up to three years. Age-grade systems were tied to these practices.

The works of African women writers whose visions spring from a viable African past continue to portray the female principle, which, like Esi Kom, has the capacity to take every new idea encountered back "into the old house" for reevaluation and initiation of consequent change processes. Although Esi Kom "had gone to knock on the door of Yaw Mensa to ask for the hand of his daughter for [Ato]" (53), she takes to heart Ato's explanations about Eulalie's ancestral connections to theirs (48). Esi Kom later extrapolates from Ato's response and begins the work of adding another new wing to the Odumna Clan household.

Esi:
...And we must be careful with your wife
You tell us her mother is dead.
If she had any tenderness,
Her ghost must be keeping watch over
All which happens to her ...
[There is a short silence, then clearly to Eulalie.]
Come my child. (93)

Esi Kom's action involves both the (re-)claiming of the returning native, Eulalie, and the reevaluation of the new idea that is Eulalie's arrival in a household undergoing transition and growth.

INTELLECTUAL ANTHROPOLOGY AND CONCEPTS OF DEVELOPMENT

Regarding Africa's development and the female question, the conversation that takes place between Esi Kom and Eulalie has yet to be imagined. Eulalie's marriage to a confused Ato, and her departure from Harlem to become the daughter-in-law of an ambitious, illiterate woman in an underdeveloped Ghana are all part of basic development issues that African thought considered and solved in the past. Current cultural differences between continental and diaspora Africans are as significant as the communication gaps between the Western-educated Ato and the family members he returns to after his education abroad. Aidoo's suggestion at the end of *The Dilemma* is that Africans must make decisions about taking control of the changes deferred African history and Western interference have effected in Africa. Constructive return to the old house requires continuous exploration and understanding of the systems of thought from which both the old house and its builders derived their existence. Intense and continuous engagement of African traditions and customs remains the essential, but missing, element; mere revivals and displays of cultural artifacts encourage the maintenance of communities of observers and consumers. This means that realistic avenues should be (re-)created for the immersion of Africans in their birth cultures as a route to critical rethinking to a viable African future. Western Christian and political practices require baptism and voter registration, respectively, to ensure continuity through sustained enrollment and inauguration of youth.

Contemporary Africa's retention of African thought is evident in African languages and oral narrative traditions. One of the most difficult and least used ideas within the African worldview is that of the relationship between narrative land and the world of the living. Narrative land or spirit land, festival drama, and religious rituals were shelved from the colonial encounter and onto contemporary

Africa. Susan Preston Blier's discussion of the impact of the use of terms like "fetish," "magic," and "custom" during the shelving process is illuminating (143-66). Blier's exploration facilitates understanding of "the longstanding separation of Africa and its arts from Europe and [Africa's] taxonomic proximity with the Pacific Islands and Native America." She asserts that, "what is important is that ... this sense of deprivation or lack is an assumption of ... qualities of *heightened sensitivity (emotional power) and danger*" (149; emphasis added). Comparing the Art Historian's use of language and psychoanalytical frames to separate Africa, Africans, and African art from their European parallels with the portrayal of women in film, Blier contends that "illogic (and indeed magic) ... support ... these premises of simultaneous lack, longing, repulsion and attraction" (150). The obstacle to the use of African ways of knowing in its capacity to advance development strategies and projects in contemporary African life is the adoption of these postures by Africans in search of modern nationhood. Although (and because it is?) a postcolonial structure, the contemporary African nation is firmly lodged in the colonizer's imagined Africa and remains inextricable from alienating Europeans' premises of their own susceptibility to heightened emotional sensitivity and danger from their contact with the African world. The task is to engage African narrative traditions such that it becomes possible again to see images of traditional African life (most of which are still in use!) as carriers of truth and relevance for African life and advancement. This suggests a need for contemporary Africa and Africanists to simultaneously reclaim the parallel universe of narrative/spirit land with the land of the living, for both have been carefully preserved by ancestral thought in African traditions, art, and culture. The bulk of Africa's parallel universe is coded in the world of the living, in African languages and African verbal arts.

Recognizing the power of language in the service of the maintenance and purposeful advancement of African life and experience, African writers, in African and non-African languages, continue to write an unmistakable trail of words that lead to ancestral legacies. While I remain in awe of the animating and impressive research and discussions about African literature in European languages (Achebe, Ngugi, Irele), it has become necessary to move research in this area to a new level. The question should no longer be about whether or not Africans write "real" African literature in European languages. Rather, we should begin to ask what should/can be done since African writers in African and European languages must continue to write. Further, they will continue to write in Roman script unless Africans develop a new, different, and viable script that will enhance participation in current international forums and markets. Some questions, aimed at facilitating the transition to new research paradigms, include, What does ancestral thought suggest/maintain with regard to transitions and adaptations to new dispensations? What suggested strategies already exist for the resolution of issues such as these in the parallel universe of the African narrative/spirit world? Do contemporary African communities maintain relational modes with this parallel world on a critical level? Is there critical, objective, cross-cultural engagement among contemporary African communities of the conflicts and contradictions that persist between the colonizer's imagined Africa and traditional African imagination couched in African verbal arts? What is the history of Africa's intellectual tradition? What are that tradition's predictions? Have any African individuals or communities achieved any of those predictions? What kind of reasoning and logic continues to make sense for contemporary Africans within that legacy?

While I am not suggesting that there exists one African approach to understanding the world, it is necessary to consider that there exist unique ways of knowing that enabled Africans to negotiate peace and war, complete cross-continental migrations, and maintain local and long-distance economic and political relationships. Among the Igbo of Nigeria, for example, most of this was accomplished "without writing and ... without *clear* forms of political hierarchy" (Feierman 1993: 177; emphasis added).

Clarification of form, content, and objectives is the task of the contemporary African intellectual involved in the discovery of the match between traditional African thought and contemporary experience such that African advancement, progress, and growth become synchronized with a parallel, traditional African universe that remains future-directed. A cyclical view of the world, an essential aspect of African cosmology, no longer needs discussion. The challenge is how to effectively transfer viable ancestral vision into usable development strategies and goals. Their later (than the African male) arrival to, and marginal position in, the production of contemporary African literature are considerations that keep African women writers cognizant of the challenges of disabling European viewpoints and the consequent male-oriented foundation of the postcolonial state. Constantly reappraising practical responses to real-life questions within traditional thought, these writers continue to point contemporary Africa to the wealth of knowledge and practical applications within African thought. Nwapa's introduction of *Uhamiri* to the new narrative tradition of the novel expands again the shelved domain of woman-as-female-and-principle, making plausible the advancement of the Oguta woman's concrete social domain. Reinforcing the idea of Efuru, the Oguta (Igbo) woman, as having access beyond (and in addition to) *Ala, the earth goddess, Uhamiri* modifies and complements the received and popular charge (to the Igbo woman) to eternal and inevitable motherhood originating from the myth of the earth mother. *Uhamiri* reaffirms the ubiquity of woman-as-female-and-principle.

References to African proverbs and Christian thought in *The Dilemma* indicate a route to intellectual anthropological excavations within African thought. Aidoo also extends the boundaries of the new practice of the comparison of texts between African thought, expressed in the proverb, and one of the colonizer's tools of control and subjugation, the Bible.

1st Woman: .... You talk, my sister,
As if the days are gone

When the left hand washed the right
And the right hand washed the left.
    2nd Woman: Perhaps they are not, my sister.
But those days are over
When it was expedient for two deer
To walk together,
Since anyone can see and remove
The beam in his eye with a mirror. (52-53)

Aidoo's background against which the village's voices are heard is the voices of the two village women who address and analyze every issue raised in the Odumna Clan house embroiled in crisis and transition. The second woman's response moves the focus from the African proverb's reference to the washing of hands, to the biblical reference to deer, eventually deducing a new order as self-help results from reflections of the self in a mirror. The implications are clear: unlike Ato, Africans cannot choose a "middle of the courtyard" (93) solution. Whether the choice is Cape Coast or Elmina, both places are in Ghana (continental Africa), with each place harboring recognizable ancestral and personal ghosts.

NOTES

    1. I use African thought and African worldview interchangeably and in the singular. This does not indicate that all African peoples think the same on all issues. It does, however, indicate that African peoples do tend to think of similar outcomes regarding issues of disengagement from persisting mechanisms of colonialism and slavery. The overall implication here, rather than one of emphasis on a series of confrontations with past oppressions from within or without, explores a purposeful intellectual African heritage committed to the establishment of harmony and advancement in the precolonial environment. Some of these have been carried over to contemporary life and experience.

    2. The author was granted a personal interview with Flora Nwapa at the African Literature Association Conference, New Orleans, March 23, 1991. References here to "discussions" and "conversations" with her are to this interview.

    3. The author was granted a telephone interview with Ama Ata Aidoo on October 20 and 21, 1996. References here to "discussions" and "conversations" with her are to this interview.

    4. *Efuru*, a short story by Nwapa, is set in Oguta, Nwapa's hometown. Because of the proposal for intellectual anthropological excavations in the real Igbo world made in this chapter, I will use "Oguta" rather than the fictional "Ugwuta" to avoid confusion.

    5. Ikemefuna is used in a similar manner when his people give him to the people of Umuofia as part compensation for murdering Udo's wife and to avoid war. The virgin given along with him becomes Udo's wife (Achebe 1959; 29).

REFERENCES

Achebe, Chinua. 1959. *Things Fall Apart*. New York: Fawcett Crest.

―――. 1975. *Morning Yet on Creation Day*. New York: Anchor Press/Doubleday.

Aidoo, Christiana Ama Ata. 1965. *The Dilemma of a Ghost*. New York: Collier Books.

―――. 1996. Telephone interview, October 20, 21.

Andrade, Susan. 1990. "Rewriting History, Motherhood and Rebellion: Naming an African Woman's Literary Tradition." *Research in African Literatures* 21 (1) (Summer): 91-110.

Ba, Mariama. 1981. *So Long a Letter*. Trans. Modupe Bode-Thomas. Oxford: Heinemann Educational.

Blier, Susan Preston. 1993. "Truth and Seeing: Magic, Custom and Fetish in Art History." In *Africa and the Disciplines*, ed. Robert H. Bates, V. Y. Mudimbe, and Jean O'Barr. Chicago and London: University of Chicago Press, 139-66.

Chilcote, Ronald H., and Dale L. Johnson, eds. 1983. *Theories of Underdevelopment: Mode of Production or Dependence?* Beverly Hills, CA: Sage.

Emecheta, Buchi. 1979. *The Joys of Motherhood*. Oxford: Heinemann Educational Books.

Feierman, Steven. 1993. "African Histories and the Dissolution of World History." In *Africa and the Disciplines*, ed. Robert H. Bates, V. Y. Mudimbe, and Jean O'Barr. Chicago and London: The University of Chicago Press, 167-212.

Frank, Andre Gunder. 1969. *Latin America: Underdevelopment or Revolution*. New York: Monthly Review Press.

Head, Bessie. 1977. *The Collector of Treasures*. Oxford: Heinemann Educational Books.

Irele, Abiola. 1981. *The African Experience in Literature and Ideology*. London: Heinemann.

Mittleman, James. 1988. *Out from Underdevelopment: Prospects for the Third World*. New York: St. Martin's Press.

Nasta, Susheila, ed. 1992. *Motherlands: Black Women's Writings From Africa, the Caribbean and South Asia*. New Brunswick, NJ: Rutgers University Press.

Nwapa, Flora. 1966. *Efuru*. Oxford: Heinemann Educational Books.

―――. 1990. Personal interview, March 23.

Ogunyemi, Chikwenye Okonjo. 1966. *African Wo/man Palava: The Nigerian Novel by Women*. Chicago: University of Chicago Press.

p'Bitek, Okot. 1966. *Song of Lawino and Song of Ocol*. London: Heinemann Educational Books.

Rodney, Walter. 1982. *How Europe Underdeveloped Africa*. Washington, DC: Howard University Press.

Rostow, Walt W. 1960. *The Stages of Economic Growth: A Non-Communist Manifesto*. Cambridge: Cambridge University Press.

Stratton, Florence. 1994. *African Literature and the Politics of Gender*. London and New York: Routledge.

Umeh, Marie. 1987. "The Poetics of Thwarted Sensitivity." In *Critical Theory and African Literature*, ed. R. Vanamalli, E. Oko, A. Iloeje, and Ernest Emenyonu. Ibadan: Heinemann.

Walker, Alice. 1983. *In Search of Our Mother's Gardens*. San Diego: Harcourt Brace Jovanovitch.

Wa Thiong'o, Ngugi. 1993. *Moving the Center: The Struggle for Cultural Freedoms.*
    London: James Curry.
———. 1964. *Weep Not Child.* London: Heinemann.

13

Development and Women's Writings from Southern and Northern Africa

Victoria Carchidi

The appalling situation of the majority of Third World women is
not a remnant of archaic systems of patriarchy, or a sign of
backwardness and underdevelopment; on the contrary, it is a sign
and product of modern development.
                                                    —Bennholdt-Thomsen 1988: 159

INTRODUCTION

"Development" is a concept widely used and variously defined. When used to
describe desired change for groups of people, however, it must be based in the
concerns and interests of those people and center on women, who
disproportionately bear the brunt of change and inculcate young children with the
values to continue development. This chapter looks at short stories written by
women from two regions of the African continent to discern the hopes and
dreams, fears and despair of women in these regions and as a source of
information for those hoping to further development projects.

Women's roles in development, while widely acknowledged today, were, for
a long time, ignored (Jabbra and Jabbra 1992: 12). Development that focuses on
technology, in tandem with Western attitudes toward men and women, has tended
to value men's contributions over women's work, often domestically centered.
Although acknowledged more clearly now, the blind spot concerning women has
not been erased in the way it structures priorities (Rathgeber 1992: 22).
Scholarship into women's issues has been "ghettoized," segregated as a special
issue, rather than seen as central to a proper reconfiguring of development to
meet the needs of all people, including women (Mona Russell 1992: 123). The
heightening of awareness made possible by forums such as this volume is a
valuable prelude to the eventual integration of men's and women's work,

reflected in a people-centered, not male-centered, theory of success, progress, and value.[1]

To paint any picture of Northern and Southern Africa requires a very broad brush indeed: both regions encompass several countries, and together they offer the contrast of a Muslim, Mediterranean, largely Francophone region led by Egypt, against a Sub-Saharan region dominated by British colonialism and the Republic of South Africa. Such extremes make a comparison fruitful—do the literary works of women in these two areas have anything in common? In addition, one commonality—that each region contains a dominant country closely allied with the First World industrial cultures—prevents a perniciously patronizing approach to what can be learned from these writers.

One approach to development is statistical: compiling tables of life expectancy, literacy, number of live births per woman, household income, and so forth. Any numbers so generated are subject, of course, to critiques about sampling, interpretation, and so on. In addition, these neat numbers provide averages that may not correspond to any person's actual experience. They also isolate factors, rather than looking at interconnections between the different data. Such general analyses demonstrate the grossness of the measurements usually applied to even the most diverse and personal life issues. Gender and development (GAD) is an approach that considers not just women's positions but the underlying questions of gender hierarchy: "It seeks to analyze culturally specific forms of social inequality and divisions, to see how gender is related to or interlocked with other forms of social hierarchy" (Young 1995: 135). For such an approach, women's literature becomes both a difficult and a crucially important source of information: difficult because the number of female writers is limited by literacy,[2] and crucially important because women's writing allows women's voices to be heard.[3] To listen to women writing creatively is to hear the song that is silenced by statistics: the song of specificity, not generality, the song of human desires in all their complexity, of confusion and compassion, of struggle and defeat. Women's literature from Northern and Southern Africa captures, as no table, graph, or other generalizing technique can, the diversity of life in these regions.[4] Only by moving away from quantified representations of life, by turning back to the stories with which people shape their lives, can development help people to flourish not simply as economic units or in predetermined social groupings, but in the ever-changing and flexible ways that human societies have forged for themselves throughout time.

NORTHERN AFRICAN STORIES

Education offers women one way to develop themselves. For example, Wedid Zenie-Ziegler writes of Egyptian women that greater knowledge about the social codes that do control women's lives could allow women more options. She bemoans that a "special, optional clause called the *Isma*" gives women "the right to seek a divorce.... Countless other women are not even informed of the existence of the *Isma*" (1988: 128). Such lack of information is common, Zenie-Ziegler points out, in a country where 75 percent are illiterate. Although she points to special status accorded an educated woman, or *muwazzafa*, "[o]nly very few women gain access to education, despite the introduction of compulsory education since the revolution of 1952" (66).[5] Even more basic information is lacking, Zenie-Zigler states: "Boys and girls—particularly the girls—sometimes come to marriage totally ignorant of sexual matters" (1988: 116).

Such lack of knowledge may contribute to cultural practices such as female circumcision, a procedure that Peter Adamson (1996) argues has led to enormous pain and suffering for women. In Alifa Rifaat's "Who'll Be the Man?" a woman explains the reason for the procedure to a young girl: "So that men will come running after you without your asking. And when your husband goes away for a long time, you won't suffer at all" (1990: 77). Critics of the practice take a less benign view, some linking it to patriarchy: "To perpetuate discriminatory systems, cultures adopt practices to control women. One of the most notorious is female genital mutilation," which threatens more than 2 million girls each year (Nelson 1996: 134).

Nawal El Saadawi, herself an educated Egyptian doctor and activist, well known for her opposition to clitoridectomy, writes indirectly about female circumcision in "She Was the Weaker" (1989). This story describes a weak young man, who is bullied by his mother and who despises his frailty. On his wedding day, the groom must demonstrate his bride's virginity by inserting his finger into her genitals and showing the blood. The bride is presented to him vaginally, but he is too feeble to push his finger through the entrance, apparently infibulated after circumcision. The groom then shows his clean hands and spits, thereby denying the "purity" of the bride. This vignette demonstrates the intolerable expectations that patriarchy places on men, as well as women. The story also shows that, ultimately, women suffer from patriarchy to a greater extent: the man protects his weakness by transferring it onto his bride's body like a scapegoat.

Some women, like the groom's mother in Saadawi's story, affiliate themselves with the powerful status quo, even against other women. The inescapability as well as the desolation of such affiliation are shown in Rifaat's "Another Evening at the Club." Samia misplaces a valuable ring her husband has given her; he accuses the maid Gazia, who is taken away by the police. Later in the day, Samia finds the ring on the floor and waits anxiously for her husband to rectify matters. He is glad the ring is found but unconcerned. Samia points out that Gazia is still being interrogated: "They've been beating up the girl—you yourself said they'd not let her be till she confessed" (1987: 192). But her husband's reputation is all-important; he decides to sell the ring so no one will know it has been found and pats Samia's cheeks: "It was a gesture ... that promised her continued security, that told her that this man who was her husband and the father of her child ... carried the responsibilities, made the decisions," while her role is "to be beautiful, happy, carefree. Now, though, for the first time in their life together, the gesture came like a slap in the face" (192-93). Samia's error is enacted on the body of Gazia, the powerless servant. Yet when Samia's husband suggests they go out to the club, Samia smiles and joins him. Her choices are few; although socioeconomic status separates her from the maid, Samia is equally subservient. It is not surprising that many women fight against such a recognition.

Men and women, however, can also join forces to oppose oppression. In "Eight Eyes," (Rifaat 1983) the central male character resists the compulsion to "be a man" and continue a blood feud, despite accusations of being weak and "spineless." Only his mother's voice has so empowered him, by criticizing "the barbarism of animals that they wanted to force on you in the name of virility" (336). In this instance, a mother helps her son oppose cultural machismo; husbands and wives, too, can oppose custom.

In Assia Djebar's delightful "My Father Writes to My Mother," a marriage of true affection and respect leads the narrator's father to send his wife a postcard:

my father had quite brazenly written his wife's name, in his own handwriting, on a postcard which was going to travel from one town to another, which was going to be exposed to so many masculine eyes ... and what is more, he had dared to refer to her in the western manner as "Madame So-and-So ...," whereas, no local man, poor or rich, ever referred to his wife and children in any other way than by the vague periphrasis: "the household" (1993: 164).

The postcard marks a turn in the marriage, allowing the wife to refer to her husband directly in her conversations with others. Their affection is strong enough to cut through local custom. The story, however, attests to more than their love: this couple's affection is like a brief flash of light that all the more brightly illuminates the stultifying customary denial of a wife's existence.

An even more surprising example of unity between husband and wife is shown in "The Long Trial," by Andree Chedid. A traveling holy man blesses a woman who offers him food and water: he calls for seven more children for her. But she has nine, who like "grasshoppers, bounded against her, encircled her, transformed her into a clod of dirt, inert. Their hundreds of hands became claws, nettles twitching her clothes, tearing her flesh" (1983: 205). The mother, stricken, demands the holy man recant the benediction. Angry at her blasphemy, he calls her mad; in her desperation she even *demands* her husband join her plea against such a blessing. To her astonishment, her husband does not beat her for her demand but instead joins his voice with hers to halt childbirth. The village turns against the holy man in violence as he refuses to take back his words. The next day the men are arrested. The long trial is over—on one level, of course, because the men are gone, the women will no longer suffer from childbirth. But on a more profound level, the story suggests, the trial of separation is over, as husbands and wives have joined together to fight an unjust construction of womanhood inappropriate to material conditions.

Another story demonstrating a moment of marital closeness, however, also limns the fragility of such unions. In "Amina" (Saad 1985) a woman has given birth to a baby daughter and lies mourning in the hospital. This is her fourth daughter, and she and her mother fear repudiation. But against all expectation, her husband, Hamid, is caring: he "looked at his wife, tried to smile and searched for something nice to say.... 'Don't cry,' he said distressed. 'The important thing is that you and the girls are in good health.'" He goes on to point out they can try again later. This story demonstrates both that happiness and kindness can exist and that the power is disproportionately the husband's and that the "shame" of the child's sex disproportionately the wife's—thereby showing an entrenched devaluing of women.

Wedid Zenie-Ziegler writes powerfully of the importance of children in marriage: "In Arab society, celibacy is despised. The aim of marriage is to perpetuate the species, therefore to procreate" (1988: 115). Furthermore, when noting the lack of interest in contraception, Zenie-Ziegler notes, "Fertility is a basic value ... and the *Quran* exalts the role of wife, and even more, that of mother" (73). Thus, women like Um Hani, who is twenty years old, has six children and is expecting the seventh (27).

Yet these women have very little access to money; Um Hani sews dresses to help support her family. Consequently, they depend on male wage earners and will accede to any demands to obtain this support: "Financial security, it is true, is a far from negligible concern in all social classes, especially the most underprivileged. Thus, many women are ready to make all sorts of concessions to obtain or preserve it. ... For Fatma and most of the women questioned, the man's fundamental role consists of assuring his family a basic material well-being and comfort" (Zenie-Ziegler 1988: 69).

Many of these works value a husband for more than food and shelter. In Rifaat's "The Kite" (1987), an old widow, Widad, is courted by her childhood sweetheart. She at first refuses him, but after a kite steals one of her chicks, she reconsiders. In the story, two advantages of a husband are manifested: he can lead the prayers that Widad longs to offer for her simple life, and he can offer protection—specifically, as a scarecrow against the kite, but metaphorically as more general physical security. This simple and lovely story's subtext, that a woman needs a man to be safe against sudden incursions of violence into her life, is a message women receive in both a rural Muslim community and in a Westernized city.

Western critics' views of the Maghreb have been colored by reactions to Islam; Zoubeida Bittari's "The Voice of Happiness" (1990) concerns a woman who tries to gain greater freedom for herself, at first by accompanying her young son on excursions. The disquiet this causes her family is shown when, after a late-night dentist visit occasioned by Ramadan, her husband refuses to let her in the house, and her parents denounce her as a whore. A sympathetic male lawyer helps her find a job as a domestic (after checking with the dentist that her story is true). Although her new life is a great pleasure to the narrator, she grieves at having had to leave her son behind because of her uncertain state.

Although Bittari depicts a son as being the innocent path to his mother's freedom, that situation is quite unusual: the mother is young, this is her only child, and, although sad at the separation, she gives up her son. A more brutal depiction of the role of children is presented in Noha Radwan's "The Silk Bands" (1990), in which the mother endures marital abuse amounting to rape and sees her little children binding her with silk bands to the bed of torment.

Fatima Mernissi (1990) recounts a traditional folktale that also attests to the imprisonment of women. In the tale, a prince and a carpenter's daughter engage in verbal and sexual sparring; he then asks to marry her. Her father is reluctant but agrees when his daughter persuades him. But the prince asks the woman whether men or women are smarter, and when she replies, "women," locks her in the cellar. Thanks to her father, who has dug a tunnel to the cellar, the heroine continues happily enough, appearing in the cellar only to give her nonsubmissive reply every day. Meanwhile, the prince travels about and on three occasions meets a mysterious woman with whom he spends a week and sires a child. These are, of course, all his wife, who cleverly contrives these encounters and finally appears with the three children and wins her rightful place as wife, the prince finally acknowledging—and accepting—her cleverness. Yet this tale indicates the huge disparity in power, if not in cleverness: the prince is free and can seek out sexual partners; he is also free to acquire and incarcerate a woman because of some words she utters, threatening his assumption of superiority. The woman must rely on her father's sympathy and wealth to dig tunnels, set up luxurious tents, care for her children, and so forth, in addition to her enormous cunning and self-control.

Outside the realm of the folk story, however, women's cunning acquires a more desperate hue. In Rifaat's "An Incident in the Ghobashi Household" (1987), a mother discovers her daughter is pregnant and decides to disguise herself as the mother of the arriving infant. The ruse, however, requires a gamble: the pregnant daughter must go to Cairo, alone and unprepared, until her child is born and can be produced as the mother's own.[6]

Djebar's bored and restricted girls in "Three Cloistered Girls" (1993) play a dangerous game, writing to pen-pal lovers with the most unrealistic dreams of escape, which leave them vulnerable.

SOUTHERN AFRICAN STORIES

Understandably, Southern African stories touch on different topics than the ones mentioned before. However, although treated differently, some themes recur: specific oppressions are highlighted, as are universal themes of partnership and parenthood, albeit inflected by local concerns.

An example of the general and specific can be seen in Barbara Makalisa's poem "Fight On!" (Kitson 1994: 71-74). It identifies pressures facing both

Northern and Southern African women—if not all women. However, these material restrictions are felt differently given local conditions, as shown in the obstacles confronting three generations of Southern African women. For example, the poet's grandmother faces resistance to education: her father tells her, "School is for lads" and that now that she can write her name and read the Bible, that is all he will undertake, as soon she will marry and leave her family.

The poet's mother, in turn, faces the double bind that allocates women's responsibility for child care on top of their other work and then blames them for children's behavior: "When I excelled, Dad sang a song./ When I failed, Mama was to blame." In the third generation, the speaker herself faces lower pay for the same work, as well as the contempt showered on any woman seeking to control her fertility and develop abilities. She and her friends face fixed and stereotypical expectations of women; as she points out, she is paid less because her "main task should be baby production." Her efforts to control her fertility, for her own health and that of her children's, are described as a prostitute's behavior. The same imputation of prostitution accompanies any efforts by these women to assert their abilities.

Rather than give in to this form of coercion, the speaker urges women to struggle on in the war against such little attitudes, returning to her pioneering grandmother's efforts. She cries that education can provide a spear in the battle, and knowledge a shield (74).

That education can act as a weapon for preventing oppression is suggested both in Northern and Southern African writing. Of note in South Africa is the apartheid regime, which has been felt throughout Southern Africa as efforts to deracinate the black population and relocate it to homelands influenced by family structure. Women, seen as a particular danger by the apartheid government, were disproportionately affected by pass-law restrictions (Bernstein 1985: 16-17). The literature of this region, written from exile both within and outside the continent, reflects writers with a range of backgrounds and affiliations.[7]

Race as a political opposition creates one sort of chasm in women's solidarity.[8] In Agnes Sam's "Two Women" (1989) a white woman arrests a black female guerrilla fighter she finds on her farm. The fighter manipulatively tries to create fellow feeling, but their polarization is too great. However, once the fighter is able to disable the car in which they are traveling, the situation changes. They hear a car approaching, and the captor points out their common vulnerability: "Whichever way—one of us will be raped." The fighter suddenly fears, "If she were caught with me now, I would be a party of whatever was done to her." As in Rifaat's "Another Evening at the Club," here each woman, fighting for her side of a racial battle, is suddenly united with the other: upon their bodies will be enacted the violent struggle of racial dominance. The story illustrates that, although guerrilla warfare may seem an absolute split, women on either side are equally subject to incursions of male violence: women become the site for the acting out of political violence at the very same time that they are prevented from meaningful participation in public life.[9]

The effect of racial segregation on human intimacy is revealed in stories concerned with sexuality across the "color bar," in violation of South Africa's notorious immorality act. Nadine Gordimer's "Country Lovers" (1990) looks at the effects of racial segregation on a rural couple. In the country, a childhood partnership turns sexual at adolescence. In due course, a baby arrives; in due course, its father kills it. The social conventions of apartheid destroy and render inhuman the communion of the closest human connections.

The combination of race and violence against women can further erode the strongest human affections. In "Milk," a middle-aged woman is raped repeatedly while her family is held at gunpoint. She becomes pregnant and does not know whether the baby's father is her husband or the rapist's. She watches the infant for racial characteristics: "The third day the small face peering from its covers showed a dark tint, as though a shadow had fallen over it" (Joubert 1987: 308). On the fourth day, the mother notes "the new black shadow that had spread over the skin, the structure of the nose was more apparent. It was wide, broad-flanged, like that of the man who had dragged her from the car, while her husband sat with the barrel of a pistol against his temple" (309). Therefore, the mother suffocates her baby while it is nursing. A reporter comes to inquire into the story, looking at the "unattractive ... old and tired" woman and asks, "How does it feel to have smothered your baby?" "She gestures at her breasts. The moisture seeps through the nightdress. "What do I do with the milk? she asks wordlessly. Who do I feed with the milk?" (310).

This story demonstrates the "shadow" that falls over human relationships under racism: the violence it unleashes between people, the invidious concern with color and facial characteristics that dries up humanity. This story's poignancy rests in the woman's repleteness—she is full of milk for her child yet, given her circumstances, there is no place for the milk of human kindness. The pain that comes from the inability to be kind and express humanity is equated with the terrible pressure of a milk-filled breast that cannot be nursed.

The effect of such starvation of humanity extends even beyond racially strained relationships, as shown in Ferreira's "The Lover" (1987). The first-person male narrator recounts how his mistress asked him for a private beachside location at which to meet her lover. The reader discovers the tryst was with death—the mistress shot herself at the beach. Furthermore, (a married man's) possessive jealousy characteristic and lack of understanding emerge as part of the suicide's motivation.

More self-aware but just as anesthetized, in Marquard's "Regina's Baby" the narrator watches her servant bewail the death of her baby daughter and admits, "I can't cope with this; emotion, turmoil, confrontation" (1993: 117). When she grieves over the emptiness of her own, well-kept, middle-class life, she prides herself that "[m]y grief is a silent, dignified, poised emotion" (123). The rigid construction of identities along racial strata strips these white characters of real human emotion.

"Regina's Baby" bridges the gulf between rich and poor. The narrator's grief is controlled because it is, after all, unhappiness, not desperation. Bessie Head evokes a more basic concern. "Looking for a Rain God" depicts a rural family[10] pushed to the edge. For seven years there has been a drought; then rain falls, and the family heads out to plant. But the drought returns. "Only the children, Neo and Boseyong, were quite happy in their little-girl world.... They made children from sticks around which they tied rags, and scolded them severely in an exact imitation of their own mother." The women begin to wail; the men stay silent: "It was important for men to maintain their self-control at all times but their nerve was breaking too" (1996: 92). Then the oldest man, Mokgoba, begins to recall an ancient "rain god who accepted only the sacrifice of the bodies of children" (92). The little girls are sacrificed, and the family flees back to town. There await the police and the death penalty for the men. The narrator comments, "The subtle story of strain and starvation and breakdown was inadmissible evidence at court; but all the people who lived off crops knew in their hearts that only a hair's breadth had saved them from sharing a fate similar to that of the Mokgoba family. They could have killed something to make the rain fall." (93)[11]

The direness of the local conditions presented by Head moves the story out of the local and into an international arena. Global environmental and food production and distribution strategies can avert such tragedy, and the story thus indicts the complicit global community. An equally global concern is violence against women[12]: the 1996 issue of *Vital Signs* addresses violence against women around the world and points out, "Gender-specific forms of violence ... occur where male dominance is institutionalized in social, political, and economic systems" (Nelson 1996: 134). Rape as racially motivated has already been touched on; Gcina Mhlope presents it as almost normal in "Nokolunga's Wedding" (1987).

Young Nokolunga is one day suddenly seized by a party of men from a neighboring village and taken to the hut of her future husband, Xolani. The first night she fights him viciously, biting his arm, so the next night the men help in her defloration: "They roughly pulled her back on to the bed, and Xolani was placed on top of her. Her legs were each pulled by a man. Others held her arms. Men were cheering and clapping hands while Xolani jumped high, now enjoying the rape ... she heard roars of laughter before she fainted" (43). This violence goes beyond the physical. Nokolunga has been stripped of her community in fact and in emotion—she wonders why her community let her go, if they cared about her. Such deracination accounts for women's alienation.

Olive Schreiner demonstrates how even seemingly benign treatment can reinforce such isolation for women. "The Woman's Rose" shows two women forced apart, despite their very similarities of class and position. The tale is narrated by a woman of twenty-seven, remembering her arrival in a village twelve years earlier. There had been a reigning beauty there, whom all the men worshiped, but on the narrator's arrival, they deserted her and turned to the narrator, maligning their previous object of attention. The narrator is flattered and delighted by the unaccustomed attention: "Only one thing took from my pleasure; I could not bear that they had deserted her for me.... I would have given all their compliments if she would once have smiled at me.... But I knew it never could be; I felt sure she hated me; that she wished I was dead, that she wished I had never come to the village" (71). But at the narrator's farewell party her rival gives her a rare midwinter rose for her hair. The adult narrator still cherishes the rose in a wooden box. This brief story indicates the barriers set between people even outside racial and material concerns: it links the issues of "development in the Third World" back to the concerns that confront even "First World" citizens. We all share the same world; these discursive divisions simply attempt to defy the parallels that cut across specific and local conditions: apartheid, sexism, economic exploitation—all similarly function by pitting against each other people who might otherwise find common purpose. In "A Woman's Rose," the women are a striking minority. Certainly, there are plenty of men to court both, but instead one woman is selected to demonstrate that the power to privilege and distinguish belongs to the men.

In the face of these many intersecting oppressions that deform women's lives, it is not surprising that both Northern and Southern African literature celebrates activism. As in Chedid's "The Long Trial" (1983) people can work against oppression. In Gordimer's "A Chip of Glass Ruby" (1982) an Indian wife and mother's commitment to printing protest pamphlets leads to her arrest. Her husband feels confused: "He had married a good plain Moslem woman who bore children and stamped her own chilies. He had a sudden vision of her at the duplicating machine, that night just before she was taken away, and he felt himself maddened, baffled and hopeless" (45). This story shows the uneasy ways in which people must negotiate their conflicting identity positions, as he exclaims, "I don't understand how she can do the things she does when her mind is always full of woman's nonsense at the same time" (47). But, as his daughter reminds him, and as he recognizes, his wife's ability to unite the disparate parts of her world, to see humanity across the bars set up in a divide-and rule state, makes her so central to her family even while in jail. In Tlali's "Point of No Return" (1983) the rift again cuts across a family: S'bongile both understands and resists the need for her partner, Mojalefa, to leave her and fight the pass laws and racism in South Africa. Mojalefa risks death, as well as jail. The story ends simply: "He lifted her chin slightly with his forefinger and looked into her eyes. They seemed to smile at him. They parted" (141). As with the end of "A Long Trial," separation here attests to a common purpose—but also comes at the painful wrenching apart of lives and loves.

CONCLUSION

These stories present no simple answers, because life—especially, many lives—are not simple. So, to the extent that this literature forestalls facile solutions, its effect is beneficial. The women[13] here discussed live in a variety of material conditions—rural and urban, poor and rich, and so on. Their lives are shaped by patriarchal and economic forces, as well as by religious and cultural structures that have imposed caste divisions across women.

The difficulty of writing itself attests to the importance of what is written. In Mhlope's "The Toilet" (1987) a young woman finds the "room of her own" that Virginia Woolf asserts is a writer's essential haven only in the public toilet, where she shelters from the rain while waiting to sneak back to an illegal room. In an eerie parallel, when Alifa Rifaat's husband forbade her creative career, she obeyed him by not publishing. But to continue writing, giving voice to her perceptions of the world, she retreated, like Mhlope's narrator, to the bathroom (Badran and Cooke 1990: 72). Jean Dejeux points out that women still take noms de plume to protect their husbands and families (1994: 8). The difficulty women can have not simply in having their writing published or read or kept in print but in finding time, space, and acceptance within their own families shows how much development is still required.

The literature here discussed invites Western readers not only to view these regions in African as plural and various but to turn that recognition on ourselves—and see that "we" are not one but similarly divided by concerns of class, ethnicity, religion, and other differences. Recognition of the plurality of so-called developing countries can help Western readers see how much still needs to be developed in our countries—literacy, health care, and access to the basic requirements for life like clean water and good sanitation. By so breaking down the subject-object position of the West to help the "other," the literature of Africa can also help Western readers learn from the cultures we presume to "develop."

NOTES

1. Many of my thoughts on development and women's literature first became articulated while supervising Hannah Nash's master's thesis on women and development. Hannah's work has enhanced my own understanding considerably.

2. This does not mean orature is not practiced by those women but that material reaches an outside audience only with difficulty.

3. Just as in development studies, in literary studies women's work has traditionally been ignored and devalued. The change in interest in, and valuing of, women's perspectives has been quite recent; except for exceptional women such as Jane Austen and Virginia Woolf, only the last few decades have begun to accord women's writing the respect and exploration routinely given to men's writing.

4. I discuss short stories here; the time and resources needed to nurture and shape a fully developed novel have been found by African women, but more have been able to find the space of time in which to pen a story. In addition, the narrative form is more useful for development questions, as lyric poetry and drama, two other genres that allow a writer to speak quickly and lastingly, focus more on subjective states of emotion and on performative action. The short story's form by its nature asks for a linear account building to a climax that resonates beyond the events of its

story—thus, I have found it most useful for conveying both information about women's circumstances and the emotional, psychological reactions to those events.

5. In contrast, Mona Russell points out that upper-class Egyptian women conventionally receive very good levels of education (1992: 124).

6. The risk involved is more evident in Saadawi's (1989) darker version of such a scenario: the mother pushes her daughter onto a train in the dead of night so she won't be killed for becoming pregnant by a relative's rape of her ("Circling Song" 17).

7. The temptation to identify writers as "black or colored or white" needs to be resisted, to avoid endorsing the apartheid practice, questionable since its inception, of categorizing people by arbitrary and superficial standards.

8. See my essays "Whither Feminism?" (1994) and "Assuming the Position" (forthcoming) for discussion of other ways feminisms and feminists can become polarized and how we can come together across theoretical and other oppositions, rather than fracturing into factions.

9. Until the 1980s, both black and white women were legal minors (Diana Russell, 1989: 13).

10. This story also addresses the complex family structure: "Mokgoba—who was over seventy years old; two little girls, Neo and Boseyong; their mother Tiro and an unmarried sister, Nesta; and the father and supporter of the family, Ramadi" (90). Kate Young points to the difficulty development studies have with generating methodologies appropriate to the varied kinds of family units in which people live (1995: 114-15).

11. Equally distressing are urban stories of dislocation. For example, the homelands policy that leaves grandparents looking after their grandchildren while parents must work in the cities shows one disruption of life; another is the policy of relocation itself. In Farida Karodia's "Cardboard Mansions," (1993) an elderly woman and her grandson travel to find a remembered community of friends—but it is gone, all she knew removed. The grandson's sudden insecurity makes clear how such changes shatter one's foundations.

12. It is not coincidental that the sacrificed children are girls in Head's story.

13. The term "woman" itself is neither uniform nor hegemonic; there is no single event that is sure to have occurred to every woman and only to women.

REFERENCES

Adamson, Peter. 1996. "Deaf to the Screams." *The New Internationalist*, Contents page issue 287, NI Home Page.

Badran, Margot, and Miriam Cooke, eds. 1990. *Opening the Gates: A Century of Arab Feminist Writing*. Bloomington: Indiana University Press.

Bennholdt-Thomsen, Veronika. 1988. "Why Do Housewives Continue to Be Created in the Third World Too?" In *Women: The Last Colony*. Ed. Maria Mies, Veronika Bennholdt-Thomsen, and Claudia von Werlhof. London: Zed, 159-67.

Bernstein, Hilda. 1985. *For Their Triumphs and for Their Tears: Women in Apartheid South Africa*. Johannesburg: International Defence and Aid Fund for Southern Africa.

Bittari, Zoubeida. 1990. "The Voice of Happiness." In Badran and Cooke, 282-95.

Bruner, Charlotte, ed. 1993. *The Heinemann Book of African Women's Writing*. London: Heinemann.

———. 1983. *Unwinding Threads: Writing by Women in Africa*. London: Heinemann.

Carchidi, Victoria. Forthcoming. "Assuming the Position: Maryse Conde', Ama Ata Aidoo and the Postmodern." *Feminism. Postmodernism. Postfeminism*. Ed. Lynne Star and Lynne Alice.

———. 1994. "Whither Feminism? A Literary Tack." *FMST: Feminist Studies in Aotearoa [New Zealand] An Electronic Journal* 29 (Sept. 9), 7-15.

Chedid, Andree. 1983. "The Long Trial." In Bruner, *Unwinding Threads*, 202-8.

Davis, Susan Schaefer. "Impediments to Empowerment: Moroccan Women and the Agencies." In Jabbra and Jabbra, 111-21.

Dejeux, Jean. 1994. *La Litterature Feminine de Langue Francais au Maghreb*. Paris: Karthala.

Djebar, Assia. 1993. "My Father Writes to My Mother." In Bruner, *Heinemann*, 162-65.

———. 1993. "Three Cloistered Girls." In Bruner, *Heinemann*, 157-61.

Duly, Margot. 1986. "Women in the Islamic Middle East and North Africa." In *The Cross-Cultural Study of Women*. Ed. Margot I. Duley and Mary I. Edwards. New York: Feminist Press, 406-37.

Ferreira, Jeanette. 1987. "The Lover." In *A Land Apart: A Contemporary South African Reader*. Ed. Andre' Brink and J. M. Coetzee. London: Penguin, 137-39.

Gordimer, Nadine. 1982. "A Chip of Glass Ruby." *Six Feet of the Country*. London: Penguin, 36-47.

———. 1982. "Country Lovers." *Six Feet of the Country*. London: Penguin, 61-70.

Head, Bessie. "Looking for a Rain God." In *Looking for a Rain God: An Anthology of Contemporary African Short Stories*. Ed. Nadezda Obradovic. New York: Simon and Schuster, 89-93.

House, Amelia. 1983. "Conspiracy." In Bruner, *Unwinding Threads*, 142-55.

Jabbra, Joseph G., and Nancy W. Jabbra. 1992. "Introduction, Women and Development in the Middle East and North Africa." In Jabbra and Jabbra, 1-10.

———. eds. 1992. *Women and Development in the Middle East and North Africa*. Leiden: Brill.

Joubert, EIsa. 1987. "Milk." Trans. Mark Swift. In *The Penguin Book of Southern African Stories*. Ed. Stephen Gray. London: Penguin, 306-10.

Karodia, Farida. 1993. "Cardboard Mansions." In Bruner, *Heinemann*, 136-46.

Kitson, Norma, ed. 1994. *Anthology No. 1—English—1994*. Harare: Zimbabwe Women Writers.

Marquard, Jean. 1993. "Regina's Baby." In Bruner, *Heinemann*, 113-23.

Mernissi, Fatima. 1990. "Who's Cleverer, Man or Woman?" In Badran and Cooke, 317-27.

Mhlope Gcina. 1987a. "Nokolunga's Wedding." In *A Land Apart: A Contemporary South African Reader*. Ed. Andre' Brink and J. M. Coetzee. London: Penguin, 38-45.

———. 1987b. "The Toilet." In *Sometimes When It Rains: Writings by South African Women*. Ed. Ann Oosthuizen. London: Pandora, 1-7.

Momsen, Janet Henshall, and Janet Townshend. 1987. "Toward a Geography of Gender in Developing Market Economies." *Geography and Gender in the Third World.* Albany, NY: SUNY Press, 27-81.

Nash, Hannah. 1997. "A Novel Approach to Education and Development: Insights from African Women Writers." M.A. thesis. Massey University.

Nelson, Toni. 1996. "Violence Stalks Women Worldwide." *Vital Signs 1996.* New York: Norton, 134-35.

Radwan, Noha. 1990. "The Silk Bands." In Badran and Cooke, 120-21.

Rathgeber, Eva M. 1992. "Integrating Gender into Development: Research and Action Agendas for the 1990s." In Jabbra and Jabbra, 11-29.

Rifaat, Alifa. 1983. "Another Evening at the Club." In Bruner, *Unwinding Threads,* Oxford: Heinemann, 188-93.

———. 1983. "Distant View of a Minaret and Other Stories." *Distant View of a Minaret and Other Stories.* Oxford: Heinemann, 1-4.

———. 1983. "An Incident at the Ghobashi Household." *Distant View of a Minaret and Other Stories.* Oxford: Heinemann, 23-28.

———. 1983. "The Kite." *Distant View of a Minaret and Other Stories.* Oxford: Heinemann, 107-12.

———.1990. "Who'll Be the Man?" In Badran and Cooke, 74-77.

Russell, Diana E. H. 1989. *Lives of Courage: Women for a New South Africa.* New York: Basic Books.

Russell, Mona L. 1992. "The Female Brain Drain, the State and Development in Egypt." In Jabbra and Jabbra, 122-43.

Saad, Shirley. 1990. "Amina." In Badran and Cooke, 49-53.

Saadawi, Nawal el. 1989. *The Circling Song.* London: Zed.

———. 1989. "She Was the Weaker." *She Has No Place in Paradise.* Trans. Shirley Eber. London: Minerva, 9-15.

Sam, Agnes. 1989. "Two Women." *Jesus Is Indian and Other South African Stories.* London, Women's Press, 70-78.

Schreiner, Olive. 1987. "The Woman's Rose." In *The Penguin Book of South African Stories.* Ed. Stephen Grey. London: Penguin.

Tlali, Miriam. 1983. "Point of No Return." In Bruner, *Unwinding Threads,* 129-41.

Tlemcani, R. 1992. "The Rise of Algerian Women: Cultural Dualism and Multi-Party Politics." In Jabbra and Jabbra, 69-81.

Young, Kate. 1995. *Planning Development with Women: Making a World of Difference.* London: Macmillan.

Zenie-Ziegler, Wedid. 1988. *In Search of Shadows: Conversations with Egyptian Women.* London: Zed.

Index

About the Contributors

AMY BEER worked for a number of years as a human rights attorney and has also served as a producer on several human rights documentaries. Her publications include a number of articles on global communications.

VICTORIA CARCHIDI is Lecturer of English at Massey University in Palmerston North, New Zealand. Several of her writings have appeared in international journals.

FELIX K. EKECHI is a renowned Professor in the Department of History at Kent State University in Ohio. He has contributed extensively to the African studies literature through his books and numerous articles.

ALICE ETIM has worked with small business entrepreneurs both in the Mississippi Delta and in Jos, Nigeria and in the banking system in Nigeria.

JAMES S. ETIM, Associate Professor of English at Mississippi Valley State University, has authored and edited several books and refereed articles. He has taught for many years at Nigerian and American universities.

VALENTINE UDOH JAMES is Director of African Studies and Associate Professor of Social Science at Kalamazoo College in Michigan. He has authored and edited ten books and is the recipient of the Fulbright-Hays Faculty Research Abroad Award and was selected by the American Association for the Advancement of Science as a Diplomacy fellow. He is the editor-in-chief of the *Journal of Sustainable Development in Africa* (JSDA).

KOFI JOHNSON is Associate Professor of Political Science at North Carolina Central University. He is a Ghanian native with extensive field experience in Africa.

ANTHONIA C. KALU is Associate Professor of Black Studies and Chair of the Africana Studies Department at the University of Northern Colorado, Greeley. She is the recipient of several distinguished awards and has published widely in refereed journals.

CHRISTINE LIST is Professor of Communications at Chicago State University. She serves on the editorial board of the *Democratic Communique*, a journal that focuses on political economy of international media. She has directed a number of documentaries about human rights in Guatemala and publishes in the area of global communications.

ESTER IGANDU NJIRO is a native of Kenya and is affiliated with the African Mountain Research and Evaluation (AMRE) Organization as a researcher. She has been a consultant for many nongovernmental organizations for several years and was previously affiliated with the University of Nairobi.

AMBE J. NJOH is Assistant Professor in the Public Administration Program at the University of South Florida in St. Petersburg.

NOBLE J. NWEZE is senior research fellow at the Center for Rural Development and Cooperatives at the University of Nigeria in Nsuka, Nigeria. He also holds a Senior Lecturer position in the Department of Agricultural Economics at the same university. His publications have appeared in such journals as *Oxford Agrarian Studies* and the *Journal of Rural Development and Cooperative Studies*.

R. BABATUNDE OYINADE is Assistant Professor of Communications at Shaw University. Several of his publications have appeared in edited volumes dealing with issues of governance and sustainable development.

IFEYINWA E. UMERAH-UDEZULU is Assistant Professor of Political Science at Morris College in South Carolina. She has published several articles and book chapters pertaining to women's health and sustainable development issues.

ISBN 0-275-95946-5

9 780275 959463

HARDCOVER BAR CODE